2000 YEARS OF JAPANESE ART

Author's dedication

This work is respectfully dedicated to Bernard Berenson who in my youth guided me through my Italian studies, opening for me the door to Western art, and whose inspiration has illuminated and enriched my work in Eastern fields

YUKIO YASHIRO

2000 YEARS OF JAPANESE ART

Edited by Peter C. Swann

with 135 photogravure plates and 42 plates in colour

HARRY N. ABRAMS, INC. NEW YORK

LIBRARY OF CONGRESS CATALOG CARD NUMBER: 58-13478

PRINTED IN THE UNITED KINGDOM

In editing Professor Yashiro's text, I have tried to remain as faithful as possible to his original meanings. His assistance and his most kind confidence in my discretion have greatly eased what is always a difficult and can be a dangerous task.

The editing of a text of this nature requires some knowledge of the subject. This creates its own difficulties in so far as it is almost inevitable that the editor will disagree with some of the writer's opinions. He may be tempted, perhaps unconsciously, to change meanings, to interpret in a manner which produces a sense contrary to the intention of the writer. I have tried to obviate the intrusion of personal opinions. For what they are worth, they are included in my 'Introduction to the Arts of Japan' recently published.

It has been a pleasure to work with such an eminent authority as Professor Yashiro and to be associated with such a magnificently produced volume. Its timely appearance, coinciding with the exhibition of Japanese National Treasures, will do much to quicken the appreciation of Japanese art in this country and will serve as a permanent record when the masterpieces are returned to their native home.

I wish to thank Mr Phillip Rawson for reading my text and for many valuable suggestions.

PETER C. SWANN
MUSEUM OF EASTERN ART, OXFORD

Author's Foreword

When I was in Europe in 1956, representing the Japanese Government in the discussions that took place on the problem of holding an Exhibition of Japanese Art in the West, I was asked to write a book on Japanese art, in which its main historical developments and their special characteristics would be systematically elucidated with ample illustration. I welcomed the idea because of all the great regional arts of the world, the true aspects of Japanese art are surprisingly little known in the West.

Before 1868 Japanese contacts with the West had been slight. Moreover, since the sixteenth century, when the ships of the West penetrated the Eastern seas, the military government of Hideyoshi and, later, the Tokugawa Shogunate Government adopted a strong isolation-policy, which forbade the entry of nearly all foreigners for almost three hundred years. When at last the Tokugawa rule collapsed, and the New Japan was born in 1868, Japan was eager to have communication with the West and to absorb its science and its industrial techniques. Foreigners were welcomed and tourists began to visit the country. Slowly Japanese art became known in Europe and America, in the beginning through Ukiyo-e colour-prints, which had a seminal effect on the Impressionist movement.

But when Japanese art-objects began to be exported abroad, the conservative elements in Japan issued the 'Law of National Treasures', which prevented nearly all important works of art from leaving the country. This was in a way a good thing, because Japanese art is preserved almost intact in its place of origin, a situation which does not occur in any other civilization. At the same time, however, Japanese art, being kept so completely within its geographical frontiers, where public museums are few and the finest pieces preserved in private collections, which are not always easily accessible, especially for foreign visitors, inevitably suffered in the appreciation of the West. Except for the Museum of Fine Arts, Boston, and the Freer Gallery, Washington, whose Japanese collections had been mostly formed before the 'Law of National Treasures' was rigidly enforced, there are to be found only very few examples of Japanese art in European and American museums which can be considered as really first-class. After visiting nearly all the Japanese collections abroad I have come to the conclusion that, as Japanese art is so inadequately represented in other countries, it is natural that the real merit of Japanese art is neither recognized nor understood.

When after the defeat of Japan in the Second World War the National Commission for the Protection of Cultural Properties was created as the Government body in charge of National Treasures, Monuments, and Museums, I was appointed its Deputy Chairman. I thought that the isolated position of Japanese art should be ended and that a proper appreciation of it in the West was a way of explaining another and more enduring aspect of the Japanese character. The 'Law of National Treasures' itself is not easy to change, but so far as is possible in both my official and personal capacity I have tried to make the essentials of Japanese art better known and appreciated abroad. With such a motive, humanistic as well as patriotic, I have with other members of the National Commission tried hard to materialize the long-cherished plan of holding a very fine Exhibition of Japanese Art at least once outside Japan. With the same motive, but with the freer and more personal interest of the scholar, I accepted the request of the publishers of this book to produce what I sincerely hope offers to Western readers an opportunity to get a new and more valid view, historical as well as aesthetic, of Japanese art, so often misinterpreted.

When I returned to Japan, after concluding the arrangements for the coming Exhibition in Europe, I began my preparations for this book. A special photographer, Mrs Wachsmann, was sent by the publishers to Japan to make under my direction colour-photographs from the original paintings, and I would like to take this opportunity of paying tribute to her excellent work. As the time approached, however, when I ought to begin to write the text, I fell seriously ill, and it was obvious that I would be in ill-health for some time. As the only way to finish the book in time for the Exhibition, I decided to dictate my ideas for the text in Japanese and to have them translated into English. When this first English draft was produced by the heroic efforts of Mrs T. Yoshino, I read through it with as much concentration as was possible for a sick man in a hospital. What irritated me most during this work of correcting was that I could not look up reference-books in order to check the English equivalents of Japanese names and many other things. My former pupil and friend, Professor C. Yamada, kindly offered his help in this work and also for the large volume of correspondence with my publishers in London. Of course, such is not the usual way to produce an important book, and when the English text was finally looked through and corrected by me I found that it was still so inadequate both in substance and in language that I asked my publishers to have the whole text re-examined and, if necessary, rewritten—naturally leaving my main arguments unchanged—by an English scholar. When I was told that Mr Peter C. Swann, Curator of the Museum of Eastern Art, Oxford, was willing to do the work, I was immensely relieved, because I knew that during his stay in Japan a few years ago he had studied Japanese and other Eastern art and that he was a scholar of growing reputation with the right knowledge and sympathy. Indeed, Mr Swann has accomplished a most difficult task with tact and discretion and I am very grateful to him. When I examined his rewritten text, I sympathized with him, because the editing of the work of an author who was not only many thousands of miles away but also in ill-health, must have been very trying and often very awkward. How I wished that I were in London, so that I could talk over problems directly with Mr Swann. Anyway, under such unusually difficult circumstances we have done our best, and thanks to Mr Swann's sincere collaboration and help, it is possible to publish this study.

In this book I have used the method of treatment by subjects as in the Introduction to the small Catalogue of the 'Japanische Malerei der Gegenwar', published in Berlin in 1930, when I brought to Germany an Exhibition of Contemporary Japanese Painting. In this Introduction I tried to make clear the special features of Japanese Painting inherited by the present. After this successful experiment, I have decided to adopt the same method here again, because the main purpose of this book is to make the essential features and special beauties of Japanese art understood as easily as possible, with actual examples of similar subjects arranged in historical order.

Japanese and Chinese names have always presented problems of transliteration. In Japan the same persons and things are often called by different names. Here I have used the simplest and most familiar. In the names of the artists, I have generally used only the first names, which are often their pseudonyms as artists, but as we approach modern times I have given the family-names in addition, in order to prevent confusion. When I refer to Chinese artists, I have generally given their names in the Japanese manner, because they are always quoted as such in the histories of Japanese art, although I have given their original Chinese form as well.

YUKIO YASHIRO

TOKYO, SPRING 1958

Contents and List of Plates

III JAPANESE SCULPTURE

I INTRODUCTION

Hitherto, many factors have contributed to prevent the west appreciating the arts of the east purely as art. The majority of westerners still regard eastern cultures as strange and alien. The civilizations of the east, nurtured in a remote part of the world, have remained objects of curiosity rather than subjects worthy of serious study. Seldom have the arts they produced been considered simply as manifestations of the human spirit which could have a universal appeal.

Why was this so? There are certainly many contributory factors. The east, of course, is far removed from the west. In the east, man and nature have produced a different environment with totally different ways of life, religions, customs, languages, literature, and history. The materials and techniques of their arts differ radically from those of the west. It is easy to understand that anybody who bases his ideas of art on those of the west should feel that the products of eastern artists are somewhat unfamiliar. The result has been to create a large body of specialists in the fields of eastern folklore, geography, religion, language, literature, anthropology, and history whose duties have been to interpret the east to the west. Their specialized studies were, without doubt, of the greatest value and interest.

However, eastern art is art as much as any other art. It is equally an intimate expression of the human soul. Its fundamental characteristics spring from the same eternal values which make it appeal to all men. Like truth and goodness, which are also manifestations of our highest aims, so beauty, regardless of its place of origin, must make a universal appeal. This is not to deny the fact that many elements of geography, history and race play a vital part, but fundamentally the values which give an object beauty, life, and reason, are universal. Anybody with a keen perception and an open mind can understand their true character. It has, in a sense, been a misfortune that the great differences of cultural background and historical development have invited only the attention of scholars and that the difficulties of these studies have tended to obscure the fundamental artistic values of eastern art. Indeed, deep research into the background of eastern art requires so much specialist effort that it rarely enables a man to appreciate fully the basic artistic qualities of a work of art; as one would say in English it is difficult for specialists 'to see the wood for the trees'. The result has been that those who concern themselves with oriental art are, for the most part, orientalists, that is to say scholars devoted to *research* in oriental subjects. They are seldom artists and critics whose main function is to assess art in terms of human values. Thus, the idea is current in the west that eastern art is a *recherché* subject which demands a great deal of preliminary knowledge. The courage to look at eastern art with one's own eyes, and to respond naturally to it, is still greatly lacking.

The arts of the east have shared in the great strides made in recent years in all branches of oriental studies, but one important step remains to be taken. They must be rescued from the hands of specialists and brought back into the realm of art studies. Having spent many years as a specialist, I should be the last to deny the importance of oriental studies. However, I feel that inquiries into the historical and linguistic backgrounds are only means to an end—which is the true knowledge of art. We must realize that, if we base our appreciation of all art on an assessment of its fundamental quality of beauty, then there should be no difference between east and west.

The problem was brought home to me as long ago as 1935–6 on the occasion of the great exhibition of Chinese Art held in London. This exhibition aroused wide interest among art lovers, and experts from all over the world delivered lectures designed to enlighten the general public. As a member of the committee in charge of the exhibition I stayed in London and contributed to this lecture series. Two good friends approached me with their doubts. Sir Gerald Kelly, then a Member and later President of the Royal Academy which sponsored the exhibition, remarked how interesting he found the exhibition and how scholarly the lectures and articles on it. Yet he could not help feeling that the impressions the exhibits made on him often differed very strongly from the views expressed by the scholars. For example, many of the pictures which the scholars were at great pains to explain and praise seemed to him dull by comparison with some of the less-noticed works. He had discussed this problem with some of his painter friends and they felt that, as painters preoccupied with the search for beauty, they had the right to express an opinion. He wondered whether he should trust to his own immediate reaction or submit meekly to the opinions of the orientalists. The doubts which he voiced were of significance in view of his eminence as a practising artist and in view of the fact that he was very interested in eastern art and had considerable experience of it gained in the east itself. I told Sir Gerald that in my opinion, although learned explanations threw light on the subject-matter of a painting or on the life of the artist and his cultural background, the intrinsic merit of a work of art depended entirely on the aesthetic taste of the spectator and that a mind open to beauty would immediately understand whatever deep and lasting values it might contain. I felt that a scholar deeply immersed in the biographical details of Rembrandt's life might not necessarily be the best to appreciate his work and that, by the same token, scholarly research does not automatically ensure for the scholar an undisputed position of being the best judge of the artistic qualities of an eastern work of art. I told him that, as artists, they might well learn from the experts but that they should not hesitate to trust their own impressions and judgments. I felt that the western world would be the richer if they frankly and fearlessly stated their opinions.

At about the same time, another old friend, Sir Kenneth Clark, then Director of the National Gallery, approached me with similar doubts. He, too, found that his own immediate impressions differed radically from those of the experts. He was interested in their findings but found it difficult to agree with their aesthetic judgments. In view of Sir Kenneth's long interest in oriental art and his undisputed position as a critic and historian I felt that his opinion was of some significance. I replied that his lack of background knowledge of the arts of the east might well be for the good. The fundamental criterion of eastern as of western art is beauty, and if his opinions on this aspect of eastern art differed from those of the orientalists so much the better. I hoped that he, too, would frankly state his reactions to the objects shown at the exhibition and I told him that it was his duty as a critic to approach the works of eastern art directly, to find beauty in them where he could, regardless of the knowledge contributed by the experts. I assured him that his conclusions would not only both greatly interest me and help in the cause of rescuing oriental art from the grip of the orientalists, but that they would also encourage the public to understand it in its rightful role as art, pure and simple. When Sir Kenneth broadcast his impressions of the exhibition he did just this. He described the paintings he most enjoyed and his opinions were all the fresher and more interesting for their freedom from the usual mass of obscuring learned comment.

Many years have passed since the great London exhibition but the arts of the east still remain for the most part in the hands of orientalists. They have still not become the concern of legitimate art criticism. I wish to make it clear that I do not intend in any way to imply that all specialist scholars are insensitive to beauty; one must merely admit that the difficulties of oriental scholarship do not tend to foster a sense of beauty in those who pursue them. Among the many outstanding scholars produced in this century, few approach the arts of the east with that same open heart and unsophisticated readiness to appreciate beauty that they would employ when faced with the works of Botticelli, Rembrandt, Cézanne or Renoir. In such conditions it is difficult to reach a clear understanding of the aesthetic values of eastern art. My sincerest hope is that, with the spread of knowledge concerning the east, the general public will not be intimidated by any feeling that abstruse, specialized knowledge is essential but that they will look on eastern art simply as art. Indeed, it does not differ from any other art of the world and the only requirement for its appreciation is that freedom and receptiveness of spirit which should characterize the lover of beauty.

Unfortunately, Japanese art has shared the custom of being regarded as the exclusive domain of specialists. In all fairness, it must be admitted that Japanese scholars themselves have encouraged this misconception by stressing what is unusual in our art, i.e. the peculiarities resulting from our historical background. Japanese art came to the notice of the west only in the mid-nineteenth century and through only one peculiar manifestation, namely the art of the colour-print. This particular art of *Ukiyo-e* depicts the popular pleasures of the commoners of Edo, the present-day Tokyo, at its most decadent period, when the citizens of the capital revelled in the theatres and the gay quarters. Without doubt, this art has its own charm and beauty; its decadent atmosphere as well as its technique appealed strongly to European *fin de siècle* artists. Indeed, the Japanese colour-print acted as a powerful stimulus for artists dissatisfied with conventional academic modes and it was a considerable factor in the emergence of Impressionism. However, the peculiar charms of this art do demand special knowledge of its historical background and of the social customs of Edo Society. Seen in this light, one can understand why such emphasis was placed on research into the customs and manners of the theatre and gay world. The colour-print has maintained its tremendous popularity in America and Europe but it is an abnormal manifestation of Japanese art and to dwell exclusively on it can give a false idea of the centuries of art which lie behind it. Without in any way decrying the achievements of the colour-print, one should be aware of the fact that to see the whole of Japanese art through this particular form produces a picture as distorted as that provided by *Madame Butterfly*.

When, after about three hundred years of isolation, Japan was opened to the world, her contacts with the west suddenly greatly increased. Exhibitions in Vienna, Paris, and London provided a more comprehensive view of Japanese art and its ancient past than the west had hitherto seen. Later such museums as the Museum of Fine Arts, Boston, and the Freer Gallery, Washington, assembled large and carefully chosen collections of our arts. Unfortunately such institutions are very few, but through their activities Japanese art slowly reached a wider public. In this spread of understanding Japanese scholars have had a great influence, although in a quite different direction.

The most outstanding disseminator of knowledge of Japanese art was the eminent Okakura Kakuzō. The writings of this immensely gifted man were widely read in Europe and greatly helped to provide a more enlightened view of our art. However, he was a passionate believer in the supremacy of oriental culture over that of the west and he stoutly defended all eastern concepts against those of the west. His books are very enlightening but they tend to stress too much the peculiarities of our art, i.e. those special characteristics in which it differs from western art. He emphasized the importance of *Zen*, and its influence in the formation of *suiboku* (black-and-white ink painting), and the parts played by the *Noh* drama and the tea ceremony. He pointed out, with all the persuasiveness at his command (and he was an excellent writer), the role that these features of our life played in creating a uniquely Japanese sense of beauty. Understandably enough, his readers were induced to feel that without some knowledge of *Zen* Buddhism, the *Noh* drama and the tea ceremony, they would never fully understand Japanese art.

Zen Buddhism, it is true, has left a deep mark on Japanese thought. It was introduced during the Kamakura and Muromachi periods from China of the Sung and Yüan Dynasties. Its severe, ascetic spirit appealed to the warrior classes of Kamakura who governed the country by a strict feudal system. From that time the Japanese imposed on *Zen* some peculiarly national characteristics. It has continued to influence our life and culture ever since. The tea ceremony was developed by *Zen* adherents and attained a tremendous vogue during the Muromachi and Momoyama periods. It became an arbiter of taste and developed a system of art-appreciation based on *Zen* principles. One cannot deny that, from the Momoyama period to the present day, the tea ceremony has greatly influenced architecture, painting, and the applied arts. Nor can one ignore the unique aesthetics produced by the tea ceremony with its sensitive appreciation of many evanescent aspects of beauty. But to interpret all Japanese art on the basis of 'tea-ism', as so eloquently set forth in Okakura's well-known *Book of Tea*, is to go to the extreme. Both the tea ceremony and the taste it fostered have their individual merits but they do not provide the essential key to an appreciation of Japanaese art. It is high time that Japanese art was freed from such philosophical and literary ideas and was seen clearly and in a balanced manner, simply as art.

As previously stated, the arts most affected by *Zen* Buddhism and the cult of tea were black-and-white ink painting, architecture, and gardens, and all the applied arts used in the tea-ceremony rooms. The spirituality of *Zen* was of particular importance for painting. Yet these arts did not appear before the Kamakura period and their finest products were made during the Ashikaga, Momoyama, and later periods. However, the greatest periods of Japanese art came before the birth of these art forms—they were the Asuka, Nara, and Heian periods. Even in the centuries following the Kamakura period, the proportion of art which requires knowledge of *Zen* and the tea cult is relatively small.

Okakura himself did not interpret *all* Japanese art in the light of *Zen* and 'tea-ism'. His knowledge of oriental art in general and Japanese art in particular was too wide and sound. His judgments on the whole were correct. However, one sees in his English writings an emphasis on just those unusual aspects of Japanese art which were calculated to impress the western amateur. His literary talent, and also, it must be admitted, a certain nationalistic spirit, gained for him a wide audience, but his very success created the danger of his presenting a somewhat warped or incomplete picture.

The conclusions stated above are the outcome of long experience with the arts of the world and of comparisons made with Japanese art. When I first came to Europe some forty years ago, I approached the arts of the west with no preconceived ideas and, it must be admitted, with only little knowledge to guide me. I was immediately and deeply moved by the soul of Leonardo da Vinci, by the wonderful sense of beauty of Piero della Francesca and Botticelli. The high quality of the work of such masters requires no art-historical or aesthetic introduction. On the contrary, I often wonder if the knowledge of the painters' lives and cultural backgrounds which I later acquired really enabled me to understand their art any better or whether the studious preoccupation with technical details and circumstantial evidence has not detracted from my pure, human judgment. I often wonder also, when reading the works of other scholars renowned for their grasp of detail, if their judgments have not been impaired. In its essence the study of art ought to be based on the direct impression a work creates and the enthusiasms it arouses. However, constantly one encounters the difficulty of reconciling the spontaneous reaction with the technicalities of research. Long years of study have taught me how precious are the moments of first impression and how vital it is to try to keep them alive in the absorbing intellectual interests which research into the background of works of art provides.

I remember clearly how, when I first returned to Japan after my years of art study in Europe, I hastened to see again the art treasures of my native country. I was anxious to compare them with the great works of the west which were still fresh in my memory. At that time, thanks to a stay in Florence and to the guidance of my teacher Bernard Berenson, I had some knowledge of Italian art but I was almost completely ignorant of oriental art in general and Japanese art in particular. As I looked at the masterpieces of Japanese art, I realized that I was seeing them with the same openness with which I had first approached western art. I was a simple lover of art, content merely with experiencing their beauty. I can remember most vividly the joy and enthusiasm which this experience gave me. With no preconceptions or historical data to encumber my senses, this moment of search for pure beauty was one of the most treasured moments of my life. It was of value that I could look at them without any thought of whether they belonged to the east or west. I saw them from a higher spiritual plane where only beauty reigned and place of origin was unimportant. I felt that these great works of my own country could compare with any of the masterpieces of Italian art which I had so long been studying.

If, at the risk of repetition, I may be allowed to summarize, I should like to reaffirm that my international training in the arts and the constant comparisons I have made over the years have led me to conclude that the only criterion in judging art is beauty. I firmly believe that the essence of beauty is human and universal. Research is only a tool—a means to an end. Works of art were not made for art historians—they were created for the enjoyment, and sometimes for the salvation, of ordinary people. The vital quality required of a lover of art is that he possesses sensibility and an awareness and love of beauty. Actual experience has strengthened my opinion in this matter.

In the year 1953, on behalf of my government, I brought an exhibition of Japanese painting and sculpture to the United States. This was the first important cultural project which Japan had undertaken since the end of the sad events of the Second World War. We were mindful of the importance of this exhibition and we made every effort to provide outstanding works which would reveal Japanese art as faithfully as possible. Japan's long isolation has resulted in her preserving the art of the islands within her boundaries.

I have previously dwelt upon the esoteric nature of Japanese art which our scholars have fostered, how they insist that the mastery of difficult religious or philosophical ideas must precede any appreciation of art. My conscious aim in assembling the first great post-war exhibition of Japanese art was to break down this misconception and to bring together a body of Japanese works of art which would provide a clear picture of its essential character. We chose works of the highest artistic quality regardless of the superficial impressions of tourists or the involved philosophical commentaries of the scholars. We hoped that, by merely showing them without attempting to interpret them, they would be received and recognized primarily as art. With this purpose in mind we omitted the small and elaborate objects of applied art which usually attract the foreign tourist and restricted the exhibits to the finest paintings and sculptures. An exhibition on such lines was new, and its high standards distinguished it from all previous exhibitions in the west.

When the exhibition opened in the United States, its effect surpassed my hopes. This was particularly so in the Metropolitan Museum of Art, New York, in whose spacious galleries the Japanese paintings and sculptures, shown with ample space and in the best possible conditions, gave the impression of an unexpected grandeur. The conception of Japanese art as being exclusively curios such as lacquer objects, ivory carvings, *inrō* and *netsuke* was dispelled completely. The Metropolitan Museum houses masterpieces from the whole world and these Japanese works placed by their side provided a valuable opportunity for close comparison. To choose a simile from another activity, one felt that Japan had sent its champions to the Olympics of art. I was able to prove conclusively to myself that Japanese art objects, without explanations attached, could compare in their immediate artistic impact with the arts of the world.

In these surroundings, two types of Japanese painting, the Buddhist works of the Heian and Kamakura periods and the screen-paintings of the Momoyama period, made a particularly strong impression. Their grand style was particularly effective even from a distance. In these works bold outlines, rich colours, and spiritual power combined to provide an unforgettable experience. It was but a few steps from the gallery housing the Japanese Buddhist paintings to the rooms where the Italian masters were hung. To return from the Italians to the Japanese, the visitor immediately felt that the religious paintings of Japan had lost none of their impressiveness. Slightly farther away were the galleries devoted to the display of paintings by Delacroix, Courbet, Renoir, and other great modern masters. To see them and then look at the Japanese masterpieces of the Edo period did not create an impression of returning to a small, dainty and over-decorated art form which is the common, mistaken idea of modern Japanese art. The thirteenth-century portrait of Yoritomo (Plate 72) stood comparison with the masterpieces of Rembrandt in the Altman collection. Repeatedly I questioned my own judgment and made the comparison, but my conclusion remained unchanged.

In comparison with the arts of the world, Japanese art reflects the same most important element, that exalted human quality which one might call 'the universality of beauty', the final value of art.

The fusion of this universal quality with the indigenous Japanese racial characteristics gives our works of art their interest and their appeal. For example, the *E-makimono* (scroll-paintings) evolved in Japan in a unique manner. Their pictorial form has affinities with the compositions round the Roman triumphal columns and with the predellas of Italian altar-pieces. Japanese artists developed these scrolls as a means of illustrating stories in a most dynamic manner unparalleled until the invention of the modern moving-picture technique. This art of scroll-painting, which we shall discuss at greater length later in the text, is an outstanding example of a unique Japanese development with a universal appeal.

Suiboku painting provides another example. This form of painting in ink dispenses completely with the use of colour, yet the subtle black-and-white tones it creates can be compared with Rembrandt's wonderful effects of light and shade. There is even a possibility that Rembrandt was influenced by oriental black-and-white drawing which he could have seen in Holland, a country active in trade with the east from early times. The question is too complicated to be dealt with here and such a connection in no way detracts from Rembrandt's greatness as a master of light and shade. It is illuminating to be able to see black-and-white paintings from the east in close proximity with the works of Rembrandt. The experiences of this exhibition produced in me a sense of freedom—as if Japanese art was for the first time released from the bonds created by the superficial impressions of tourists and the theorizing of the art historians. I do not deny the individualities of Japanese art and I was delighted to see the interest this touring exhibition aroused among the experts but, for me, its greatest success was the response it drew from ordinary lovers of art who had no specialized knowledge of the arts of the east.

The success of our venture in the United States did not pass unnoticed in Europe where various countries expressed their desire to have a similar exhibition of outstanding works. Their wishes, I am happy to say, are about to be fulfilled. However, in contrast to the United States, orientalism in Europe has deep roots. The *chinoiserie* so popular during the seventeenth and eighteenth centuries has there created its own ideas of eastern art. These preconceptions make it even more difficult to provide a comprehensive survey of true eastern art in general and Japanese art in particular.

All exhibitions of Japanese art in Europe with only one exception have hitherto included the applied arts in addition to painting and sculpture. The Japanese were quite willing to comply with this custom if the European countries so desired. In April of last year I discussed in Paris the practical problems with the representatives of the various countries concerned. Mr Philip James of the Arts Council of Great Britain endorsed the opinion of Sir Kenneth Clark, then Chairman of the Arts Council, that the American exhibition had amply demonstrated that traditional ideas of Japanese art had been one-sided and misleading. He strongly advocated that the European exhibition should follow the lines of the one held in America. It would provide a comprehensive view of the plastic arts of Japan and dispel the old misconceptions. The representatives from the other European countries agreed and it was decided that the exhibits would be chosen on the same principle.

I sincerely hope that the European exhibition will lead, as it did in the United States, to a revaluation of Japanese art by enabling a comparison to be made with the masterpieces of the rest of the world. The main objective of this book is to further this revaluation.

II EPOCHS OF JAPANESE ART

Japan is a chain of islands most of which are situated off the coast of China and Korea while some stretch farther to the north. As a result of its geographical situation the inhabitants of Japan probably always had some contact with the cultures of the mainland. However, it was not until A.D. 552 when, via Korea, Buddhism and the culture it brought with it were introduced on a vast scale into the islands, that Japan emerged from its prehistoric period. There are no historical records of the period prior to this time, and accordingly it can be called the Archaeological Age.

These many centuries can be subdivided into three periods according to the nature of their respective archaeological remains. The earliest period is that of the *Jōmon* culture and extends from the earliest times to about 200 B.C. This is followed by the period of the *Yayoi* culture, roughly 200 B.C.–A.D. 200. The latest of the three sub-divisions follows the *Yayoi* and extends from the middle of the third century A.D. to the mid-sixth century when Buddhism and the whole culture of the continent reached Japan. During this period Japan was already a unified nation. One of the distinguishing features of this last period was the custom whereby the people buried their eminent dead in huge tumuli; this gives the period its name, the *Kōfun* or Tumulus period.

Despite the archaeological division of these centuries into three periods, their prehistoric art shows only two main styles—those of the *Jōmon* and *Yayoi*. The *Jōmon* style has unique characteristics which bear little relation to the *Yayoi* remains. However, later Japanese art is firmly rooted in the *Yayoi* style which continued throughout the Tumulus period. The *Jōmon* and *Yayoi* artifacts seem to indicate two completely different cultures. According to an old theory the *Jōmon* peoples were overrun by the *Yayoi* who invaded Japan from the south-west. The latter drove the remnants of the *Jōmon* into the north-east of the country and occupied the central regions. They would, therefore, be the ancestors of the present-day Japanese.

However, more recent anthropological and archaeological research has produced a new and now generally accepted theory, according to which the *Jōmon* and *Yayoi* peoples belonged to the same race. This theory is based on the measurements of human bones belonging to the peoples of the respective periods.

Scholars who hold this theory, believe that the difference between the two cultures can be explained by the fact that the *Jōmon* people followed a nomadic and hunting way of life whereas the *Yayoi* had settled down to an agricultural life. This difference alone, according to the theory, produced the different cultures. Some scholars claim to be able to distinguish certain archaeological finds which belong to the transitional period.

The problems involved in the racial theories must be left to specialist research, but one wonders if the measurements of bones alone provide sufficient evidence to reconcile such remarkable differences in form and artistic spirit as exist between the two cultures. Whether such an extraordinary change would be caused simply by a change in ways of life is a problem which may well deserve further study. A number of modern archaeologists are beginning to think that the whole question of human bones should be reinvestigated. The finds from the *Yayoi* and Tumulus periods, however, show a

The Archaeological Age

quality which is akin to the sensitivity and taste of the Japanese in the historical period and there can exist no doubt that the *Yayoi* culture developed into the culture of sixth-century Japan.

Hitherto *Jōmon* and *Yayoi* artifacts have been studied mainly by archaeologists merely as material for the divisions of prehistory. However, modern interest in primitive art has aroused a great interest in prehistoric Japanese art.

The most important artistic evidence from these periods takes the form of clay pottery and clay figures and figurines. The designs on the pottery show a vitality and originality which appeal strongly to modern interests. The frank and naïve expression of the clay figures and figurines has its own particular charm. The *Jōmon* figurines probably spring from the fetishes of an unsettled mode of life which depended on the hunt. The awe reflected in their expressions appeals greatly to modern interest in the depiction of the supernatural in art.

The more settled life following the introduction of agriculture led to the beginnings of a sense of beauty and desire for decoration. This tendency to beauty becomes more marked as the historical period draws closer and it distinguishes the *Yayoi* and Tumulus remains from those of the *Jōmon* period. Outstanding in this trend are the patterns and colours of the pottery but most of all the clay figures of animals and people known as *haniwa*.

The magical intention of the *Jōmon* figurines is missing from the *haniwa*. Most of these *haniwa* were made as decorations for tombs and they express an interest and pleasure in many aspects of nature. A child-like spirit and an instinctive desire for beauty obviously inspired their makers. In a modern sophisticated world their uncomplicated and innocent appeal is irresistible.

The Asuka Period 552-645

Buddhism and the advanced culture it brought with it entered Japan via Korea. Their introduction marked the end of the types of art we have seen in the Archaeological period. This was Japan's first cultural awakening and the history of Japanese art proper can be said to begin from this momentous event.

The early years following the introduction of the new religion were marked by a religious and political conflict between those who favoured and those who opposed Buddhism. However, the greatly superior way of life which it represented overcame the opposition and Japan adopted the faith on a vast scale. As a consequence, a powerful wave of continental culture swept over Japan and Buddhism became tantamount to a State religion. It was to rule the destinies of the nation and be the chief arbiter of thought and culture for many centuries.

The beginnings of this new age were in the Asuka period (A.D. 552–645) and the famous Hōryū-ji Monastery is its greatest monument. It represents the first Japanese emulation of the architecture, sculpture, and painting of the continent as these arts in their turn had developed from the Buddhist arts which entered China from India. The sculptures of the Asuka period reflect the styles of the Six Dynasties period of China (A.D. 221–589), notably that of the Northern Wei (A.D. 386–534) which entered Japan through the Korean Kingdom of Kudara (Korean: Paekche). They show how magnificently Japan adopted and assimilated the Chinese and Korean styles. The preservation almost intact of so many fragile objects of the highest quality dating back to the seventh century is as rare in eastern as in western art and the Hōryū-ji treasures are entitled to rank among the world's most precious antiquities.

The previous Asuka period corresponded in time to the Sui Dynasty in China (A.D. 589–618). However, Asuka art reflected the styles of the previous Six Dynasties period in China (A.D. 221–589) allowing for a certain time lapse before it reached Japan due to the slowness of communications. The short-lived Sui Dynasty which reunified China was followed by the T'ang Dynasty (A.D. 618–907). The Chinese during these centuries established a vast empire and an art in keeping with its strength and grandeur. During the Nara period which followed the Asuka, Japan adopted the arts of Sui and T'ang China on a vast scale. Even the Japanese capital was planned on the lines of the great T'ang metropolis of Chōan, better known to western readers by its Chinese name Ch'ang-an. Buddhism became firmly established as the State religion and Japan witnessed a flowering of the Buddhist arts which is unparalleled in its history.

For convenience, historians generally divide the Nara period into two parts, the Early Nara period (A.D. 645–710) which is also sometimes known as the Hakuhō period, and the Nara period proper (A.D. 710–794), also known as the Tempyō period.

During the Early Nara period the arts of the Sui and Early T'ang Dynasties entered Japan where they were enthusiastically studied. The comparatively primitive style of the Asuka period—sometimes over-severe and a little stiff—was displaced by forms which brought Japanese art into direct line with the full, magnificent styles of the Sui and Early T'ang Dynasties.

During the Nara period proper, the brilliance of the mature art of the T'ang Dynasty overwhelmed Japan completely; its influence is seen in architecture, sculpture, and painting. To such an extent and so faithfully did Japan emulate her powerful neighbour that anybody wishing to gain an idea of the splendour of T'ang art must turn to the temples of Nara where it has been carefully preserved. The Nara period was Japan's 'golden age'. To refer to it, as do some critics, simply as an imitation of the culture of China is to over-simplify a very complex cultural phenomenon. It would be better just to visualize Japan moving in rhythm and harmony with the powerful forces of T'ang culture as it swept over all the nations within the cultural orbit of China.

Two important qualities distinguish the T'ang culture which entered Japan and flowered there during the Nara period. Firstly, the influences came directly from the Chinese capital of Ch'ang-an. Japan had sent her ambassadors and students to Ch'ang-an itself where they experienced the full force of the most advanced civilization of its day. Moreover, eminent Chinese priests like Ganjin (Chinese: Chien Chên) were invited to Japan where they greatly impressed the Japanese with their deep learning and noble characters. The aspects of T'ang culture which reached Japan were thus the finest that China could offer and, as a result, what it produced in Japan was in no way provincial like the arts of Tun-huang, on the western border of China. The outstanding quality of the civilization of Nara bears testimony to the purity and metropolitan nature of the Chinese influences.

Secondly, Nara culture shows the same breadth and the same international quality which characterize the culture of T'ang China. The T'ang empire reached out as far as the borders of Persia and had contacts with most of the known world of that time. This universal character of T'ang culture is reflected in that of the Japanese Nara period.

An Imperial Depository called the Shōsō-in was created in the mid-eighth century. It houses a wealth of cultural objects dating from that time and includes among its many treasures articles from Persia and other West Asian and Central Asian areas. These not only provide valuable evidence of T'ang-Nara art but also testify to a greater intercourse between east and west in these early days than one might imagine.

The Heian period lasted from A.D. 794, the year in which the capital was established in Heian-kyō (present-day Kyoto), to 1185 when the Heike clan was destroyed. It is usual to subdivide these four centuries into an Early Heian or Kōnin period (794–897) and the Heian period proper (897–1185) which is often known as the Fujiwara period.

The Early Heian period was in some respects a continuation of the Nara period, for the movement to assimilate T'ang culture continued without interruption. But, by this time, the character of the

T'ang Dynasty had changed. China was no longer the firmly united strong nation of the Early and Middle T'ang centuries whose culture had been so eagerly studied by the Japanese during the Nara period. With the decline in the internal strength of her vast empire, came the signs of a deterioration in her culture. Esoteric sects of Buddhism appeared which emphasized the importance of complicated iconography and mystical rituals. The Heian period was subject to the influences of the Late T'ang and naturally differed considerably from the Nara period. New influences guided the development of Japanese art and life.

The most far-reaching of these new influences was, without doubt, that of esoteric Buddhism. Its mysticism and ritualism was a novelty which made an immediate strong appeal to the Japanese. The new *Tendai* and *Shingon* sects which stressed the esoteric aspects of Buddhism rapidly gained a wide following. From these sects, in later times sprang others which, as we shall see, were peculiarly Japanese interpretations of the faith. Esoteric Buddhism had a profound effect on the art of Japan. The mystical aspects of the sect resulted in a style of sculpture unknown in the Nara period and for which wood was the principal material. They also stimulated the creation of a new type of large painting to meet its requirements. In short, the enthusiasm for the new Buddhism contributed much to the flowering of all the Buddhist arts. Another important factor in this great artistic activity was the influence of the large number of T'ang masterpieces brought back to Japan by travelling student-priests who went to China in search of knowledge. In the fifth year of the Kaishō (Chinese: *Kuai-ch'ang*) era (i.e. A.D. 845), Buddhism suffered a great persecution in China and most of the Buddhist art was destroyed. However, Japanese priests studying in China at the time were given special permission to return to Japan with a number of excellent works which would otherwise have been destroyed. These naturally served as models for the Buddhist artists of the Early Heian period in Japan.

With the decline and fall of the T'ang Dynasty, Japan no longer felt an urge to turn to China for inspiration. The system of regular *kentoshi* or embassies (which had included students) established during the Nara period, was discontinued from A.D. 894. The close contacts which Japan had preserved with China since the Asuka period were for the first time interrupted. From this time Japan was forced to rely upon her own resources and the nation had reached a point in its development when it was perfectly able to do so. This marks the beginning of the Heian period proper.

This was a period of great peace and prosperity for the Imperial court. Powerful nobles, the strongest being the Fujiwara clan, gathered round the throne. The Heian is consequently often referred to as the Fujiwara period. Its aristocratic society was characterized by luxury, refinement, and graceful relationships between the noblemen and women of the court. It was a colourful and decorative age which sometimes bordered on the effeminate. In the Asuka and Nara periods it had been difficult to draw a line between the culture of the continent and that of Japan. However, in the Heian, the culture was essentially Japanese in so far as it relied solely on native inspiration. The essentially Japanese aspects of Heian life are important but it is impossible to ignore the fact that Japan's isolation resulted in a culture which was somewhat inbred and artificial. Prolonged isolation led to a loss of vigour and to a preoccupation with trivialities which tended to degenerate into an over-refinement of taste and into sentimentality.

Women came to play an increasingly important part in this elegant, refined court life. Women of literary genius appeared like the author of the *Tale of Genji*. The feminine influence at the court encouraged the tendency to over-refinement and sentimentality.

The 'Japanization' of life had important consequences for the arts. The architecture of the Asuka and Nara periods had closely followed continental models but, during the Heian period, architects departed from this classical, grand, and symmetrical pattern. For instance the *Shinden Zukuri* style emerged, in which buildings were designed to fit into an irregularly laid-out garden and to merge into the landscape. Sculptors used wood almost exclusively instead of bronze, clay, and dry-lacquer; the artists thus turned to the material which was closest at hand. In general, the arts were gradually modified to suit Japanese taste and the Japanese way of life—particularly in so far as they were made to harmonize with the natural background.

The Early Heian period has left magnificent works which reflect Late T'ang Buddhist painting in the same way as, in the Nara period, Buddhist sculpture faithfully reflected the finest T'ang style. As the period progressed, Buddhist images lost their spiritual strength and became ephemeral reflections of imagined beauty.

E-makimono (scroll-paintings) were the most important development in the painting of the period. This form grew out of the pictorial illustrations to Buddhist sutras. The increased demand for this type of painting was partly due to the popularity of the romances written by the authoresses of the time. The form originated in China but it ideally satisfied the Japanese love of narrative and developed in a manner which is uniquely Japanese. E-makimono were particularly popular during the Heian and Kamakura periods when a number of masterpieces were painted.

The Kamakura Period 1185-1392

The effeminacy and sentimentality of the Heian court were swept away by a new class of fighting men who ruled the country through a Baku-fu (military government) with a Shōgun at its head. This new government which had seized power through force alone avoided setting up their headquarters at the old capital of Kyoto, the former centre of court-life, traditional customs, and learning. They established their capital in Kamakura some three hundred miles to the north-east. In contrast to the Heian period, the spirit of the régime was vigorous, masculine, and realistic in keeping with the militaristic nature of the new rulers. Their world was ruthless and their vision clear; their taste in the arts was essentially naturalistic. It was in complete contrast to the elegance, lyricism, and decorative ideals of the Fujiwara court.

Contacts with China were re-established; new influences entered the country from the Chinese Sung (A.D. 960–1280) and Yüan (A.D. 1280–1368) Dynasties. These two periods in China are remarkable for their spiritual qualities and their arts differed completely from those of the T'ang period. In Buddhism the influence of the Zen (Chinese: Ch'an) sect was paramount. Other sects had erected towering pagodas, which are monuments dedicated to the worship of relics, or beautiful Buddha Halls for the adoration of images. The Zen sect rejected both relic and image worship and substituted stern spiritual discipline. It taught that true religious experience should be sought in everyday life. This attitude profoundly influenced art. Whereas the other sects painted in splendid rich colours pictures of the glories of paradise where Buddhas and Bodhisattvas enjoyed an other-worldly happiness, the Zen sect produced severe drawings in black-and-white which showed such subjects as the rigours of Shakyamuni's life as an ascetic in the wilderness, or the self-discipline of Bodhidharma meditating for nine years before a cliff face. At other times the Zen artist would ignore altogether any reference to a Buddhist subject and simply draw a very simple scene taken from nature. By this he would suggest that the truth behind the universe resided in any such casually selected simple natural scene.

Allied with the fervent spiritual outlook of Zen was a powerful realistic mode of thought. The Zen adepts opposed the ideal world of the imagination. In their belief that wisdom and tranquillity of soul could only be found in a humble life amidst the more severe aspects of nature, the Zen followers aimed always at being as close as possible to nature. The spiritual aspect of this creed and the realism it encouraged agreed well with the emphasis on discipline and the keen observation of nature of the new Kamakura ruling class. This Buddhist outlook united with the masculine qualities of the fighting men to produce an art completely different from that of the Heian period. The desire for realism showed itself mainly in the development of a portrait art which was one of the most significant achievements of the Kamakura period. Japanese art had hitherto tended towards idealism, lyricism, and decoration. The strict realism of the Kamakura is a completely new departure. Both in painting and sculpture some superb portraits were created.

However, in other forms of art the new realism did not always produce such fortunate results. For instance, it tended to weaken the other-worldly expression of religious figures. To take another example, the *e-makimono* (scroll-paintings) gained in truth to nature and in accuracy of detail but they lost the poetic feeling which distinguishes the Heian period examples. The natural flow of Japanese lyricism was impeded and, as always with realism, a danger arose of art falling into the prosaic.

The greatest contribution which the new spirit made to art was in the field of *suiboku* or black-and-white ink painting. This had been imported from China during the Sung and Yüan Dynasties and has always been extremely popular in Japan. Hitherto the monopoly was held by *Yamato-e*, the polychromatic and highly decorative school of painting which had developed during the Heian period from the Chinese T'ang paintings introduced during the Nara period. The new *suiboku* style, which was completely different from *Yamato-e*, was a revolutionary introduction which has changed the whole pattern of Japanese painting. In the following Muromachi period it achieved its full Japanese expression.

The Muromachi Period 1392-1573

The new spirit born in the Kamakura period came to flower in the culture of the succeeding Muromachi period. Japan was still ruled by a class of fighting men but the Ashikaga *Shōguns* of the Muromachi period came to differ greatly from their Kamakura predecessors. For during the two hundred years this class had undisputed control of Japan, it had gradually adopted many of the qualities which distinguished the aristocratic rulers of previous periods. Prosperity and peace created conditions which fostered a life of leisure and enjoyment. With the government removed to Kyoto, the old capital of Heian times, the Ashikaga *Shōguns* rapidly became victims to its traditions, and adopted the way of life and the tastes of the old Kyoto nobility.

It is easy to understand how the Ashikaga *Shōguns*, preoccupied with the traditions and pleasures of Kyoto, came to surrender their effective power and prestige. Powerless to check the civil wars and general unrest which were the consequence of their loss of influence, they tended to retire from the active world of politics into a life of increasing decadence and aestheticism. Although Muromachi culture was, in a sense, a continuation of that of the Kamakura period, the whole of life looked as if it had become subject to an aesthetic code. In this sense the period is a landmark in the development of Japanese taste, and had far-reaching consequences.

Zen Buddhism became even more popular now than in the Kamakura period and it lies at the root of all the arts of the time. Henceforth it sometimes looked more like an expression of aesthetic taste than a severe disciplinary teaching. The most striking example of its new character is seen in the cult of tea. This widespread fashion can be called *Zen* spirituality adapted to art and social enjoyment. The cult was popular with *Shōguns* and commoners alike. In its original and purest manifestation it was what it purported to be—a form of *Zen* Buddhism which emphasized the importance of a simple, ascetic life. However, over the centuries it developed into little more than an aesthetic game with exaggerated and sophisticated rules which are the very reverse of those high and simple principles for which it once stood.

The homes of the fighting men and *Zen* priests of this period are distinguished by a new architectural feature called the *tokonoma*. This is a little alcove in a room where paintings and other precious objects were displayed and which formed the centre of its decoration. The tea room, another special architectural form, was created to satisfy the needs of the small parties at which the intellectual élite conversed and sipped tea. These architectural innovations—the *tokonoma*, the tea room and others were to have a great influence on art forms in later times. Thus in the sense that the lives of the Muromachi nobility were governed by taste, they resembled the Fujiwara aristocracy whose lives had been shaped by poetry and art. Both societies were ruled by aesthetic standards. The essential difference is that, whereas Heian period taste indulged in lavish use of colour, the *Zen* spirit of the Muromachi aristocracy encouraged the use of black-and-white ink painting, along with other characteristics of Sung and Yüan culture, and contacts were maintained with the Chinese Ming Dynasty (A.D. 1368-1644).

So there was much interest in all things Chinese but, broadly speaking, the Muromachi period was a great period of Japanese taste, when many specifically Japanese arts such as *Renga* poetry, the *Noh* play and the tea cult were firmly established. They greatly influenced the subsequent arts of Japan.

The Momoyama Period 1573-1615

Although this period lasted for only forty-two years, it was an extremely important formative period for Japanese art. Its very individual characteristics merit the usual practice of treating it as a separate period. It might be more accurate to regard it as a splendid introduction to the following Edo period.

By the end of the preceding period, when *Zen* had lost its purity and driving force, and the *Shōguns* their political power, the country was plunged into a period of civil wars which brought great suffering to the population.

The unrest and confusion were terminated by two outstanding military leaders, Nobunaga (died 1582) and his successor Hideyoshi (died 1598). They ruthlessly brought the warring factions under control and laid the foundations for the peace and prosperity of the long Edo period. To impress the feudal lords whom they controlled with the sense of their power and prestige, Nobunaga and Hideyoshi built massive castles and palaces which they decorated to suit their own flamboyant taste.

The demand for a lavish form of art was stimulated also by the wealthy merchant classes who had grown rich and powerful during the civil wars. As the power of the central government slowly diminished, the commoners found increasing opportunities for trade and commerce. During the previous régime some enterprising merchants had already begun to trade with foreign countries. Through their contacts abroad they not only amassed great wealth but also came into contact with new and stimulating ideas. During this period Japan made her first contacts with the west which were later fundamentally to influence her development.

In 1543 some Portuguese were shipwrecked on the island of Tanegashima and as a consequence western firearms first entered Japan, radically changing Japanese methods of warfare. The advent of the Christian missionaries was no less significant, for through them Japan gained her first real knowledge of western culture and civilization. Many Japanese became Catholic converts and churches were built in many places. For a time it looked as if Japan was about to make a completely new departure. However, Christianity soon came under suspicion and the Edo rulers banned it completely. Centuries were to elapse before western culture would be allowed to enter Japan again and introduce a new and powerful living force. It would be difficult to explain the freshness and vitality of Momoyama art without taking into account the impressions made on the Japanese by the western art which reached Japan during this half century.

The most representative works which show the new vigour and breadth of Momoyama art are the large screen-paintings used to decorate the castles and palaces of the time. Artists lavishly decorated them with gold and brilliant colour. The practice of using screens for interior decoration was, of course, not first invented in this period but the energetic spirit and heroic scale of the Momoyama period screens gives them a breadth and brilliance seen only rarely in Japanese art. The costumes and household objects used by the occupiers of these magnificent rooms were designed to match the brilliance of the screens and consequently the Momoyama period produced many superb works of applied and textile art.

Thus the splendour and impressiveness of the arts of the short Momoyama period were due in part to a reaction against the over-refinement of the preceding Muromachi culture, which was based on *Zen* spirituality, and also in part to various other positive influences which were later to usher in a new age.

The pacification and unification of Japan begun by Nobunaga and Hideyoshi was completed by Tokugawa-Ieyasu (1542–1616) who established the headquarters of his feudal governmen in Edo,

The Edo Period
1615-1867

the present-day Tokyo. His firmness and astute policy laid the foundations for the three hundred years of unbroken peace known as the Edo or Tokugawa period.

During the first two decades Japan remained open to Western influences as she had been during the Momoyama period. When the *Shōguns* began to suspect that the Christian missionaries harboured political ambitions, they ruthlessly suppressed Christianity and closed Japan to all contact with foreign countries. Complete isolation was the foundation-stone of the country's policy and it remained so until the end of the nineteenth century. The decision to make Japan into a hermit kingdom was all the more unfortunate in so far as Japan had just begun to experience the stimulus provided by contacts with other nations and was eager to make experiments in every field. Henceforth, the energies and inventiveness of the Japanese people were turned inwards with the inevitable consequence that Japan's development was inbred.

Meanwhile, outside Japan, these centuries saw a great expansion of trade and travel. Even the strict laws of the Edo government could not prevent the slow infiltration of western knowledge into Japan. The Japanese were hungry for such knowledge, and in one way or another western scientific and cultural ideas found their way into Japan, where they had a powerful influence on her art.

The bureaucratic system of government of the Tokugawa *Shōgunate* created an official position even for art. The Kano school of artists became accredited painters to the military government in Edo while the Tosa and Sumiyoshi schools of *Yamato-e* became official painters to the Imperial court in Kyoto. It seemed for a while as if these three schools would dominate the art world but they rapidly lost their vitality and their official positions became little more than empty titles. The true vitality of Tokugawa art is to be found in the art of the commoners.

The most interesting manifestation of this new art was, of course, the well-known *Ukiyo-e*. Figure painting had always been practised to some extent in Japanese art, but hitherto it was restricted to portraiture or to illustrations of historical narratives. The custom of seeking inspiration from the everyday pursuits of the common people which provide the subjects of *Ukiyo-e* was a completely new departure in the arts of the Momoyama and Early Edo periods. Previously a long and powerful tradition had always restricted the subject-matter of painting, and the realistic representation of the human form or genre painting inspired solely by considerations of beauty were not considered worthy subjects for a serious artist. It was not until the citizens of Edo and Kyoto began to demand an art form which suited their own simple and naïve tastes that true figure painting emerged. They were ignorant of or disinterested in the religious, historical, and literary themes of traditional painting and hence free from the pedantic approach which classical painting demanded. They wanted little more than charming representations of the world they saw around them. Such figure paintings began to appear from the Momoyama period onwards and flourished during the Edo period when the wealth and prosperity which the régime brought to Japan created a class of people with money to patronize such an art. Gradually they became so popular with less exalted classes of society that the supply could not meet the demand, and from the eighteenth century the technique of wood-block prints, popularly called *Ukiyo-e* prints, was developed and perfected to try to satisfy an insatiable public.

These prints have long been considered as trifles in Japan; in much the same way westerners would hardly treasure their picture post-cards. However, when they reached Europe in the nineteenth century they created a sensation and, as is well known, their instinctive and impressionistic approach to nature, their skill of line and subtle colouring strongly influenced a number of European artists.

Japanese wood-block prints are a specialized form of art now familiar to the western public. Collections in Europe and America are better than in Japan itself. We shall, therefore, omit them here and concentrate on the early hand-painted *Ukiyo-e* which preceded the colour-prints. These date back to the Momoyama and Early Edo periods, i.e. to the beginning of the seventeenth century when figure painting first began to appear on Japanese screens. They reflect the grand style of the Momoyama period and show a firm grasp of the human form and a masterly appreciation of decorative costume. The vigour of these early examples contrasts most strongly with the nervous and delicate line of the later *Ukiyo-e* prints. The sudden emergence in the Momoyama years of such large-scale and richly-coloured figure paintings may well be due to the influences entering Japan from the west.

Perhaps the most important artistic development during the Early Edo period was the rise of the Sōtatsu decorative school of painting. This was the product of the combined talents of the calligrapher Kōetsu and his relative and pupil the eminent painter Sōtatsu. These two remarkable artists passed their youth in the Momoyama period and deeply assimilated the splendour of its screens and decorative arts. In the Early Edo period they established a school based on *Yamato-e*, the most Japanese of all art forms, to which they added bold decorative elements. The movement they founded suited Japanese taste and gained great popularity. It influenced not only painting but also lacquer-work, pottery, and other branches of the applied arts throughout the Edo period. After Sōtatsu's time the finest period of this movement were the Genroku years (1688–1703) when Kōrin, the outstanding decorative painter of Edo times, and his no less famous brother, the potter Kenzan, took over the leadership of the movement.

The development of realistic painting was also of great importance during the Edo period. As we have previously mentioned, even the strict policies of the *Shōguns* were unable to exclude completely all knowledge of western sciences, particularly of the medical sciences. Japanese intellectuals gradually began to adopt a scientific approach to natural phenomena. Realism had never played such a large part in Japanese painting as it had in western art, but Japan could not escape the tendency which was sweeping the whole world to observe nature objectively. Ōkyo was the outstanding artistic representative of the movement to study nature in a scientific western manner but he was by no means the only artist to do so. Modern realism affected Japanese art in many ways and these will be discussed in their proper place.

It is typical of Japanese art that the popularity of realism created a reaction against it. A new *Bunjin-ga* (poet-painter) school in the Late Edo period opposed the popularity of realism. The *Bunjin-ga* ideal had its origins in the Chinese painting of the Yüan Dynasty and became extremely popular in China during the Ming and Ch'ing Dynasties. The theory behind it is that painting should above all reveal the exalted spirit of a cultured man. Poet-painters considered realistic representation of nature as suitable work only for craftsmen; art they felt should transcend such matters and be an expression of the spirit. The protagonists of anti-realism claimed to be the real supporters of the fundamental concepts of eastern art and they always assumed the duty of warning artists against losing sight of the true objects of art, to which they felt an undue emphasis on realism blinded them. The reaction can thus be seen as a reassertion of the basic artistic ideals of the orient.

The long years of feudal government had bred general discontent and the now powerful commoners were growing restive under an outdated military type of government. In a world where travel and communications were becoming increasingly easy it was no longer possible for Japan to continue her policy of strict isolation. The Meiji Restoration of 1868, which began a new age for Japan, was born of a widespread dissatisfaction with the decaying feudal government. The Tokugawa government was overthrown and replaced by a government headed by the Emperor and backed by democratic institutions. Japan opened her doors to the world and a new and vigorous age began.

The natural death and dissolution of the Tokugawa *Shōgunate* allowed a flood of western culture to enter the country where the Japanese eagerly welcomed and absorbed it. The life of the nation seemed to pulse with new energy and the whole atmosphere was imbued with enthusiasm. Japan began to assimilate western culture with the appetite of an adolescent. The awakening of Japan and the development of the country along western lines had much in common with the years following the introduction of Chinese civilization in the Asuka and Nara periods. The same intensity and zeal for knowledge characterized the period. If at times the emulation appeared excessive, the fault came not so much from

*The New Japan
1868*

a desire to imitate as from an over-eagerness to learn. The excesses of the Asuka and Nara periods had been gradually corrected in the Heian period as Chinese culture was better understood and assimilated; the same has been true of the modern age. With the emergence of modern Japan after the Meiji Restoration, Japanese life, scholarship, art, and letters experienced many changes. Here we shall be concerned only with significant developments in the arts.

Artists eagerly adopted western techniques of oil painting and sculpture in stone or plaster. The study of anatomy and 'scientific' perspective, hitherto unknown in Japan, became integral parts in the curricula of art schools. The custom of holding exhibitions as a means of consciously stimulating interest in art was introduced. This had hardly existed in old Japan where the appreciation of art meant the leisurely perusal of a single work of art at a time. There had been occasions when many paintings had been assembled and their relative merits discussed, but the typical western custom of regular art shows intended to foster interest was new to Japan. For good or ill the new influences have been considerable.

It seemed for a time as if Japan was to be completely swamped by western culture but, in fact, she was going through a process which, as we have seen, was by no means new to her. A period of reflection and reassessment was bound to follow. Slowly, judgment and selection based on a national taste and tradition asserted themselves and many forms of western art were explored in an effort to discover the artistic modes best suited to express the Japanese artistic spirit.

With this study of western art, the Japanese also began to see their own arts from a different view-point. Mention must be made here of an American scholar, Ernest Fenollosa. He came to Japan in these early years to teach European philosophy at a newly-established Japanese university. He immediately recognized the qualities of Japanese art at a time when most Japanese were ready to disown their past. Through Fenollosa, the Japanese began once more to appreciate the values of their own arts and took steps to preserve their treasures from harm. Thus, fortunately for Japan, the new art movements were well grounded in the appreciation of past traditions. The process is one which continues to this day.

The new art of the Meiji period is usually ignored and most histories of Japanese art end with the art of *Ukiyo-e*. In the opinion of the author this new art reflecting the sudden development of a nation after a period of long seclusion has a breadth and vitality which are more significant than the decadent arts of the Late Edo period.

It reflects the enthusiasm and creative power of a people quickened into activity after centuries of suppression under a feudal régime. Time must pass before it can be adequately assessed but meanwhile a few of the most outstanding works of these decades are here reproduced in order that the work of this significant period may not go unnoticed.

III JAPANESE SCULPTURE

The inherent plastic sense of the Japanese already showed itself in the *haniwa* clay figures produced in the primitive period of Japanese art at the dawn of the historical age. In the period preceding that which produced the *haniwa*, i.e. in the Archaeological or *Jōmon* period, clay figurines were produced which were crude representations of the human body. These figurines probably had some religious or magical meaning; their fantastic but very powerful forms appeal to something beyond our conscious understanding; they speak, as it were, to the residual 'primitive' in us all. For this reason, these prehistoric figurines have been highly appreciated in recent years. They have much in common with the sources of inspiration of some modern art trends. However, as explained in the introduction, the relationship between the makers of this art and the present Japanese race is by no means firmly established. Two examples of the art are here reproduced (Plates 1, 2).

However, the doubts concerning the identity of the makers of the *Jōmon* statuettes do not apply to the people who developed the *Yayoi* culture which followed. This is certainly the precursor of all subsequent Japanese civilization. It developed directly into the Tumulus period and thence into the historical periods. The *haniwa* (Plates, 3, 4, 5) of the Tumulus period reflect the Japanese plastic sense as yet untouched by influences from the highly developed continental civilization. They were mostly used as ornaments on or around the huge grave mounds and, according to legend, they were intended to take the place of faithful retainers who were once buried with their dead masters. The simplicity and innocence which inspired these early modellers gives their products the charm found in the art of children.

The greatest output of *haniwa* was in the fifth century. Japan does seem to have had some contact with China from the mid-Han period (about the beginning of the Christian era) but the influx of continental civilization was at that time negligible and the great period of the introduction of plastic art from China was still to come. There is hardly any Chinese influence in the *haniwa*.

They were intended merely as grave decorations and casually modelled with little attention to technical perfection. Their simplicity and naïvety give them their peculiar attraction. The traditional emphasis on technique and theory has tended to overwhelm modern artists, who have often turned back to primitive art for inspiration and escape. The recent popularity of *haniwa* both in Japan and abroad is just another sign of this modern tendency. It is very similar to the vogue in Europe for Etruscan art which had long been considered as crude and unpolished and completely overshadowed by the brilliance of Greek sculpture.

For all their charm, *haniwa* are simple products of a primitive stage in the artistic development of Japan. Continental culture introduced in the sixth century was so obviously superior in every way that it had no difficulty in establishing itself there. The Buddhist sculpture which entered Japan was refined in material and technique and extremely sensitive in its portrayal of spiritual qualities. The assimilation of this culture was the basis for all later developments of Japanese culture. The influx of Buddhist art during this first period was little less than a complete cultural migration. The learned monks, who in the fervour of their faith came to Japan to proselytize the new country, were accompanied by skilled artists. They brought with them fine Buddhist paintings and sculptures as well as the materials and the knowledge of techniques required to produce them in Japan. The impact of this new civilization completely overwhelmed what opposition there was and won over the Japanese by its obvious superiority. Buddhism became a State religion and Buddhist art was paramount.

The building of temples and the manufacture of images for them occupied the first stage of this new movement. During the Asuka and Nara periods every type of continental Buddhist sculpture was introduced and eagerly studied. In many other countries Buddhism over the centuries suffered persecutions but in Japan the Buddhist tradition has remained unbroken. Consequently many of these earliest Buddhist images have survived to this day. The care which the Japanese have shown in preserving them is in marked contrast to the Chinese attitude. In China numerous wars and attacks on the faith have resulted in the destruction of the vast majority of works of ancient Buddhist art. The only exceptions are the cave-temples in distant places and the stone carvings they contain. Thus, the Buddhist sculptures of the Asuka and Nara periods provide evidence not only of a golden age of Japanese sculpture but also of the splendour of Korean art during the Three Kingdoms period and of the art of China throughout the Six Dynasties, the Sui and the T'ang periods. All students of Korean and Chinese art are indebted to the care with which the Japanese have preserved their Buddhist art over so many centuries.

The sculptures of the Asuka and Nara periods are in bronze, clay, dry-lacquer, and wood. These materials were also popular on the continent. Those who study Chinese sculpture sometimes gain the false idea that early Chinese sculpture was mainly in stone, for the most important specimens of Chinese sculpture on display in museums throughout the world are stone images recovered from such sites as the cave-temples of Yün-kang, Lung-mên, and T'ien-lung Shan. The idea of establishing cave-temples in remote places or on steep cliff-sides where man could dwell apart from the distractions of life in contemplation of the religious images around him, came from India through Central Asia to China, and when the persecutions of Buddhism resulted in the destruction of the statues in the capital cities which were made of more fragile materials, the images in the distant cave-temples were often overlooked. Stone also has the virtue of being less perishable in its own right.

The records testify that in the great days of Buddhist art from the Six Dynasties to the T'ang Dynasty, artists in China often used bronze, clay, dry-lacquer, and wood. This same range of materials was also exploited by the Japanese Buddhist sculptors of the Asuka and Nara periods. It is of interest to trace the steps by which Japanese artists assimilated the continental sculptural techniques and gradually adapted them to suit native conditions. They gradually modified the foreign materials and techniques until they found those most suited to Japan. The material which best fitted the Japanese artistic genius was wood.

Let us first consider bronze. This material was prized both for its durability and beauty. Chinese artists frequently used it. However, bronze has an intrinsic value as metal and such statues in time of war or economic stress were often melted down. Thus, little remains of the large Chinese bronze statues. In Japan, bronze images from the Asuka and later periods have been splendidly preserved to provide evidence of the skilled technique of the bronze casters of the time. They also give an idea of the grandeur of Chinese bronze sculpture in these early centuries.

The *Shaka Triad* in the Hōryū-ji (Plate 6) takes first place among the early masterpieces of Japanese bronze sculpture. It is the work of a certain artist called Tori, the descendant of a line of sculptors who emigrated from China to the Korean Kingdom of Kudara (Korean: Paekche) and thence to Japan. The triad was cast in the year A.D. 623 and follows the style of the Six Dynasties which had its beginnings in the Northern Wei Dynasty. It is the largest and most important of the works in this material and style. A number of bronzes in the Six Dynasties style have survived but, with the exception of a few from Siragi (Korean: Silla) in the Three Kingdoms period of Korea, the majority of the continental bronzes are small gilt-bronze statuettes. The histories refer to many large and imposing bronze statues existing on the continent in these early days but it is almost impossible to find any, and their past glory can only be imagined from such works as this *Shaka Triad* and from other large bronze works of the Japanese Asuka period. The halo of the triad originally had a surround of flying angels now lost. They must have added considerably to its appearance. One can see such haloes surrounded by flying angels on Chinese gilt-bronze statuettes of the Six Dynasties period.

During the Asuka and Nara periods also many small gilt-bronze figures were made. These are generally called in Japanese *Suikobutsu* (Suiko Statuettes). They include the famous *Shijū Hattai Butsu* (Forty-Eight Buddhist Statuettes) which are of outstanding quality. These formerly belonged to the Hōryū-ji, but were presented to the Imperial household and became Imperial treasures. The group was probably originally used as images for private worship by the Imperial family or by other powerful court families. Their execution, workmanship, and spiritual expression place them far above the bronze statuettes of the Six Dynasties in China and those of the Three Kingdoms period in Korea, which are highly prized by the world's museums. They show not only the high quality of Japanese workmanship but also the splendour of the continental prototypes on which they were based.

The world-famous *Yakushi Triad* (Plates 15, 16) of the Yakushi-ji Temple was cast in the Early Nara period. These images follow the style of the Sui or Early T'ang Dynasty and, in my opinion, they are without doubt the most beautiful bronze statues in the world. Their magnificent design, powerful modelling and divine dignity of expression attest a faultless standard of workmanship and a great depth of inspiration. Over the centuries the bronze has acquired a deep black lustre which shines with a mysterious light and gives the statues an indefinable other-worldly beauty. Such marvels of the caster's craft and sculptor's inspiration provide evidence of the heights to which artists of the cultural circle of the T'ang could reach.

To turn now to clay sculpture, we find that in this medium also fine Chinese examples are equally rare. The statues at Tonko (Chinese: *Tun-huang*) in the remote west of China are made of clay but they are comparatively rough provincial workmanship. Again, we know from the records that clay was a popular material for such religious sculptures but, due to its fragility and its perishable nature, the Chinese have been unable to preserve their early examples. In Japan, however, a number of these fine statues were preserved with great care in the ancient temples. These, too, provide valuable evidence of a Chinese art which is now almost entirely lost in the country of its origin. Perhaps the most striking qualities of these statues are the manner in which the soft-textured clay has been skilfully used for the harmonious modelling of body and drapery and the beauty of the rich colours which decorate the surfaces. Such artistic achievements provide some evidence to support the reputation of the T'ang sculptor Yokeishi (Chinese: *Yang Hui-chih*) whose fame for clay statuary and reliefs rivalled that of Wu Tao-tzu for wall painting.

The Buddhist sculptures of the Nara period include many in dry-lacquer. Why was this unusual and difficult technique so popular in the Nara period? My own theory is as follows: Dry-lacquer statues are hollow inside. The surface modelling is obtained by applying a paste made from the dust of incense-wood mixed with lacquer on layers of hemp which have also been impregnated with lacquer. This process gave the statues great durability, although being hollow they were comparatively light and easily transportable. Thus, they were very suitable for use as travelling images in the Buddhist festivals of the T'ang Dynasty. They were carried on carts through the streets in order that all the people might pay homage to them. This ease of transportation made them ideal for export to Japan. The Japanese, for their part, in their enthusiasm for all things Chinese and also because most of the images arriving from China were in dry-lacquer, may well have thought in view of the inherent conservatism of religious art that it was the principal medium for Buddhist sculpture. This view would be substantiated by the existence in Japan of some Chinese dry-lacquer statues and I believe that such examples as the Four Guardians of the Taema-ji can be interpreted as such.

Among the many dry-lacquer statues of the Nara period are such masterpieces as the *Kannon* in the Shōrin-ji Temple (Plate 19) which ably demonstrates the skill with which the Japanese had mastered this difficult technique. Very few dry-lacquer statues have been preserved in China, and American museums own a few authentic examples.

Wood was a popular material for sculpture in China from early times but again examples are very rare. The Chinese wood sculptures in American and European museums seldom date to such early times as the T'ang Dynasty. As with dry-lacquer, the lightness and durability of wood sculptures facilitated their transport to Japan where the sculptors studied and copied their forms and techniques. A considerable number of early Chinese wood sculptures exist in Japan and some of them have impressive records to prove that they arrived at an early date. A great opportunity awaits the scholar who will make a new study of ancient Chinese wood sculpture, basing his researches on the remnants of Chinese works preserved in Japan and on the Japanese works which faithfully followed the Chinese models. Hitherto, unfortunately, little attention has been paid to this interesting field of study and our knowledge is still very confused.

Japan is a mountainous country surrounded by semi-tropical seas and consequently produces a plentiful supply of wood suitable for carving. With the advent of Buddhism, artists naturally turned to a material which lay close at hand and was a suitable plastic medium. During the Asuka period, Japan had still not made direct contact with China and all Buddhist sculpture was imported via Korea. A number of old wooden statues in Japan are said to be of Korean origin but, on examining them more closely, we find that they are made from the wood of the camphor tree which, according to the botanists, did not grow in Korea at that time. Their continental style suggests that they must have been fashioned in Japan on Korean models. Wood-carving suited the Japanese taste. A number of outstanding Asuka sculptures based on Korean models are reproduced to illustrate the trends of the period.

The *Kannon* of the Dream Hall in the Hōryū-ji (Plates 7, 8) is considered so sacred that it is still kept almost secret and is generally hidden from the common gaze. This statue must be given pride of place among the works of the Asuka period. The style closely follows that of the gilt-bronze sculpture of the Six Dynasties period but has here been interpreted in wood. The sharp metallic lines of its prototype are softened by the texture of the material and through it achieve a unique beauty.

Perhaps the best-loved wood statue of the Asuka period is the renowned *Kudara Kannon* (Plate 9). Legend ascribes it to the Kingdom of Kudara (Korean: Paekche) but it, too, must have been made in Japan as it is of camphor wood. Stylistically, in its distinctive grace, it shows a Japanese artistic characteristic. The tall, ethereal figure, elegant and serene, seems to embody the spiritual aspirations of mankind and recalls the figures of apostles in Early Gothic sculpture.

A popular form of divinity was the seated, meditating Bodhisattva probably intended to represent *Miroku* (Sanskrit: *Maitreya*) and also sometimes identified with the young Prince Shaka, before his complete enlightenment. The popularity of these statues followed the continental fashion. The most outstanding are the famous *Kōryū-ji Miroku* (Plates 12, 13) and the *Chūgū-ji* figure (Plate 11). These representations, sometimes understood to be portraits of the young Prince Shaka, who fled to the mountains to meditate on the sorrows of mankind, have a quality which is at once tender and beautiful. The softness and pliancy possible in wood-carving give perfect expression to these half-human, half-divine figures of Suiko sculpture.

We have seen how in the Asuka and Nara periods almost all the techniques in common practice on the continent were introduced into Japan. Good stone, however, is rare in our volcanic islands and some of the other materials, though faithfully used by the Japanese in emulation of Chinese models, neither suited the native taste and talent nor were readily available. Thus natural conditions and the character of the Japanese themselves modified sculptural techniques. Bronze and dry-lacquer were very costly and slowly fell out of use. The humid Japanese climate was inimical to clay. Thus, during the last years of the Nara period, wood-carving took the place of works in the other materials. With the complete Japanization of culture during the Heian period, wood sculpture came into its own and reached unsurpassed heights.

Sculpture in wood, however, demands not only a plentiful supply of suitable wood but also good steel for the carvers' tools. The Japanese had already developed an advanced technique of tempering steel and, therefore, Japanese sculptors had all the necessary technical conditions for raising Japanese sculpture in wood to heights unexcelled throughout the world.

However, wood is not a material which is easy to carve. Unlike marble, it does not come in an even quality throughout; its grain and unevenness create their own difficulties. In its natural state it cracks very easily. The texture is uneven and the grain is more beautiful in some sections than in others. This renders some parts of a block easier to carve than others. During the Asuka, Nara, and Early Heian periods sculptors used the early method of carving statues from a single block of wood. However, these large pieces were not only clumsy in shape but had a strong tendency to split. Gradually the Japanese developed a technique whereby they hollowed the core of the wood to prevent cracking. Later, during the Heian period, many methods were evolved for the actual choice and handling of wood. These were known as the *Kidori* (method for choosing the suitable parts of the wood) and the *Kiyose* (method for assembling the various parts of wood). The invention of these special techniques is attributed to the sculptor Jōchō who carved the *Amida* figure in the Hōō-dō (Phoenix Hall) at Uji (Plate 37). The primitive system of using a single block of wood was here replaced by joining various smaller pieces together to form the basic structure of the body. This enabled sculptors to choose the best wood with the finest grain which would facilitate the carving of the body surface. The core was made hollow to prevent cracks. These techniques are of Japanese origin. The complicated nature of wood-carving took sculpture into the realms of craftsmanship rather than art and led to an emphasis on neat, smooth, somewhat superficial carving of beautiful wood rather than on the plastic qualities of the body which are the main interest of pure sculpture.

The 'assembled-block' technique has the inherent danger that it can easily degenerate into mere manipulative skill and superficiality. These dangers were already present in Heian work in the medium. The Early Heian period produced the finest wood sculpture even though the technique had not developed into the involved art it later became. At this time the single block method was still in use and occasional experiments were being made with hollowing out the inner core. These works occasionally cracked but they are noble figures with all the volume and grandeur of the continental styles emulated during the Nara period. Through the bold and decisive use of the chisel they show that unique plastic beauty possible in wood-carving. The Japanese carvers with a bold and free use of their knives achieved a highly plastic line and mass which were lost in the later neat and dexterous carving of the surface.

We must now turn to the development of sculpture in the various periods. The Asuka sculptures reflect the simplicity of approach and the innocence of expression of the Chinese styles of the Six Dynasties, yet at the same time they embody the characteristic Japanese qualities of beauty and tenderness. However, their beauty is of the spirit and they are surely some of the finest art the world has produced. The *Suiko Statuettes* (Plate 10), for example, are as yet untouched by any realistic conception of the human body. In their concern for purity and holiness of spirit the artists reflect the fantasy of innocent children's dreams. In type and expression they may recall to western readers the goddesses and maidens from the Acropolis in Athens which date to the sixth century B.C. They also remind one of some products of the Romanesque and Early Gothic periods, in particular the tall figures of saints at the entrance to Chartres Cathedral.

With the Nara period, we seem to enter a different world. The full influence of the arts of the Chinese Sui (589–618) and T'ang (618–907) Dynasties is reflected in the Nara masterpieces. These mature human figures show a magnificence combined with deep spirit and power. They express a perfect unity of body and spirit. But in marked contrast to the ideal and imaginative nature of Asuka art, their beauty is of *this* world. The dignity and majesty of the Nara period was once typified by the Great Buddha of Nara, intended to represent the ruler of the universe and the protector of the State. This colossal statue is entirely gone. In its present form it has suffered badly from clumsy restoration. However, the fine incised line drawings of the Buddhist universe on the lotus petals of its huge pedestal (all that remains of the original), provide some idea of its former splendour. The same qualities of expression and modelling are seen in other images of the period, in the *Kannon* of the Shōrin-ji (Plate 19), the *Kannon* of the Hokke-dō of the Tōdai-ji (Plate 18), and the *Nikkō* and *Gakkō* (Plate 23) figures in the same building. In addition to these calm, meditative figures intended to impress their worshippers by a tranquil nobility which surpasses mere beauty, the Nara period produced some fierce figures of militant guardians of the Buddhist faith. Outstanding among these are the *Four Guardians* of the Kaidan-in (Plate 26) and the *Shitsukongōshin* of the Hokke-dō (Plate 24). The creation of such images presents great difficulty for an artist. They must reflect not only a heavenly wrath intended to awe and terrify a wrong-doer, but also an underlying capacity for infinite compassion and a deep love of humanity. Also notable products of this period are a number of outstanding portrait sculptures, such as that of Gyōshin in the Dream Hall of the Hōryū-ji and Ganjin (Chinese: Chien Chên) in the Tōshōdai-ji (Plate 28).

The sculpture of the Early Heian or Kōnin period was mainly in wood. The dominant religious influence was that of esoteric Buddhism newly introduced from the Late T'ang Dynasty. The images it inspired show a strange combination of sensuous beauty and mystical depth which is of great interest in the history of religious art. They sought to create their effect by an overpowering sense of mystical ecstasy. Their almost hypnotic quality brings esoteric Buddhism close to magic. A typical example of this tendency is the *Kannon* in the Hokke-ji Temple (Plates 32, 33) which, according to tradition, was carved in the image of Empress Kōmyō, the 'Empress Radiant', by a foreign priest who was overwhelmed by her beauty. Alas, the charming tradition cannot be true since the statue belongs to a period much later than that of the Empress. Nevertheless, the voluptuous body and sensuous face produce a fascination which is partly an intoxication of the senses and partly religious ecstasy. The same sensuous beauty is seen in its most highly developed form in the *Nyōirin Kannon*, the most sacred image of the Kanshin-ji Temple (Plate 34).

Some of the finest examples of the newly-mastered wood-carving techniques in this period are housed in the Muro-ji Temple, a stronghold of the esoteric faith built deep in the mountains of Muro. The *Shaka* is outstanding for the flow of its drapery, of which the fluency and harmony of line compare with the best Japanese line drawing. The deep, free chisel cuts are masterly. However, as previously mentioned, technique became more important than inspiration and Late Heian sculpture, though superficially beautiful, lacked the basic strength of earlier works. In the same way, the Buddhist faith itself, under the feminine influences of the time, degenerated into sentimentality. An increasingly decorative approach to religious sculpture was the natural product of an artificial age. But before the art declined completely, it produced the *Amida* by Jōchō in the Phoenix Hall at Uji (Plate 37), showing the inspiration and technique at their best. Even the Buddhist images made during this climax of Heian culture are intended to be little more than integral parts of the brilliant background of an aristocratic world. They are far removed from the atmosphere of the Nara and Early Heian periods in which Buddhist images, in either their august or terrifying manifestations, were intended as spiritual supports of the nation. The same process is seen in Buddhist paintings of the Heian period.

One of the most interesting aspects of Heian sculpture was the beginning of the custom of making Shintō images. Shintōism, the native religion of the Japanese people, is closely connected with ancestor worship, and the shrines themselves retain architectural elements derived from primitive Japanese dwellings. However, until this time, a belief that the gods were too holy to be represented in visual form had prevented the creation of a popular imagery. So the oldest Shintō shrines are just empty buildings, where the gods are supposed to dwell. The introduction of Buddhism popularized image worship and stimulated the Shintō believers to create their own icons. According to Shintō beliefs, the gods are ancestors of the Japanese people, and consequently the images were made in the form of Japanese men and women in national dress. They contrast strongly with the idealized representations of foreign deities which constitute the Buddhist pantheon. Despite their genre quality, Shintō worshippers demanded a supernatural dignity in their statues. Plate 35, a goddess of the Natsuno-o shrine, shows the unique qualities of this essentially Japanese form of sculpture.

The forces which had reduced carving to a mere exercise in decoration were strongly countered in the Kamakura period. The reaction took the form of a powerful realism. During the civil wars which brought the Heian period to an inglorious end, the forces of the Heike clan had destroyed the Great Buddha at Nara as well as a number of other important Buddhist temples in the old capital. A great enthusiasm for their restoration inspired the Kamakura years. It naturally led to a reappraisal and a fresh study of the Nara masterpieces. The Kamakura period was, in fact, the 'Renaissance' of the great art of ancient Nara. The reaction against the decadent beauty of Heian times and the study of old works produced great sculptors like Unkei and initiated a new and brilliant epoch in the history of Japanese sculpture. The most characteristic works of the period are the two colossal *Kongō Rikishi* in the Nandaimon Gate of the Tōdai-ji Temple (Plate 39). Bulging muscles and fierce expressions give these statues, the largest in wood in the world, a most impressive effect. They were made by the joint efforts of the two most talented sculptors of the period, Unkei and Kaikei.

The Kamakura period injected new life into Buddhist sculpture but the revival was to be short-lived. From the Kamakura period onwards, the *Zen* sects took over the leadership of Buddhism. *Zen* had been introduced from China in the Sung and Yüan Dynasties and gained great popularity with the fighting men of Kamakura. However, its beliefs dispensed with image worship and the demand for these religious icons rapidly diminished. The ascendancy of the *Zen* sect marked the end of a long line of Buddhist sculpture.

The realism which inspired Kamakura art was another contributory factor in the decline of Buddhist imagery. Chinese Sung art, which lay at the root of the products of the Kamakura period, was characterized by a strong spirituality which sprang from the philosophical nature of Chinese culture especially during the Sung centuries. Yet at the same time Sung art had a strong realistic tendency. This realism was not always conducive to the creation of fine Buddhist images which should be conceived as idealized spiritual beings. Any emphasis on realism detracts from their divine qualities and brings them too close to the everyday world. An instance of the realistic tendency can be seen in the custom of inserting eyes made of rock-crystal. This may have been derived from Sung models and indeed it produced a very life-like effect. It served the art of portraiture very effectively, but it hardly increased the idealistic and spiritual qualities of Buddhist images. The new realism may have been effective in figures like *Kongō Rikishi*, which required energetic and realistic representations but, generally speaking, it is doubtful if the trend contributed anything of value to the spiritual power of Buddhist images.

The finest sculptures of the Kamakura period were undoubtedly the portraits. Realism is a vital factor in this field of art and the Kamakura period gave it a wide scope. It had long been the custom for Buddhist temples to carve portraits of great priests, in particular of their respective founders. In the Kamakura period many masterpieces of this type were produced, notably the *Mūchaku* and *Seshin* of the Kōfuku-ji Temple (Plate 41). The vogue for *Nise-e* (likeness paintings) is a feature of the pictorial arts of the period to which we shall return later. It is interesting to mention here that the fashion created a group of professional portrait painters. The art of portraiture was not restricted to likenesses of Buddhist priests but was developed to embrace a much wider field, particularly in the representation of lay persons.

Plate 1
JŌMON FIGURINE
Jōmon Period. 4th to 3rd Century B.C.
Clay. Height 10 in.
Excavated in Yamanashi-ken, Central Japan
Tokyo National Museum

The smallness of this figurine—it is only 10 inches in height—hides its monumental qualities. It is simply moulded of clay with a stamped decoration on the shoulders which are also burnt brown. The features are powerfully represented by deep incisions. No sex is indicated in this very early figure, and it is impossible to determine its meaning. Familiar as we are with Neolithic and primitive art—and with their echoes in modern western art—this figure has a singular appeal.

Plate 2
FEMALE FIGURE OF
JŌMON TYPE
Jōmon Period. Between 2nd and
1st Century B.C.
Clay. Height 15 in.
Collection Mr Echigoya, Aomori-ken

This outstanding and most typical
example of the earliest Japanese prehistoric sculpture was excavated in
Kamegaoka, Aomori-ken, in the
northern part of Japan. It is of more
definite human proportions and a
female figure is obviously intended.
One leg and the mouth are broken.
The modelling is heavier, the decoration more involved. Nevertheless,
there is no diminution in strength. It
reflects a powerful imagination and is
the product of considerable technical
skill. It remains an open question
whether these early figurines which
show a plastic sense so different from
that of the Japanese in the historical period can be linked to the art
of historic Japan. More research is
necessary and many gaps in our knowledge remain to be filled.

Plate 3
HANIWA: FALCONER
Kōfun Period. 6th Century A.D.
Clay. Height 30 in.
Collection Mr Matsubara, Tokyo

The Jōmon period was followed in about 200 B.C. by the Yayoi period. The styles of objects from these two periods differ greatly and scholars by no means agree that they are products of the same race. After the Yayoi period, it is quite clear that the same people occupied Japan without a break, gradually developing their own artistic style and sensibility over the centuries.

The Kōfun (Tumulus) period followed the Yayoi with overlapping in places and links up with the historic period. Emperors and nobles were buried in huge tumuli, often surrounded by moats. In early times in China it was the custom to bury servants with the dead. This custom of immolation seems to have existed also in Japan. According to tradition, a wise man at the court advocated the abolition of the custom and *haniwa* figures were created to keep the dead company. Much can be learned of the customs and dress of these early people from the *haniwa*—of their houses, boats and animals, their pastimes and social structure. Indeed these clay figures are perhaps the earliest and purest manifestation of the plastic talents of the Japanese people before they received any great influence from outside the country. Their simple modelling and direct expression make an immediate appeal to the artistic sense of modern man.

Plate 4
HANIWA: FEMALE HEAD
Kōfun Period. 5th Century A.D.
Clay. Height 6½ in.
Collection Mr Matsubara, Tokyo

This woman's head has become one of the best-known examples of *haniwa* art. The modelling is of the very simplest, the features being indicated in only the barest manner; a simple headdress crowns the head. Yet, despite its brevity of means, the expression has all the poignancy which we have come to associate with this unusual art form.

Plate 5
HANIWA: WARRIOR IN ARMOUR
Kōfun Period. 6th Century A.D.
Clay. Height 25 in.
Collection Mr Negishi, Saitama-ken

This figure of a warrior in helmet and armour was excavated near Tokyo. Although still in *haniwa* style its sculptural qualities are more advanced. It is more naturalistic in its modelling and proportions. It is understandable that, having reached such an advanced stage with only their own native traditions on which to build, the Japanese were both ready and able to assimilate the flood of Chinese art about to reach them.

Plate 6
SHAKA TRIAD
By Tori Busshi. Asuka Period. Dated the equivalent of A.D. 623
Gilt-bronze. Height (central figure) 46 in.
Hōryū-ji, Nara-ken

This Buddha triad is the main devotional object in the Kondō (Golden Hall) of the ancient Hōryū-ji Monastery. According to a contemporary inscription engraved on the back of the halo, it was made by a sculptor named Tori in March of the year A.D. 623. At this time Prince Shōtoku, the great protector of the faith, was ill. His Princess together with other followers offered up prayers for the Prince's recovery and the statue was made. The large halo behind the Buddha was originally decorated with cast bronze figures of flying angels surrounding it.

This triad is the earliest and certainly the most important Japanese sculpture of the Asuka period. It was modelled on a continental prototype, and broadly speaking, is in the style of the Chinese Northern Wei Dynasty (386–418). However, this powerful style entered Japan via the Southern Dynasty of Liang in China and via the Korean Kingdom of Kudara (Paekche) and the group shows influences from the arts of those countries through which it passed. Many gilt-bronze sculptures in the Northern Wei style have survived but none match the Tori Triad either in size or importance.

7

Plates 7 and 8
KANNON
Artist Unknown. Asuka Period. Early 7th Century A.D.
Wood, gilded. Height 78 in.
Yumedono, Hōryū-ji, Nara-ken

This statue is housed in the Yumedono (Dream Hall), another building of the complex which makes up the Hōryū-ji Monastery. Here, according to tradition, in the company of visiting angels and saints, Prince Shōtoku used to retire for meditation. Ancient records claim that the statue is actually a portrait of the Prince. A thirteenth-century document states that even then it was already considered a very sacred object and that for a long period it had not been shown. Ernest Fenellosa, the American pioneer in the study of Japanese art, was in 1878 the first scholar to see it after many centuries. He found it swathed in long wrappings and covered with the accumulation of centuries of dust. It was perhaps due to such precautions that this valuable work has been preserved to this day in its perfect condition. Although the statue is of wood, the carving is so sharp and undamaged that it gives the impression of being cast in bronze—an impression increased by the rich dark colour which age has imparted to the gold flakes, covering the whole surface of the statue. Indeed, the continental model for this statue may well have been in metal and the Japanese sculptor faithfully transposed it into wood, a material which has always suited his talents better.

Plate 9
KANNON
Artist Unknown. Asuka Period. Early 7th Century A.D.
Wood, painted. Height 83 in.
Museum, Hōryū-ji, Nara-ken

This unique work is known as the Kudara *Kannon*. Kudara was the contemporary Korean Kingdom of Paekche and, as the name suggests, some scholars consider that it was either actually made in Korea and then imported to Japan or made by one of the many Korean workers who emigrated to Japan. Many such Koreans found ready employment in Japan where they satisfied the demands for Buddhist art among the newly converted Japanese. Despite the existence of small bronze figures of similar style in Korean collections, two features in particular strongly suggest its native Japanese origin. First, the camphor wood from which it is carved did not grow in Korea at that time but was a popular wood for Japanese carvers. Second, and less tangible evidence is the harmonious flow of its curved lines along the tall figure and the combination of beauty and sadness in the face, which are typical Japanese artistic qualities. An exact copy of this exquisite figure, which was specially made to the order of Laurence Binyon when he visited Japan, is on permanent exhibition in the British Museum.

10

Plate 10
MIROKU
Artist Unknown
Asuka Period. Dated the equivalent of A.D. 606
Gilt-bronze. Height 16½ in.
Tokyo National Museum

This exquisite statuette represents *Miroku* (Sanskrit: *Maitreya*), the Buddha of the Future. He is shown in the form of a young Bodhisattva in meditation. It is perhaps the best of the famous 'Forty-eight Statuettes' presented by the Hōryū-ji to the Imperial Household and now housed in the Tokyo National Museum.

The figure has particular importance in that the inscription around the pedestal gives its date of manufacture as the fourteenth year of the reign of Empress Suiko, i.e. A.D. 606. This is one of many masterpieces inspired by the cult of *Miroku* which flourished throughout East Asia at this time. Simplicity of form, solemnity of expression and religious conviction unite in this statuette to produce a work of incomparable beauty.

This statue is one of the best known and the most popular of all Japanese
sculptures. In the Chūgū-ji Nunnery and by the general public it is known
as the *Nyōirin Kannon* (Kannon with the gem and wheel which satisfy all
desires), a name given to the statue after the introduction of esoteric Buddhism
into Japan. However it is undoubtedly intended to represent *Miroku*, the
Buddha of the Future. The Asuka or, as it is more popularly known, the
Suiko style is distinguished by its severity and by the simplicity of its clear-cut
lines. These qualities are shown by works of art in metal and stone, the
materials most used for Buddhist sculpture in Korea and China from the
third century onwards. The stone and metal techniques were closely studied
in Japan and found their reflection in Japanese products. However, wood
suitable for carving is plentiful in Japan whereas good stone for sculpture is
almost completely lacking. Wooden sculpture became increasingly popular
and the transfer of the severe continental styles into this softer material led to
a relaxation and softening of expression.

The *Chūgū-ji Miroku* combines all the spirituality of its continental
prototypes with the beauty and appeal to the sentiments which are typical of
Japanese wood-carving.

Plates 12 and 13
MIROKU
Artist Unknown. Late Asuka Period. Middle of 7th Century A.D.
Wood. Height 48 in.
Kōryū-ji, Kyoto

According to the traditions of the temple which houses this *Miroku* statue, it was made in Korea. Indeed its style owes much to the art of Korea and the pine wood from which it was made is plentiful in Korea. Unlike the *Kannon* in Plate 8, we cannot derive evidence for its Japanese manufacture from the material alone. Nevertheless, the soft sweetness of expression and the immediate appeal which it makes to the senses suggest that it may well have been made in Japan towards the end of the Asuka period. At that time the broader and fuller style of the Early Nara period, itself the reflection of Chinese Sui-T'ang art, was first making its impression on the arts of Japan. The whole sculptural approach of this statue, notably in the face and drapery, seems to presage the arrival of an age with a new artistic spirit.

13

55

This elegant bronze figure retains the linear style of the Asuka period—notably in the drapery which hangs in rhythmical folds on the slender body. But the head, with its fullness of feature and its hint of human energy, betrays the sentiments of a new age with a different standard of beauty. As we have seen, the Asuka period was dominated by the continental influences which emanated from the Six Dynasties period in China. During the Nara period the achievements of the unified power and grandeur of Sui and T'ang China reached and overwhelmed Japan. The Early Nara period is the dawn of this brilliant epoch in Japan and this figure with its simple appeal to the worshipper reflects the spiritual and artistic adolescence through which Japan was passing.

Plates 15 and 16
YAKUSHI
Artist Unknown. Early Nara Period. Late 7th Century A.D.
Gilt-bronze. Height (figure only) 101 in.
Yakushi-ji, Nara

Many historians claim that this portrayal of the Buddha of Healing is the
world's finest bronze sculpture. The Yakushi-ji Triad, of which this is the
central figure, housed in its ancient site, produces an unforgettable aesthetic
impression. The date of its manufacture is disputed. According to one theory
the triad was made in A.D. 697 when the original Yakushi-ji was built, and
subsequently removed to its present site when the new temple was constructed
in 710. Other scholars claim that the triad was cast in 710, at the same time
as the building of the new temple.

Such works of art attest to the importance of the Early Nara period in the
history of Japanese art. With these large-scale masterpieces Japanese art came
of age. Histories of far eastern sculpture tell of the splendour of the bronze
figures produced in China during the Sui and T'ang Dynasties but in the
country of their origin the most important examples have all disappeared
over the centuries. The Yakushi-ji statues, therefore, provide the most valuable
evidence bearing on the art not only of Japan but also of China, whence the
inspiration came. They have even been called the most important surviving
evidence of the high standard of T'ang-type sculpture.

Plate 17
KANNON
Artist Unknown. Early Nara Period. Late 7th Century A.D.
Gilt-bronze. Height (figure only) 75 in.
Tōin-dō, Yakushi-ji, Nara

This figure, another outstanding bronze statue in the Yakushi-ji, shows the combination of skilled modelling and technical assurance achieved by the craftsmen of the period. The strong Indian influences indicate the form in which Buddhist art first entered China where it was often faithfully copied, and how it was then carried over to the newly converted Japanese outpost of the faith. The skill demanded by the casting of this figure provided excellent experience for the Japanese craftsmen for the creation of the colossal Daibutsu, the Buddha figure of the Tōdai-ji which, even without its pedestal, is just over 64 feet in height and the largest bronze sculpture in the world.

Plate 18
KANNON—detail
Artist Unknown
Nara Period. 8th Century A.D.
Dry-lacquer. Height 141 in.
Hokke-dō, Tōdai-ji, Nara

This eight-handed *Kannon*, an out-standing product of the dry-lacquer technique, is the principal devotional object in the Hokke-dō. This Nara period building, which is part of the Tōdai-ji, is filled with noble works of the eighth century; but this central figure dominates the austere atmosphere which they create. The form of this statue with its four pairs of arms is unusual for the Nara period. It seems to foreshadow the more esoteric religion which began to flourish in the suc-ceeding Heian period. The added ornamentation is as impressive as the modelling of the powerful figure and its elegant draperies. The large crown is worked in gilt-bronze open-work and hung with jewels of precious and semi-precious stones such as jade, rock-crystals, pearls and coloured glass beads. In its front is an exquisite silver Amida Buddha, as symbol of *Kannon*. The luxury of these ornaments is an indication of the veneration paid to this Deity of Compassion at the time.

Plate 19
KANNON—detail
Artist Unknown
Nara Period. 8th Century A.D.
Dry-lacquer. Height 82 in.
Shōrin-ji, Nara-ken

In my opinion, this eleven-headed *Kannon*, imposing of figure and digni-fied of feature, is one of the greatest masterpieces in the whole of Japanese sculpture. It is one that can challenge the achievements of any nation. It was made at the richest moment of Nara culture, at a time when Japan was fast absorbing the achievements of the T'ang Dynasty in its finest hour. A strong tendency has always existed among Japanese artists to be absorbed in the execution of details and thereby sometimes to overlook the plastic qualities of the whole figure. The Shōrin-ji *Kannon* is a notable exception. This magnificent work is unfortunately now housed in a very small niche where it is impossible to take a photo-graph which does justice to its overall beauty. The half-length reproduction, all that is possible in the circumstances, detracts from the impression it creates when seen in full length and from a distance.

Plate 20
ASHURA—detail
Artist Unknown. Nara Period. Made in A.D. 734
Dry-lacquer. Height 60 in.
Kōfuku-ji, Nara

This statue of *Ashura* (Sanskrit: *Asura*) is one of what was once a group of eight figures belonging to the Kōfuku-ji. Most of them, in an almost miraculous way considering their fragility, have survived the centuries to provide some of the most valuable evidence we possess of the plastic arts of the Nara period. According to tradition, they were made by an Indian sculptor named Mondōshi who worked in Japan. There is little to substantiate this traditional attribution. Nevertheless the dry-lacquer technique used for the group differs somewhat from that of other works of the period in the same medium. Apart from the different construction inside these hollow statues, the proportions of the figures and in particular the shapes of the heads and the cast of feature differ considerably from the work of Japanese sculptors. One theory suggests that the statues were made in China under strong Indian

influence; another that they were made in Japan but by one of the many foreign workmen or their descendants who had come to the country. Of interest in this respect is some recent documentary research which has brought to light the existence of a sculptor who was working in the Kōfuku-ji at that time named Manpuku the form of whose name suggests that he was Chinese. In my opinion, these striking images were made in Japan with the help of foreign artists or their descendants. This would explain the somewhat exotic appearance and expression which add to their very great artistic appeal.

The figure of *Ashura* is represented with three faces and six arms. He is a spirit of spirits, a supernatural being who achieves victory over the enemies of Buddhism not only by strength but also by charm.

Plate 21
BIBAKARA—detail
Artist Unknown
Nara Period. Made in A.D. 734
Dry-lacquer. Height 60 in.
Kōfuku-ji, Nara

This statue of *Bibakara* belongs to the same group of Eight Guardians of Buddhism as the *Ashura* figure in the previous plate. Whereas the features of *Ashura* are youthful and the expression mild, this figure is notable for the power displayed in the severe lines of the face.

Plate 22
FURUNA
Artist Unknown
Nara Period. Made in A.D. 734
Dry-lacquer. Height 59 in.
Kōfuku-ji, Nara

In addition to the Eight Guardians of Buddhism the Kōfuku-ji also housed another group of dry-lacquer sculptures, the Ten Disciples of *Shaka* (Sanskrit: *Sakyamuni*). The figure illustrated is of *Furuna* (Sanskrit: *Purna*), a priest famed for his wisdom and virtue. It is perhaps the finest of this group. The two groups originally surrounded the central image of the Buddha which was housed in the Saikondō building (Western Golden Hall) of the Kōfuku-ji. They formed, as it were, a silent audience to his sermon. Like the Eight Guardians, the Ten Disciples were traditionally attributed to the Indian sculptor Mondōshi (see Plate 20).

Plate 23
GAKKŌ—detail
Artist Unknown
Nara Period. 8th Century A.D.
Clay, coloured. Height 82 in.
Hokke-dō, Tōdai-ji, Nara

The deity intended by this statue has not been identified. It is sometimes called *Gakkō* (Sanskrit: *Candra-prabba*) and sometimes *Bonten* (Sanskrit: *Brahma*). It is now housed in the Hokke-dō building of the Tōdai-ji but it was originally intended for another unidentified temple and only later moved to the Hokke-dō.

The T'ang Dynasty in China was the great age of clay statuary. However, apart from the rough provincial work at Tun Huang, nothing of this great art has survived to support the claims made for it in the histories. The fragile material did not survive the periods of violence and the persecutions of the faith through which China passed, notably in the ninth century. The Japanese clay figures, however, were based directly on the metropolitan art of T'ang China and have survived the centuries in the comparative safety of the Nara temples. They provide that evidence of the glories of T'ang art which has mostly disappeared in the country of its origin.

Plate 24
SHITSUKONGŌSHIN
Artist Unknown. Nara Period. 8th Century A.D.
Clay, coloured. Height (figure only) 68½ in.
Hokke-dō, Tōdai-ji, Nara

Shitsukongōshin, one of the Guardian Deities of Buddhism, is always depicted in terrifying form. According to the temple tradition, this painted clay statue was made in 733 and from the awe which it inspired, it gained a reputation for miraculous powers. Popular legend claims that during a great civil war the deity changed itself into a hornet and subdued the rebels.

Even today this statue belongs to the select number of sacred images considered too holy for constant display. Its sealed shrine is opened only one day a year after solemn ceremonies—a reverence which has done much to preserve the rich colouring of the figure.

Plates 25 and 26
KŌMOKUTEN
Artist Unknown. Nara Period. 8th Century A.D.
Clay, coloured. Height 64 in.
Kaidan-in, Todai-ji, Nara

Although Guardian Deities sometimes stand alone within a temple, they are usually placed round a central Buddha figure. Their menacing attitudes and terrifying graces often form a perfect foil to the central figure whose calm and contemplative features radiate the Buddhist qualities of peace and mercy. A superb example of such an arrangement is found in the Twelve Guardian Kings, who form a circle round the Yakushi Buddha in the Shin-yakushi-ji, Nara.

Outstanding as sculpture among the Nara period Guardians are the *Shitsukongōshin* in Plate 24 and this figure of *Kōmokuten*, one of a set of four housed in the Kaidan-in building of the Tōdai-ji Temple. Whereas the previous deity seems to hurl himself in fury upon the wrongdoer, his face transfigured by a howl of rage, Kōmokuten's violence is latent but his power to impress is none the less for its restraint. To those who would harm the faith, it reflects the calm before the storm of his wrath.

Plate 27
ROSHANA-BUTSU
Artist Unknown. Nara Period. Made in A.D. 759
Dry-lacquer. Height (figure only) 134 in.
Tōshōdai-ji, Nara

The *Roshana-butsu* (Sanskrit: *Vairocana*) is the Buddha whose light is shed throughout the universe. This figure reflects one of the sagas of Japanese Buddhism. The Emperor, anxious to obtain the best possible instruction in the faith, invited the eminent Chinese priest Ganjin (Chinese: Chien Chên) to come to Japan. He, in his turn, felt that missionary work among the Japanese was his vocation. The priest and a handful of followers reached the islands only after a journey which lasted ten years, suffering set-backs and even shipwreck on the way. Among the survivors were a number of artists. Their arrival thus influenced not only the faith but also its art. The Emperor gave Ganjin a large tract of land in Nara on which to build the Tōshōdai-ji, one of the noblest architectural monuments to the Buddhist faith in Japan. The architecture of the Tōshōdai-ji undoubtedly owes something to the artists who accompanied Ganjin for it has an individual character which is the outcome of a union of Chinese and Japanese spirit and technique. Its Kondō (Golden Hall) is perhaps the finest ancient wooden building in the Far East. The Roshana Buddha it houses shows the qualities of power and grandeur befitting a Buddha conceived as the centre of the universe.

Plate 28
PORTRAIT OF GANJIN—detail
Artist Unknown
Nara Period. Made after A.D. 763
Dry-lacquer, coloured. Height 32 in.
Kaisandō, Tōshōdai-ji, Nara

This portrait of Ganjin is most out-standing among the portrait sculptures of Japan. It must have been made soon after his death in 763. During the priest's efforts to reach Japan he lost the sight of his eyes—according to tradition by the sea-water to which he was exposed during storm and ship-wreck. The sensitive modelling of this figure reveals a man calm of soul, resigned to misfortune and at the same time tireless in his missionary zeal. It is a work which has always held a special place in the affections of the Japanese and Bashō, the great *haiku* poet, composed a poem in its praise which has been celebrated ever since.

Plate 29
TORSO OF A BUDDHIST
STATUE—detail
Artist Unknown
Early Heian Period. About A.D. 800
Wood. Height 53 in.
Tōshōdai-ji, Nara

The huge Tōshōdai-ji Temple, built in the Late Nara period, was a thriving centre of Buddhist art as well as Buddhist faith. The large number of sculptures it possesses, many of them unfortunately damaged, is evidence of the tremendous artistic activity centred on the temple during the Late Nara—Early Heian period. The torso illustrated is an outstanding example of one of the damaged works. Many of the statues in the Tōshōdai-ji were made by the Chinese who accompanied Ganjin and they are mainly either of wood or in the dry-lacquer technique. The wooden figures are of particular interest for the light they throw on the transitional period between the Late Nara and Early Heian period. These decades were marked by the increasing popularity of wood which finally completely displaced dry-lacquer as the basic material for sculpture. The leadership of the Tōshōdai-ji in the artistic developments of the time must have been most influential. This torso, with its sharply carved drapery over a heavily built body, retains the plastic qualities of Nara style but to this is added the linear treatment in the carving of wood which is characteristic of the Early Heian period.

Plate 30
NICHIRA
Artist Unknown
Early Heian Period
Early 9th Century A.D.
Wood. Height 57 in.
Tachibana-dera, Nara-ken

That this statue is popularly known as *Nichira* comes from an interesting tradition associated with it. The temple authorities claim that it is a portrait of the Korean priest *Nichira* who came to Japan during the Asuka period. He once met Prince Shōtoku and, overwhelmed by his holy appearance, immediately knelt down before him in admiration. However, the correct interpretation is that the statue is of the Bodhisattva *Jizō* (Sanskrit: *Ksitigarbha*). Since this Bodhisattva is usually represented in the form of a priest, and since also it is housed in the Tachibana-dera, a temple founded by Prince Shōtoku, it has understandably been identified with the Korean priest.

The statue, with its well-proportioned body and smooth flow of drapery, is one of the finest wooden figures in Japan.

Plate 31
PORTRAIT OF PRIEST RŌBEN
Artist Unknown
Early Heian Period
Early 9th Century A.D.
Wood, coloured. Height 36 in.
Kaisando, Tōdai-ji, Nara

The priest *Rōben* here portrayed was the founder of the Tōdai-ji, the largest Buddhist temple in Japan. With its colossal Buddha as its main devotional figure, it has maintained a central position in the development of Japanese Buddhism. Rōben died in 773 towards the end of the Nara period. However, this statue shows unmistakable characteristics of the succeeding Early Heian period and, therefore, it cannot have been carved during his lifetime. As a portrait it is a remarkable feat of memory; its life-like qualities demonstrate the high realism which the artists of the time could achieve in wood sculpture.

Plates 32 and 33
KANNON
Artist Unknown. Early Heian Period. Early 9th Century A.D.
Wood. Height 39 in.
Hokke-ji (Nunnery), Nara

The traditions concerning many ancient Japanese sculptures are often more charming than the facts. One such tradition concerning the statue illustrated tells of an Indian sculptor who came to Japan. Deeply impressed by the beauty of Kōmyō Kōgyō (A.D. 700–760), (called 'Empress Radiant' because of her incomparable beauty), he carved this *Kannon* in her image. Stylistically, however, it belongs to a later age than that in which the famed Empress lived. The once important nunnery which houses this image was founded by the Empress herself but it is no longer as flourishing as in previous centuries. The occasional visitor finds this exquisite figure standing alone in a large dark hall attended with great devotion by the nuns. The temptation to believe the old tradition is almost irresistible.

Plate 34
NYŌIRIN KANNON
Artist Unknown. Early Heian Period. Early 9th Century A.D.
Wood, coloured. Height (figure only) 43 in.
Kanshin-ji, Osaka-fu

This famous image, which is the main Buddha of the Kanshin-ji Temple, must have been made at the same time as the foundation of the temple, i.e. between A.D. 824 and 827. Like the figure in Plate 21 it enjoys the status of 'sacred secrecy' and even today permission to see it can only be obtained from the temple authorities with the greatest difficulty. This no doubt explains how, after nearly eleven hundred years, the rich yet elegant colouring retains its extraordinary freshness. It is an image in the full spirit of esoteric Buddhism. The aim of esoteric art may be defined as the tangible realization in art of the intangible and transcendental. This six-armed *Nyōirin Kannon* is seated quietly in meditation, with eyes half-opened as if in a day-dream. Of course, obviously this is quite impossible, but to see this statue by candle-light within its closed shrine plays strange tricks on the eyes and the mind. The limbs seem to move in mysterious rhythms, pulsating with warm blood beneath the white skin of the plump arms. It produces an unforgettable mixture of sensuous enchantment and spiritual mystery. In my opinion it marks the climax of esoteric art in Japan.

Plate 35
SHINTŌ GODDESS
Artist Unknown
Early Heian Period. 9th Century A.D.
Wood, coloured. Height 34 in.
Natsuno-o Jinsha, Kyoto

In the original native religion of Japan, Shintōism, there were no sacred images which the adherents might worship. But from the beginning of the Early Heian period the Shintō shrines adopted the Buddhist custom, and began to make images which might appeal to the public. By this means they hoped to counter the popularity of the Buddhist icons. This is one of the earliest examples of such images. Most Shintō deities are conceived as mythical ancestors of the Japanese race and are therefore represented as human beings but in the costumes of the various periods in which they were made. At the same time the artists tried through gesture or expression to give them a god-like dignity. To this combination is due their character and their charm.

Plate 36
SHINTŌ GODDESS NAKATSUHIME
Artist Unknown
Early Heian Period
Late 9th Century A.D.
Wood, coloured. Height 14 in.
Yakushi-ji, Nara

After the restoration of the Emperor Meiji in 1868 a law was passed to separate Shintō shrines from Buddhist temples. This put an end to a custom which had grown up in earlier times whereby the two were sometimes closely connected. The Hachiman Shrine, for instance, adjoins the Yakushi-ji Temple compound even today. This shrine was first built between 889 and 897 and the statues it contains must be approximately contemporaneous. The Japanese predilection for rich ornament is seen in the elegant skirt worn by this very human goddess Nakatsuhime. Although still in the Early Heian period, the delicate design of birds and flowers painted in gold on a plain white background foreshadows the decorative taste of the Later Heian and indicates the trends to be followed in its art.

36

Plate 37
AMIDA
By Jōchō (Died A.D. 1057). Heian Period
Wood, gilded. Height (figure only) 112 in.
Byōdō-in, Kyoto

The graceful Byōdō-in, the most elegant of all Japanese temples, is situated amidst beautiful natural surroundings in the valley of the River Uji. It was completed in 1053 and is popularly known as the Hōōdō (Phoenix Hall) from the gilt-bronze phoenix which surmounts the roof. Originally the villa of the Prime Minister Yorimichi, it was later turned into a small temple dedicated to the worship of the *Amida Buddha*. Its architecture is intended to realize on earth the splendour of a Buddhist paradise, the home of the blessed. The golden Buddha figure, which is its main object of worship, is an authentic work by a sculptor named Jōchō, the perfector of the technique of wood-carving and the greatest artist of the Heian period. In its combination of nobility and gentleness, it reflects the ideals of Heian aristocratic taste. The expression differs from that of older statues in that it is directed downwards towards the worshipper and, softened by an understanding of his problems, is in sympathy with him. This ideal of intimacy, direct and close, between the Buddha and his worshippers was created by Japanese art in this period and it reflects the sentimental vein in the faith of Heian society, an attitude often attributed to the powerful influence of women in court life. Perhaps this same influence accounts for the rich decorative treatment of the surroundings of the *Amida* figure as seen particularly in the ornate halo and canopy. Jōchō and his pupils carved also the numerous celestial musicians on the halo and the walls of the hall. The vision of the Buddha which this great artist created influenced the work of all subsequent sculptors.

Kichijō-ten is a Buddhist goddess who has the power to bestow on her devotees happiness in this world. She is always portrayed as a handsome girl dressed in splendid robes and richly ornamented—the symbol of wealth and worldly happiness. Buddhist iconography defines her appearance as a girl of fifteen years of age with clear white skin and heavily bejewelled. Such a goddess figure was always sympathetically treated by Buddhist artists, but particularly so in the Late Heian period when the real power resided in the hands of the noble and pleasure-loving ladies of the court. Indeed, were it not for the Buddhist attributes, this statue might be mistaken for the portrait of a beautiful woman of the time. A document concerning the temple gives its date as 1212 which year falls into the beginning of the Kamakura period. Nevertheless it is the most perfect illustration of Late Heian taste.

Plate 39
KONGŌ RIKISHI
By Unkei (active 1176–1223) and Kaikei
Kamakura Period. Dated A.D. 1203
Wood. Height 333 in.
Nandai-mon, Tōdai-ji, Nara

Kongō Rikishi, or Warrior Guardians of the Faith, are frequently placed on each side of the main gate of a temple. These menacing figures, intended to deter the evil-doer, provided Buddhist sculptors with perfect opportunities for the display of their skill in the representation of movement and muscular violence. The type was particularly popular in the Kamakura period when the more vigorous taste of the newly triumphant *samurai* or warrior class replaced the feminity and gentleness of the Heian nobility. The huge pair in the Nandai-mon of the Tōdai-ji Temple are the finest *Kongō Rikishi* in Japan and incidentally the world's largest wooden sculptures. Twenty artists under the direction of Unkei and Kaikei began their commission for these statues on 24 July 1203 and completed them in only seventy-two days—a remarkable feat of inspired virtuosity and technique.

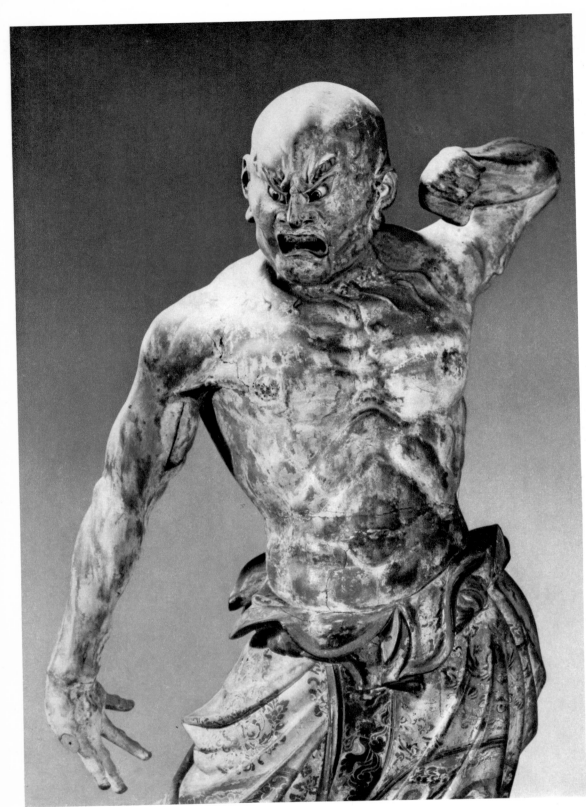

Plate 40
KONGŌ RIKISHI—detail
By Jōkei
Kamakura Period. Dated A.D. 1190–1198
Wood, highly coloured. Height 64 in.
Kōfuku-ji, Nara

A document found inside this statue records the fact that it was made by the eminent sculptor Jōkei during the Kenkyū era (1190–1198). However, at this time there were three artists with the same name and it is difficult to determine which of the three made this work. Although it is on a much smaller scale than the previous figure (Plate 39), the realism is even more exaggerated in detail. The veins swelled with anger, the bulging muscles and the surface of the skin which looks wet with perspiration emphasize the very life-like representation. It cannot of course match the former *Kongō Rikishi* in plastic conception and technique on a grand scale, but the qualities of carving and its power of expression entitle it to a high place among the masterpieces of Japanese sculpture.

Plate 41
MŪCHAKU—detail
By Unkei and his followers
Kamakura Period. Early 13th Century A.D.
Wood, coloured. Height 75 in.
Hokuen-dō, Kōfuku-ji, Nara

Sufficient documentary evidence exists to prove that the numerous Buddhist statues in the Hokuen-dō building of the Kōfuku-ji Temple were made *c.* 1208 by Unkei and his sons and pupils. Each member of this most famous school of Japanese sculpture made one statue under the general direction of Unkei. The subject of the large sculpture illustrated is Muchaku, an Indian priest who founded the *Hossō* sect of Buddhism. This sect entered Japan in the Asuka period and was particularly popular during the Nara centuries. The Kōfuku-ji Temple was the great Nara centre of the *Hossō* sect and provided a fitting setting for these idealized portraits. Realism is the dominating theme of Kamakura art and these over-life-sized statues are certainly its finest expression. Yet for all their idealism, it is inconceivable that Unkei in creating them could have dispensed with models. They could spring neither from the imagination alone nor from dry iconographical drawings. The features show no Indian characteristics; the Japanese sculptor of the Kamakura period had probably never even seen an Indian. Realism in art is the enemy of the spiritual and supernatural. From the Kamakura period truth to nature became the guiding principle of sculpture and the great days of the plastic Buddhist arts of Japan were numbered.

Plate 42
TENTŌKI
By Kōben. Kamakura Period
Made in A.D. 1215
Wood, coloured. Height 30 in.
Kōfuku-ji, Nara

This lantern-bearing goblin is one of a pair in the Kōfuku-ji Temple. An inscription found inside its companion piece records that they were carved in 1215 by Kōben, the third son of Unkei. From the time of Unkei, the technique available to sculptors was so complete that no problem of representation was too great for them. Even the humour this figure shows seems to flow with effortless virtuosity from the chisels of the Kamakura artists.

IV JAPANESE PAINTING

Painting is the art which, more than any other, including sculpture, has always provided the best medium for the expression of Japanese sensibilities. The reasons for this are difficult to determine. It may be largely due to the picturesque nature of Japan itself where the landscape at times seems almost to create the impression of a bright, decorative pattern. At other times its humid atmosphere envelops the countryside in a silvery mist which dissolves mountains, forests, and trees into nuances of grey and in which the shadows and outlines are always changing. The artistic genius of the Japanese finds its most natural expression in painting. In sculpture, except for those periods when Japan was in close contact with China and engaged in the earnest assimilation of continental styles, her plastic sense tended to lose a three-dimensional quality and to fall into frontality and flatness. The sculpture of the Heian period when Japan was intent on the Japanization of her cultural life shows this tendency most clearly.

However, Japanese painters, always show a freedom and ease which reflects the artists' complete independence and confidence in their powers. Of course, the materials and basic techniques again came from China. Water-colours and ink on paper or silk are fundamental methods that have been employed in Japan for twelve hundred years and are still very much alive. They have given Japanese painting characteristics which distinguish it from the rest of the world's painting. Much of its beauty can be attributed to the unique combination of individual national character, materials, and techniques.

Basically two techniques predominate—first, painting in water-colours and second, painting in *sumi* (Chinese ink), which produces all its effects purely in black and white and in intermediate nuances of grey. Painting in colour started in the Nara period with the introduction of the colourful Buddhist paintings of the T'ang Dynasty, from which the Japanese imitated both their materials and technique. During the Heian period this type of painting was used in Japan for large-scale Buddhist paintings. From these gradually developed a secular art with a distinctly Japanese character which is distinguished by the name *Yamato-e* or quite simply 'Japanese painting'. It became extremely popular and has always remained the main current of Japanese painting.

It is important here to dwell on the nature of these water-colours in more detail. The westerner immediately thinks of water-colours as British water-colours. These, however, are quite different from the water-colours of the east. Water is indeed used as a solvent, but the colours are much more akin to *tempera*, more correctly speaking to the *tempera a secco* of the early Italian Renaissance. It is interesting to observe how the similarity of material has even resulted in a similarity of feeling and expression. The art of wall-painting provides an excellent example. In the east, as in Italy, the ground is prepared with a white plaster and the colours applied on it have an opaque quality which is produced by the white with which they are mixed. Unlike oil painting, these tempera-like colours dry quickly and tend to produce forms which emphasize line and particularly outline. When applied to silk or paper the same linear emphasis prevails. Line thus plays a most important part in eastern water-colour painting in contrast to western oil painting which stresses tone and chiaroscuro. The mixture of opaque white with colours produces a distinctive soft and hazy effect. This is quite different from the brilliance and transparent clarity of oils. Thus, painting in the east tends to be delicate, subdued, and decorative in colour. The similarities between the early Italian and the eastern modes struck me forcibly when, in 1921, I first saw Quattrocento paintings in the original. The polychromatic decorative effects and the nuances of colour of painters like Masolino, Fra Angelico, and Piero della Francesca and the emphasis on line and rhythm in the works of Simone Martini and Botticelli are certainly the result of their training in tempera, a very different technique from oils. They are so close to eastern art, and particularly to Japanese art, that I felt when I first stood before them that they might well have been painted by and for Japanese.

When I returned to Japan after my first stay in Italy, I revisited the Hōryū-ji to see the famous eighth-century frescoes (some years later to be so tragically destroyed by fire) and also saw other great paintings of the Early Heian period. My express intention was to compare them with the great Italian masters which for some years had been my daily study in Florence and elsewhere. I was deeply struck by the affinities of Japanese painting and that of the Italian Quattrocento. This impression has been shared by many Japanese who visited Italy and by many Italians who came to Japan.

To turn to the other great mode of Japanese painting which is in ink. This form, sometimes called *suiboku*, was introduced from China during the Sung and Yüan Dynasties after the Kamakura régime had restored diplomatic relations with the mainland. The ink is a medium capable of an infinite range from the palest tones of grey to the deepest black. Unlike the T'ang polychromatic style, it relies for its effects on the skilful use of the brush. The strength of the brush provides the vitality of the outlines, the nuances of tone and the chiaroscuro which produces the atmosphere. Ink (Japanese: *sumi*; Chinese: *mo*) was invented in China in very ancient times and has always been the principal material of calligraphy. In painting it was mainly restricted in early times to outlines. The early Chinese paintings of which we have definite evidence, dating from the Han Dynasty (206 B.C.–A.D. 220) onwards, were all finished in colour. This practice continued through the Six Dynasties, the Sui Dynasty, and until about the mid-T'ang period when, according to tradition, the genius of Wu Tao-tzu effected a technical revolution. This famed artist was a great master of brushwork and the superb bravura of his brush gave a new significance to ink-drawing, although most paintings were still in colour. We do not know how far Wu Tao-tzu was, in fact, responsible for this revolution but we can say that from about the mid-T'ang period, ink-drawing played an increasingly important part in painting. Finally in the Sung Dynasty painting entirely in ink—called in Japanese *suiboku* or *sumi*-painting—became definitely established. During the Sung Dynasty, when Chinese culture took a strong spiritual turn, pure ink painting became the best mode of expression for ideas. The two fundamental modes of eastern painting were thus established in the Sung period—the polychrome style dating from ancient times and the new ink style.

It is important also to remember the importance of calligraphy in the development of ink painting during the Sung Dynasty. From ancient times the Chinese have considered calligraphy the most vital means whereby a man might express his personality. The spiritual qualities of Sung culture reinforced this idea, and encouraged a hitherto unknown free and vigorous style. The greater freedom of the brush may be due in part to a change in its shape which took place towards the end of the T'ang period. The hairs of the brush were thenceforth made much longer, giving it a greater flexibility and hence, more freedom and power of expression. The new vitality and freedom of Sung calligraphy in its turn had a powerful influence on the development of ink painting which was based on the expressive line of Sung calligraphy and the infinite gradations of tone possible with ink.

Ink painting developed greatly throughout the Sung and the succeeding Yüan periods. It was introduced into Japan in the thirteenth century together with *Zen* Buddhism, the most spiritual of all the interpretations of Buddhism. It was no coincidence that the two came together for they were very akin in spirit. *Zen* priests often turned to ink painting as a means of purging their souls of base thoughts. It is significant that both entered Japan during the Kamakura era, when a warrior class had overthrown the old aristocratic government and established an administration based on force. The simple, strict outlook of the Kamakura fighting men was in sympathy with ink painting, and the political shift of power from the Heian aristocracy to the Kamakura *samurai* was paralleled by a decline in the popularity of the colourful decorative art of the lyrical *Yamato-e* in favour of the expressive spirituality of ink painting. In contrast to *Yamato-e* (Japanese style), the new style was often referred to as *Kara-e* or *Kanga* which can be translated quite literally as 'Chinese painting'. We shall have more to say of this later in this outline of the history of Japanese art.

Despite the power of ink painting, *Yamato-e* never entirely disappeared. The two styles co-existed. Sometimes artists mixed the two to produce interesting combinations. The two contrasting styles reflect conflicting qualities in the character of the Japanese landscape—bright and beautiful in the sunlight, grey and desolate in the rain and snow. They also reflect the Japanese temperament which is a combination of the gay and grave, the cheerful and the melancholy. The history of Japanese painting can be seen as the interaction of these two traditions which are deeply rooted in the nature of the country and its people.

1 Buddhist Painting

In the first centuries following the introduction of Buddhism, although sculpture was the dominant art form, Buddhist painting was not neglected. One of the most important relics of the Asuka period is the painting on the pedestal of the Tamamushi Shrine in the Hōryū-ji Monastery. In the same way that the study of Japanese sculpture can provide vital information regarding continental work which is now lost, so also some of the early paintings preserved in Japan are most valuable for an understanding of very early Chinese painting. The lacquer pictures on this famous shrine are in the style used in China during the Six Dynasties period and then modified by their transit through Korea. Of even greater interest is the fact that they retain traces of Chinese Han Dynasty painting styles of which otherwise so little remains. It is difficult to say whether the preservation of these early styles is due to an inherent conservatism in Buddhist painting or to the time-lag involved in their journey to Japan.

Realism is quite unknown in such ancient paintings. However, its absence does not detract in any way from their effectiveness as illustrations to Buddhist legends. One side of the Tamamushi pedestal shows the story of how Prince Shaka, in a former life, sacrificed himself to a tigress (Plate 44). It tells how he once met a starving tigress and her cubs, and out of compassion for all living creatures offered his own body to feed her. The Prince is shown three times at three different stages in the action in the same picture, this providing a continuous composition. It is interesting to see in this earliest surviving Japanese painting the same predilection for continuous narrative which was to reappear so effectively in the e-makimono of later times.

Paintings inspired by direct contact with China are less numerous than the sculptures but they are of great interest. No words can express the tragedy to art of the loss by fire in 1949 of the Hōryū-ji frescoes. They were the outstanding examples of Buddhist painting in Japan and among the greatest art treasures of the world. Chinese T'ang Dynasty frescoes, according to the histories, were some of the finest products of an altogether brilliant age. However, as the result of persecution of Buddhism in A.D. 845, most of these paintings were destroyed. The Hōryū-ji wall-paintings represented metropolitan T'ang art at its best. They were of a higher artistic quality than the provincial Tun-huang paintings, the only other remnants of this great art.

The eagerness with which Japan welcomed, studied, and emulated the T'ang paintings makes it extremely difficult to distinguish between Chinese and early Japanese works. The *Hokke-dō Konpon Mandara* (Sanskrit: *Mandala*) (Plate 47) in the Museum of Fine Arts, Boston, is an outstanding example of this difficulty. The museum labels it 'Chinese, T'ang Dynasty'. However, it came from the Tōdai-ji in Nara and is painted on hemp (or a hemp-like weave of rough silk). We know that this type of material was occasionally used in Japan during the Nara period but there is no evidence of such a material being used in China during this time. This provides evidence for its Japanese manufacture. The many precious objects preserved in the Imperial Depository known as the Shōsō-in, which was established in the Nara period, are all in T'ang style and previously historians thought that they were of Chinese manufacture brought to Japan at that time. Recent studies have revealed that a considerable proportion of the Shōsō-in objects were made in Japan from indigenous materials. These studies have shown that the actual materials of which an object is made often provide clues to place of origin which cannot be obtained from artistic styles. However, apart from the material, the style of the *Hokke-dō Konpon Mandara* also suggests a Japanese hand. In general, of course, it is in T'ang style but recent infra-red photographs have revealed details of brushwork in the landscape elements which resemble the brushwork of the *Ingakyō* sutra scrolls, other Japanese paintings of the Nara period in T'ang style. The *Hokke-dō Konpon Mandara* is far larger and a much more important painting and its brushwork is infinitely more carefully executed and more involved. It is impossible here to enter into a lengthy discussion of this difficult problem but in my opinion, from its place of discovery, material, and style, it should be attributed to Japan.

After about ten years of careful study, the late Okakura Kakuzō decided that it was Chinese of the T'ang Dynasty and he labelled it accordingly in the museum. However, in the Bulletin of the Museum of Fine Arts for July 1906 he published the painting as a mid-sixth-century Japanese work, and I feel sure that his first reaction was correct. Something similar can be said of the Hōryū-ji frescoes (Plates 45, 46). They are based on the T'ang style but their delicacy of line and elegance of colour betray a Japanese sense of rhythm and beauty. I, personally, am convinced that they were painted by Japanese under the guidance of continental artists, who came to Japan at the time. An even more striking example is provided by another Nara period masterpiece, the *Kichijō-ten* of the Yakushi-ji Temple (Plate 49). The sensuous charm which fills this small painting is typical of the rich T'ang style. At the same time one detects a Japanese approach to beauty in the delicate and flexible contours of the goddess and in the exquisite colouring and shading of her robes. This *Kichijō-ten*, incidentally, is also painted on hemp.

The Shōsō-in, that vast storehouse of Nara art, houses many interesting examples of painting, among which the large ink drawing of a *Bodhisattva Flying on a Cloud* (Plate 48) is both of outstanding artistic merit and most significant for the history of far eastern painting. The figure is drawn with most spirited brushwork in strong black lines on hemp. It is not possible to say whether this was a pre-liminary sketch which was intended to be coloured or whether it was complete in itself. Disregarding such questions, it is significant for the history of the development of brushwork to appreciate that such fine line-drawing in free, vital brushstrokes was possible in mid-eighth-century Japan (i.e. in mid-T'ang times). The ink monochrome painting of the Sung Dynasty is justly famous but it is seldom realized that such brushwork already existed in the T'ang Dynasty, and that the foundations of ink painting were laid in these early centuries. This would provide evidence to prove that the T'ang artist Jodoshi (Chinese: *Wu Tao-tzu*) did indeed express that bravura in his brushwork for which he is famous and which so greatly influenced all subsequent Chinese art.

Under the influence of esoteric Buddhism, Japan in the Heian period produced some of the greatest Buddhist pictures which have survived. Due to their frequent use in special rituals associated with esoteric Buddhism they have been darkened by incense smoke and are, unfortunately, in bad condition. They were made in Japan at a time when the T'ang Dynasty had already lost much of its power but they have inherited its style and retain the ideas and plastic sense of the golden age of T'ang art. The works of religious art which this type of Buddhism inspired have an almost magical mysticism which aimed at both charming and aweing the worshipper. It was an art which tried to produce an effect of religious ecstasy and to persuade the worshipper that he actually saw the divine beings in front of him. Such religious aims are clearly seen in sculptural works like the *Nyōirin Kannon* of the Kanshin-ji Temple (Plate 34), but they found an even more effective form of expression in painting. Here the imagination of the artist had freer play than in sculpture. The *Jūni-ten* (Twelve Devas) of the Saidai-ji Temple, of which we reproduce the *Suiten* (Plate 50) in colour, provide a striking illustration of the power of these paintings to create an impression of their living beauty and awesomeness.

The finest esoteric Buddhist paintings came to Japan in the Early Heian period when priests brought the new faith from China. It ruled the arts of the whole Heian period but, as the aristocratic society of the time developed its own way of life, its mystical power was replaced by a more decorative taste in harmony with the age. The arts in general were feminized, beautified, and sentimentalized. Religion was reduced to little more than an aesthetic pastime of noblemen and women.

The grace and gentleness of this new painting developed into what we know as the Fujiwara style. Although it lacks the fervour and power of the preceding period it has its own qualities of perfection and beauty. Fujiwara Buddhism may almost be called a 'religion of beauty'. It influenced all the arts of the period.

The finest examples of this new approach to religious images are the *Fūgen* (Frontispiece and Plate 64) of the Tokyo National Museum and the *Shaka* of the Jingo-ji (Plate 63) commonly known as the 'Red Shaka' on account of its red draperies. Irrespective of the actual deities represented, these Fujiwara Buddhas and Bodhisattvas show a sweet, compassionate expression. The figures are feminine and willowy. Painters used rich colours and in particular *kiri-kane*, a technique of applied cut gold-leaf to decorate the robes. Another interesting development in this period is the artists' practice of depicting

Buddhist deities and great priests as lovely children. They represented the Bodhisattva Monjū as a lovely child and Kōbō Daishi as a most intelligent-looking boy in a painting called *Dōgyō Daishi* or *Chigo Daishi* (Plate 76). These tendencies indicate a movement to combine religious worship with maternal love.

Perhaps the most remarkable manifestation of the sentimentalizing of the Buddhist faith in Japan was the vogue during the Late Heian and Kamakura periods for the so-called *Raigō* paintings. The *Raigō* conception is attributed to the eminent priest Eshin (A.D. 941–1017) who was inspired by the conviction that Amida, the King of the West, not only waits for the arrival of the souls of the departed, but was prepared to come down to earth at the moment of their death, personally to escort them to paradise. The calm assumption that a god would deign to come down to earth for such a purpose was the height of sentimentality. But, in an age which brought everything down to a human level, such a belief in intimate contacts between god and worshipper found ready acceptance. A large number of such paintings were produced. The *Amida Triptych* of the Hokke-ji Temple (Plates 54, 55 and 56), the *Amida Coming to this World* at Kōyasan (Plate 59), the *Yamagoshi no Amida* owned by the Zenrin-ji Temple (Plate 57), and the so-called 'Swift Raigō' of the Chion-in are well-known masterpieces.

The themes of *Raigō* paintings were conducive to lively, dramatic treatment. Amida is shown sometimes flanked by his two attendants Kannon and Seishi or more often surrounded by a colourful retinue of twenty-five Bodhisattva-musicians riding on clouds. To indicate the bliss that worshippers might expect in paradise, the deities and their attendants have joyful expressions. Even the mountainous landscapes which form the settings for these scenes are attractive, with forests full of flowering cherry-trees. It is as if the whole of nature expressed its happiness in the events leading to a soul's entry to heaven. Indeed these *Raigō* paintings often have an effect rather like grand opera, and the theme became popular for religious dramas performed by priests and devotees in old Buddhist temples. This *Raigō* art with its dramatic content was an important innovation in Japanese Buddhist painting and marked a departure from the customary forms of religious painting in which single deities were generally represented in calm postures of meditation.

In addition to the uniquely Japanese *Raigō* compositions, some of the old continental themes called for large-scale compositions. Perhaps the most important of these was the Death or *Nirvāna* of the Buddha, a subject which produced masterpieces in all Buddhist countries. The finest Japanese example is the *Nehan* (Sanskrit: *Nirvāna*) at Kōyasan (Plate 58) painted in 1086. Its powerful composition and the touching manner in which it depicts the sorrow of all earthly creatures as they gather round the death-bed are most impressive. But perhaps the *Kinkan Shitsugen* in the Chōhō-ji Temple (Plate 60) is the greatest of all such Japanese religious paintings inspired by continental examples. It is based on a legend according to which the Buddha rose from his golden coffin to preach words of comfort to his sorrowing mother. This is a magnificent theme for religious painting. No worthy examples are known from China, but from Japan there is a splendid version, one of the finest paintings in the world. It shows the grief of the multitude gathered to mourn the Buddha's death and their sudden joy as he appeared with golden rays of light emanating from his body. The beholder is swept into the glory of this dramatic moment by the overpowering force of artistic magic.

The Heian was a most prolific period for Buddhist painting. The feminine taste of the aristocracy shows itself in numerous paintings which, for sheer beauty, must be numbered among the world's finest. However, not all the paintings of the period were effeminate and sentimental. Although most Buddhist deities are by their very nature compassionate and gentle, the fearful expressions of a group of *Myō-ō* or militant protectors of the faith are definitely intended to intimidate the spectator. As we have frequently mentioned, esoteric Buddhism, which contains much of the magic and mysticism of indigenous Indian religious belief, was a powerful force in this period, and these esoteric Buddhist images of the Heian period, terrifying in mien, were often worshipped in order to pray for revenge on enemies. The *Godaison* (Five Evil-Subduing Deities) of the Tō-ji Temple (Plate 52) are strange combinations of charm and power. Similarly the *Daitoku Myō-ō* in the Museum of Fine Arts, Boston (Plate 65), is one of the finest images created by esoteric Buddhism. The wrathful deity is seated on a blue ox with flames rising behind it. In the dead of night the worshippers would gather in the temple, light a sacrificial fire before it, intone the sutras and burn incense as they prayed for vengeance. I once attended such a midnight ceremony and it left a very deep impression. To see esoteric Buddhist images worshipped in this way helps one to understand why they were painted with such an emphasis on strange colours and exaggerated contrasts of light and dark. The coiling flames painted behind the figure, the glittering *kiri-kane* (cut gold-leaf decorations), and the rich varied colours on its body and robes, produced a play of light and shade in the fire-light which created a terrifying mystical atmosphere. Such a setting for esoteric paintings is, needless to say, quite alien to the flat, even light of the modern museum galleries where they are now seen.

The chief guardian of the Buddhist faith was the *Fudō Myō-ō*. From the Heian period onwards he was the most popular deity and he inspired many masterpieces in painting and sculpture. The most remarkable is the *Ao Fudō* (Blue Fudō) in the Shōren-in Monastery (Plate 53). The flames and smoke behind the blue figure are most realistically represented. Other outstanding works are the *Yellow Fudō* of the Mii-dera Temple and the *Red Fudō* at Kōyasan which are often compared to it. These paintings with their spiritual power to strike fear into the minds of their beholders were not the work of ordinary professional painters. They were painted by pious priests who devoted their lives to meditation and produced them under deep religious inspiration. One of the most important disciplines of esoteric Buddhism demanded that the adept should always keep the Buddha in the forefront of his mind. For this purpose the practice of drawing images in ink was considered very suitable. As a result these Buddhist sects produced some outstanding priest-painters with a fine sense of draughtsmanship. The daily practice in drawing, which their faith demanded, gave them a great dexterity which is exemplified in such fine works as the *Fudō* dated 1282 (Plate 67). It was painted by the priest-painter Shinkai, the son of the eminent painter Nobuzane, and he lived in the Daigo-ji Temple which has remained a great centre of esoteric Buddhism.

The Kamakura period which followed the Heian was, as we have already remarked, an age of realism in the arts. On the one hand it served to check the effeminate and sentimental taste of the Late Heian period and on the other it breathed a new life and energy into the arts. In a sense the Kamakura period can be called the Renaissance of Japanese art. However, realism is not compatible with the imaginative and supernatural character of Buddhist art. For although Buddhist painting seems to have flourished for a short time after the Kamakura period, its importance as religious art was gradually declining. This reflected a change in the faith in itself. The *Zen* sect introduced, it will be remembered, from China during the Sung and Yüan Dynasties, was becoming very popular. We have already seen how *Zen* attached little importance to images of the Buddha. It laid stress on the veneration of the founders and high priests of the sect, portraits of whom were revered as models for a good religious life. This sect emphasized the human values of a strict spiritual discipline which could be gained in communion with nature and away from the everyday world. In such circumstances the traditional forms of Buddhist art gradually declined and their place was taken by portraiture and landscape painting.

Plates 43 and 44
SHASHIN SHIKO (SHAKA GIVING HIS OWN BODY TO
FEED THE HUNGRY TIGERS)
Artist Unknown. Asuka Period. About A.D. 600
Lacquer painting in colour on wooden panel of the pedestal of
the Tamamushi Shrine
Height of shrine 92 in.
Museum, Hōryū-ji, Nara-ken

The subject of this painting is taken from the Jataka stories which recount
events in the previous lives of the Buddha. In this incident the Buddha, a
prince in a former life, one day found a hungry tigress and her cubs in a
deserted ravine. Out of compassion for all living creatures, he threw himself
down, sacrificing his own body in order to feed them. The style is that of the
Chinese Six Dynasties period with residual traces of Han style painting. The
interesting use of space and the consecutive series of scenes on the one painting
rely for their effectiveness on a fine sense of line and a sensitive rhythm.
Although this early painting is still entirely continental in style, it seems to
foreshadow the future development of Japanese painting. One of Japan's
greatest achievements in later periods was in illustrating stories with pictures
which by the skilful use of line produce an impression of dynamic action. It
culminated in the development of the unique Japanese *e-makimono* (scroll-
paintings), (see Plates 88–103).

Plates 45 and 46
AMIDA TRIAD
Artist Unknown. Early Nara Period. About the middle
of 7th Century A.D.
Wall-painting in colour on plaster
Size 120 in. × 103 in.
Formerly in Kondō, Hōryū-ji, Nara-ken
The remains of the original are preserved in the Hōryū-ji Museum

The destruction of the Hōryū-ji frescoes by fire in 1949 was
the greatest loss suffered by Japanese art in recent times. The
Hōryū-ji was built in the early years of the seventh century
but destroyed by fire in 670. The wall-paintings must have
been painted after this first disaster, i.e. in the Early Nara
period when the temple was rebuilt. This dating is supported
by the style of the paintings which reflect the full T'ang
spirit. Indeed, before their destruction, the Hōryū-ji frescoes
were considered the finest examples of T'ang wall-painting of
which so much is said in the histories but of which almost
nothing has survived. Historians claim them for both
Chinese and Japanese art but they are certainly Japanese
work based on Chinese prototypes. They show the distinct
Japanese sense of beauty expressed through the marked
rhythm of line and harmony of movement. The colours,
richly polychromatic and yet at the same time discreet and
soft in their opaque greys, are essentially Japanese in taste. In
my opinion they were painted by Japanese under the
guidance of continental artists who emigrated to Japan in
considerable numbers at this time.

Plate 47
HOKKE-DŌ KONPON MANDARA
Artist Unknown. Nara Period. Late 8th Century A.D.
Colour on hemp-like cloth. Size 43 in. × 59 in.
Museum of Fine Arts, Boston

Hokke-dō Konpon Mandara means that this painting was the 'most fundamental Mandala of the Hokkedo Hall' of the Tōdai-ji, Nara, where it was before being exported to the United States in the late nineteenth century.

This important work raises the controversial problem of whether it was painted in China during the T'ang period or in Japan during the Nara period. The styles of the two are very alike since Nara painting closely followed T'ang prototypes. The problem is complicated by a document dated 1148, affixed to the painting, which states that the painting came originally from India, was greatly damaged over the centuries, and restored by a priest-painter named Chin Kai (1091–1152) of the Tōdai-ji. It is not necessary to consider the Indian attribution seriously since similar claims are made for several paintings; such attributions were made no doubt to give them added sanctity in the popular mind. However Chin Kai's repairs and restorations which extend over the whole picture complicate any decisions made on stylistic grounds. I have discussed this subject in detail in separate articles devoted to this important painting. It is necessary here only to repeat the conclusion that it is a very important Japanese painting of the Nara period, probably of the late eighth century; that the composition is based on a T'ang model but that the details of brushwork and in particular the linear rhythms are Japanese. The material is significant for it was painted not on silk which was usual for Chinese painting but on a much coarser hemp-like material which was often used in the Nara period in Japan. Analyses based on criteria of style could only be expressed in vague terms and would sound after all inconclusive. In my opinion, the material on which it was painted is an important clue to its Japanese origin, besides the fact that the painting was discovered in Nara.

If one accepts this work as a Japanese painting, it provides the most valuable evidence of the sensibilities and technique of Japanese artists in the Nara period, the first golden age of Japanese art. The subject is Shakyamuni's sermon to his followers before the Ryōjusen (Vulture Peak). The Buddhist figures in the foreground, the baldachin over Shakyamuni, the buildings in the background with their volute-like clouds were all repainted in 1148 over the old outlines. The parts which most interest art historians, in addition to the general composition, are the dark forest and the valleys and mountains in the background. The infra-red photographs recently made of details from this part of the painting brought out very clearly the original brushwork, in ink, delineating tall trees, foliage and rocks in the valley. These brushstrokes are very similar to those in examples of Nara drawings in Japan.

Mr K. Tomita, Curator of Oriental Art in the Museum of Fine Arts, Boston, informed me recently that his predecessor, Okakura Kakuzō, published this painting as a Japanese work in the Bulletin of the Museum for July 1906. Later, however, he changed his opinion and from that time the painting, attributed to the T'ang Dynasty, formed an important exhibit in the Chinese gallery of the Museum.

Plate 48
BODHISATTVA FLYING ON A CLOUD
Artist Unknown. Nara Period. 8th Century A.D.
Ink on hemp. Size 52 in. × 54 in.
Shōsō-in, Nara

The Imperial Depository, known as the Shōsō-in was created in A.D. 756 to house all the many personal effects of Emperor Shōmu which his consort, the 'Empress Radiant' (Kōmyō Kōgyō), deposited there after his death. This historic building also contains a large variety of objects used in the inauguration ceremony of the *Daibutsu*, the Great Buddha of the Tōdai-ji, which was held in 752. The building has always been sealed with the Emperor's personal seal and for over twelve hundred years has remained inviolate. Thus many hundreds of precious relics are preserved to this day almost intact and provide the most reliable evidence we possess of the fine and applied arts prior to the mid-eighth century.

The masterly drawing illustrated here was done in free-hand black lines on hemp cloth. Its fluent, lively strokes are significant for the future development of both Chinese T'ang and Japanese Nara period painting.

Plate 49
KICHIJŌ-TEN
Artist Unknown. Nara Period. 8th Century A.D.
Colour on hemp. Size 21 in. × 12 in.
Yakushi-ji, Nara

Nara society, like that of the Chinese T'ang Dynasty from which it drew its inspiration was frankly luxury loving. Thus *Kichijō-ten*, the Buddhist Goddess of Wealth, was a popular deity of the time. But this gem of Nara period painting is more than just a picture of a deity who bestows worldly goods on her devotees; it also clearly portrays the T'ang and Nara ideal of feminine beauty—a woman of warm, full figure, her rich robes crowned with an elaborate headdress. Her elegant clothes are covered with floral designs which stand out strongly by the use of chiaroscuro. Transparent gauzes hang from her shoulders and drape down over her arms; gold necklaces and bracelets decorate her neck and arms. No clearer picture of the luxury of the brilliant T'ang-Nara Age could remain to us.

Plate 50
SUITEN
Artist Unknown. Early Heian Period. 9th Century A.D.
Colour on silk. Size 62 in. × 54 in.
Saidai-ji, Nara

Suiten, the Water King, is one of the Twelve Guardian Deities of Buddhism; his function is to hold sway over the waters. Water is of primary importance in a rice-growing culture like that of Japan and drought constitutes a national disaster. In such times special ceremonies are held before images of this deity to invoke his help in bringing rain. The poor condition of this early painting may well be due to its frequent use over the centuries for this very purpose. The esoteric Buddhism of the *Shingon* and *Tendai* sects entered Japan from China in the Early Heian period. Its mysterious ceremonies, with their magical rituals appealed to a people by nature attracted by the concept of supernatural powers. Japanese priests who studied this form of Buddhism in China brought back with them Late T'ang period paintings on which Japanese artists modelled their work. The *Suiten* here reproduced is one of the earlier and most important examples of this Chinese-inspired art which was produced in Japan.

Plate 51
SUITEN
Artist Unknown. Heian Period. Painted in A.D. 1127
Colour on silk. Size 57 in. × 50 in.
Kyōōgokoku-ji, Kyoto

The central figure of this painting is again *Suiten*, the Water God, but it was painted some 250 years later than the preceding illustration. They provide an illuminating comparison in styles. Both are masterpieces of their respective periods but the later painting shows the progress made by Japanese painting in these formative centuries. The *Suiten* in Plate 50 is still entirely continental in concept. Its aim was to overwhelm its worshippers with the impression that a supernatural deity had deigned to make an appearance in order to receive the prayers of wretched mankind. By the time that this second *Suiten* was painted Heian culture had completely Japanized the continental prototypes. The Japanese artist has represented *Suiten* as an attractive youth dressed in colourful robes and covered with gold adornments. The attendants are little more than charming children. The mystery which this representation should suggest has not entirely disappeared. Rather has its character changed into a softer kind of mysticism—the mystique of the beautiful. This new approach to religious art illustrates the underlying spirit of Heian Buddhism.

Plate 52
GŌSANZE
Artist Unknown. Heian Period. About A.D. 1100
Colour on silk. Size 60 in. × 51 in.
Kyōōgokoku-ji, Kyoto

Gōsanze is one of the *Godaison* (Five Evil-Subduing Deities of Buddhism)
whose functions are to guard the four directions and the centre of the universe.
The deity is here represented with three faces each of which has three eyes, and
with six hands some holding weapons with which to subdue evil spirits. The
figure tramples on Daijizaiten and his wife Uma, the symbols of conceit and
covetousness. Ancient records state that this series of the Five Deities together
with the series of Twelve Guardian Deities (one of which, *Suiten,* is reproduced in Plates 50, 51) were painted in 1127. According to another theory,
the Five Deities were painted in 1040, after old models which Kōbō Daishi
himself brought back from China in 806. However, space does not allow an
adequate discussion here of the involved problem of their dating. There can
be no doubt that the unusual manner of representing the angry god indicates
that it was copied from an ancient Chinese original. The strange shaped background of flames forms an intricate linear pattern which at the same time has
a compelling power to suggest real fire. This must have been derived from a
continental model which in itself possibly reflected elements of Indian mysticism and magical beliefs.

Plate 53
FUDŌ
Artist Unknown. Heian Period. Second half of 10th Century A.D.
Colour on silk. Size 80 in. × 58 in.
Shōren-in, Kyoto

The most important in popular belief of all the Guardian Gods or Kings of Buddhism was *Fudō* (Sanskrit: *Acalanatha*). He is the subject of many Japanese paintings and sculptures. Three *Fudō* masterpieces have survived from the Heian period and are popularly known as the *Yellow*, the *Red* and the *Blue Fudō*. The *Blue Fudō* illustrated here is the oldest and most important of the three.

Esoteric Buddhist images generally follow certain iconographic rules very strictly. Nevertheless, the individual vision and inspiration of the various priest-painters who made these images greatly influenced their final form.

It may be of interest to the Western reader to add here a few words concerning the manner in which these esoteric images were seen and worshipped. The ceremony for worship of such a fearful god, the King of Wrath and Vengeance, is held in a special dark hall and generally late at night. A large fire burns before the painting, incense fills the air and priests intone the *sutras* which they handle with dramatic gestures. This atmosphere does indeed produce in the spectator a sense of religious ecstasy in which the image of *Fudō* appears to move through the flickering flames of the fire burning in front of it. In this picture the large flames and dark smoke are very realistically painted in such a way that they merge into the flames of the real fire. The setting is intended to create the illusion that this terrifying god is actually evoked from the flames and the conception is typical of the aims of esoteric Buddhist art.

Plates 55 and 56
AMIDA TRIPTYCH
Artist Unknown. Heian Period. 11th Century A.D.
Colour on silk. Size: Amida (centre) 74 in. × 57 in., Kannon and Seishi
74 in. × 68 in., Banner-bearing boy 73 in. × 21 in.
Hokke-ji (Nunnery), Nara

Some scholars consider that the central *Amida* figure of this famous triptych
is earlier than the two side paintings. The composition and execution of the
two groups are so different that they possibly belonged to different sets which
were later assembled to form this set of the *Coming of Amida*. The central
deity faces squarely to the front while his attendants in freer poses fly on each
side. Such a lack of unity in composition in the three paintings makes it
difficult to understand how otherwise they could have been combined into
a triptych.

The visualization of the religious idea of *Amida Buddha* coming down into
the world to receive the souls of the dying and to carry them back to paradise
was conceived by Eshin Sōzu (941–1017), a great priest-painter who often
had such visions. This Hokke-ji triptych is one of the oldest of its kind and
one of the greatest Buddhist paintings produced in Japan. Although they
may possibly have belonged to different sets, the quiet, immovable dignity of
Amida contrasts effectively with the movement of the *Kannon* and *Seishi*
figures as they descend gracefully on soft clouds. Falling lotus petals fill the
air with spiritual happiness and the beautiful youth bearing a banner, who
guides this august and heavenly procession to the human world, himself
evokes the image of a flower in early spring.

56

Plate 57

YAMAGŌSHI NO AMIDA (AMIDA COMING OVER THE MOUNTAIN)

Artist Unknown. Kamakura Period. 13th Century A.D.

Colour on silk. Size 49 in. × 32 in.

Zenrin-ji, Kyoto

Paintings of the *Yamagōshi No Amida* type, in which the Buddha is seen descending over mountains, are variations of the *Amida Raigō* theme. The creation of this very popular composition is again attributed to Eshin Sōzu. It denotes a further stage in the sentimentalization of Japanese Buddhism. The author is tempted to believe that the artist, while walking in a dark valley, saw the full moon rising behind a distant ridge and was inspired to visualize the moon as Amida descending over the mountains.

Plate 58

NEHAN (NIRVĀNA, OR DEATH OF SHAKA)
Artist Unknown. Heian Period. Dated on the picture A.D. 1086
Colour on silk. Size 106 in. × 107 in.
Kongobu-ji, Kōyasan, Wakayama-ken

The *Death of the Buddha*, in Japanese *Nehan* (Sanskrit: *Nirvāna*), like the Passion in Christian art, is one of the most moving subjects in Buddhist art. It has inspired many masterpieces in Buddhist countries throughout the ages. This large-scale composition shows the finest technique of the Heian period and, in it, Japan produced a masterpiece which can compare with those of any other Buddhist country. The painting has been criticized for a certain lack of organization in the figures surrounding the Buddha and for stiffness in draughtsmanship. These failings may be due to the fact that the artist might have modelled his work on an actual prototype, which came from China. Nevertheless the serene expression of the Buddha as he lies quietly in the centre and the uncontrollable grief of the earthly creatures gathered around him to lament his passing have inspired a painting of the deepest religious feeling.

Plate 59

AMIDA RAIGŌ (AMIDA COMING
TO THIS WORLD)

Artist Unknown. Heian Period. Late 11th Century A.D.
Colour on silk. Size: central painting 83 in. × 83 in.
side panels, 83 in. × 41 in.
Museum, Kōyasan, Wakayama-ken

Amida Raigō paintings are intended to depict the *Coming of the Amida
Buddha to this World*. The work here illustrated is the most famous
example of its type. It is now housed in the museum belonging to the

temples on Mount Koya but it originally belonged to the Enryaku-ji Temple situated in the Hiei mountains above Kyoto, the home of the priest-painter Eshin Sōzu who was inspired to create this composition. He is said to have had a vision of Amida surrounded by his twenty-five Bodhisattva-musicians riding on the gold and purple clouds of evening as they descended to the world of man.

Behind the *Amida* group a wide expanse of water represents a distant view of Lake Biwa as seen from the summit of the Hiei mountains. This lake is the largest in Japan and a very famous beauty spot. In my opinion the picture, in its local landscape elements, retains something of Eshin Sōzu's original composition but belongs to almost a century later than the period in which the artist lived.

Plate 60

KINKAN SHITSUGEN (SHAKA REAPPEARING FROM THE GOLDEN COFFIN)

Artist Unknown. Heian Period. Late 11th Century A.D.
Colour on silk. Size 63 in. × 90 in.
Chōhō-ji, Kyoto

On the death of the Buddha his mother fell into a mood of great sorrow. In order to comfort her and to enlighten her soul, the Buddha raised himself from his golden coffin emanating a gold light from his body in which thousands of small Buddhas reappeared. He then preached a sermon to his grief-stricken mother which consoled her.

It is surprising that this inspiring theme appears so seldom in Buddhist art. It is found in a few unimportant scenes in the wall-paintings at Tun-huang in China and occasionally elsewhere. Suddenly, in eleventh-century Japan, this unique composition was created. Its prototype may well have been brought from China but, if this was so, no traces of it have survived. The Japanese master who was inspired to create this great work was obviously deeply touched by the subject. The whole composition is concentrated with unerring power both visually and emotionally on the unexpected resurrection of the Buddha.

Plate 61

HŌRŌKAKU MANDARA

Artist Unknown. Heian Period. 12th Century A.D.
Colour on silk. Size 57 in. × 34 in.
Freer Gallery of Art, Washington

A Buddhist *sutra* recounts how a magnificent building once suddenly rose out of the ground in front of *Shaka Buddha*. As he marvelled at its beauty, a voice came from within the building calling on him to enter. The door opened to reveal the *Tahō Buddha* who welcomed *Shaka* and invited him to sit beside him. The two Buddhas seated within a splendid building became a popular theme for devotional Buddhist art and representations are frequently found in the sculpture of the Six Dynasties period in China, especially at such sites as the Yün-kang caves. In later periods the worship of the two Buddhas became less popular. A few examples survive in Japan from the Heian period.

In this work, one of the finest Japanese Buddhist paintings outside Japan, the subject is represented with all the luxury and beauty demanded by the taste of Fujiwara society.

Plate 62

KUJAKU MYŌ-Ō

Artist Unknown

Heian Period. 11th Century A.D.

Colour on silk. Size 59 in. × 39 in.

Collection of Mr Hara, Yokohama

Kujaku Myō-ō (Peacock King), a popular deity of the esoteric Buddhist *Shingon* sect, is believed to protect mankind from illness and harm. The cult of *Kujaku Myō-ō* became particularly widespread after an event which took place in A.D. 908. In that year a certain priest, Seiho, prayed for rain before an image of the deity set up in the garden of the Imperial Palace. Heaven immediately responded to his prayers and sent a heavy shower of rain. This supernatural occurrence led to the creation in the Heian period of a number of paintings of the Peacock King. The example illustrated is by far the finest. It must have been painted in the eleventh century at the height of Heian culture when perfection was the prime requisite of art. Heian culture later began to show signs of decadence, its standards of beauty declined and artists often marred their interpretations by over-sentimentality. This work preserved its form and dignity and made no concessions to the demand for excessive elegance.

Plate 63

SHAKA

Artist Unknown

Heian Period. 12th Century A.D.

Colour on silk. Size 62 in. × 34 in.

Jingo-ji, Kyoto

The attractive red tones of the drapery in this picture have led to its being known as the *Aka* or 'Red' *Shaka*. Towards the end of the twelfth century the aristocratic taste and feminine influences of the Fujiwara nobility imposed a veneer of sentimentality and artificiality even on Buddhist images. Some of the greatest works preserved much of the ancient spiritual dignity, but on the whole Buddhist images were more notable for their aesthetic than their religious appeal. This *Shaka* picture is notable for the draperies in red and other colours and for the decorative designs in *kiri-kane*, or cut gold-leaf, a technique of decoration characteristic of the period.

Plate 64

FŪGEN

Artist Unknown. Heian Period. 12th Century A.D.
Colour on silk. Size 63 in. × 29 in.
Tokyo National Museum

This *Fūgen* and the preceding *Red Shaka* in Plate 63 mark the climax of the twelfth-century search for beauty and for the expression of sentimentality in art. Thus even religion could not escape the twin desires which animated the pleasure-loving feminine society of the Late Heian or Fujiwara period. Buddhism became what one might almost call a religion of beauty in which such gentle and exquisitely dressed divinities played the principal roles. The Bodhisattva Fūgen was a particularly popular object of worship among the court ladies, a position he derived from being the protector of devotees of the Hokekyō sutra, a scripture devoted particularly to the salvation of women. The *Fūgen* images of this period take the form of handsome youths, the idealized romantic figures who perhaps filled the dreams of these noble ladies.

A detail of this *Fūgen* Bodhisattva is reproduced as frontispiece to this book.

Plate 65

DAITOKU MYŌ-Ō

Artist Unknown. Heian Period. 12th Century A.D.
Colour on silk. Size 76 in. × 46 in.
Museum of Fine Arts, Boston

Daitoku Myō-ō, one of the Five Guardian Kings of Buddhism is depicted in terrifying form with six faces, six arms and six legs, and is shown riding on an ox. He is credited with the power of summoning storms to subdue evil spirits and other enemies of mankind. This painting was made in the Late Heian period at the height of the Fujiwara taste for beauty and ornate decoration. However, even in this rarefied atmosphere, paintings of great power were occasionally made. A strong under-current of esoteric mysticism still flowed through the spiritual life of the time and was sometimes able to make itself felt through the rich ornamentation of pictures. This painting was taken to America by Okakura, the Curator of Oriental Art in the Museum of Fine Arts, Boston, and presented to the Museum in his memory. The two finest Buddhist paintings outside Japan are this work and the Freer Gallery mandara reproduced in Plate 61.

Plate 66
FUDŌ
Artist Unknown. Kamakura Period. 13th Century A.D.
Colour on silk. Size 50 in. × 23 in.
Collection Mr Inoue, Tokyo

Fudō is the principal deity among the Five Guardian
Gods of Buddhism. His name 'Immovable' describes
his main virtue. The God is generally depicted on a rock
to signify the unshakable stability of faith. This painting,
however, is the well-known *Hashiri* (Running) *Fudō*.
According to popular tradition, when the Mongols
attacked the country, even the gods were mobilized and
Fudō is shown rushing to the battlefield to save Japan
in her hour of greatest peril. Tradition attributes it to a
painter named Nagataka. Whoever the master, he
produced a vivid atmosphere of excitement and haste as
Fudō with burning eyes and irresistible force hastens to
join battle with the invaders.

Plate 67
FUDŌ
By Shinkai. Kamakura Period. Dated on the
picture A.D 1282
Ink on paper. Size 46 in. × 17 in.
Daigo-ji, Kyoto

Iconographic symbolism is an important ingredient of
esoteric Buddhism. Practice in drawing Buddhist
figures formed an important part of the religious exercises
of the priests. This aspect of religious training produced
many fine priest-painters skilled in representing
religious ideas and visions in all media. This *Fudō* was
made by Shinkai, son of Nobuzane, a great portrait
painter. The year 1282 inscribed on the work is only
one year after the repulse of the Mongols. With the
national emergency now passed, the *Fudō* could resume
his immovable pose—but the fury and excitement
remain in his expression. The wind-swept flames behind
the god, the agitated waves and his rocky pedestal
remain to recall the invasion which had only just
receded from the shores of Japan.

2 Portrait Painting

Portraiture plays a large part in the arts of the world and has been responsible for some of the most memorable works we possess. However, strangely enough, it is an art form which has never been as popular in Japan as in other countries.

In Japanese art individuality was never as strongly emphasized as in the West. Thus portraiture, whose basic function is to express what is individual, was never very highly regarded. If a man was considered worthy of respect, the feelings of others towards him tended to border on religious veneration. This attitude sprang from early Japanese nature worship and the anthropomorphic polytheism of the race which considered any remarkable object or person as being near to God and in fact likely to become a god. Shintō, the indigenous belief of Japan, is based on ancestor worship which preserves this same mental attitude. A Shintō shrine is the dwelling of a god, but the god who inhabits it was seldom personified in an image or given any tangible form.

As a result of this deep feeling that a god was either too great or too holy to be represented in visible form, the Japanese often left the inner sanctuary of their old shrines either bare or simply occupied by a mirror. When Buddhism popularized the worship of images, Shintō began in competition, to make images for its own shrines. Since the Shintō gods were distant ancestors of the race or outstanding historical figures, the Shintō artists conceived their icons as human beings dressed in contemporary costume. They were, in fact, a type of portraiture. However, being divine they had to express a supernatural dignity.

The peculiar nature of Shintō images throws light on the fundamental characteristics of Japanese portraiture. Not only in Shintō images but in all Japanese portraits, either in painting or sculpture, there is certainly some desire for realistic representation, which, of course, is indispensable. But Japanese artists always felt the additional need for idealistic or symbolic forms. The tendency to idealize and symbolize, peculiar to Japanese portraiture, gives it its rare interest.

As early as the Nara period, Buddhist art in sculpture and in painting, produced many fine portraits representing the saints and the founders of the various sects. The impulse to create images for religious purposes must have been similar to that which produced the figures of St Peter or St Francis in Catholic art. However, the tendency towards idealization was much stronger in the Japanese images than in western religious art. What began as realism was always modified by idealism.

Let us first consider the images of the great ecclesiastics. In the Nara period, the strong realism inherited from Chinese T'ang art inspired such outstanding works as the image of Gyōshin in the Hōryū-ji and that of *Ganjin* (Plate 28) in the Tōshōdai-ji. Not content to regard such images simply as commemorative portraits of great individuals, the Japanese rapidly turned them into objects of veneration and worship. Thus the founder of a sect became the principal deity of a temple's Kaisan-dō (Founder's Hall) where the faithful would worship him in his image. The resulting tendency towards the supernatural and symbolical became more marked in the Heian period when all Japanese art acquired strong national characteristics. The practice of worshipping great priests of the past became widespread. Outstanding examples are the groups of paintings such as the Seven Ancestral Priests of the *Shingon* and the great priests of the *Tendai* sects. When images were made during the life-time of the priest or soon after his death, as happened with the *Zen* priests during the Kamakura period, the forces of realism asserted themselves strongly. However, when the priests had long been dead as in the series of the founders of the *Shingon* and *Tendai* sects, the artists had very little information on which to build a faithful representation and they understandably tended to idealize their forms.

The portraits of *Ryūchi* (Plate 68) and Ryūmyō are outstanding examples of this symbolical or idealistic portraiture of the Early Heian period. They represent two great Indian priests and were painted in Japan in accordance with the strongly realistic style of the Late T'ang period and modelled on Chinese paintings brought back by Kōbō Daishi (774–835). They are not so much actual portraits of individuals as idealized representations of the personalities of two distinguished priests. They rank among the world's finest religious images.

For portraits of contemporary subjects the artist may occasionally have used a living model in order to increase the realistic effect. Such masterpieces as the portrait of the priest *Gonzō* (Plate 69) and *Jion Daishi* (Plate 70), made during the Late Heian period, suggest very strongly that the artist must have referred to some sort of contemporary representation or at least to a copy of one. For realistic elements intruded into even the most idealistic of the fashionable portraits of the Heian period.

In the Kamakura period, which was dominated by a strongly realistic spirit, we find another aspect of this dual nature of portrait art. In these centuries an emphasized realism tended to overwhelm the idealism of the work of previous periods. The Kōfuku-ji figures of *Seshin* and *Mūchaku* (Plate 41) by Unkei (active 1176–1223) and his school or the Tōdai-ji *Sōgyōhachiman* by Kaikei (active 1183– c. 1236), are outstanding examples of this type of realistic sculpture. Their extremely life-like qualities inevitably detracted from their value as objects of worship.

Despite the decline of the idealistic in art during the Kamakura period, the art of portraiture experienced a development unknown in previous periods. *Zen* Buddhists condemning the worship of images venerated instead the founders or the high priests of their temples, and the main energy of their art went into the portrayal of their spiritual leaders. These portraits of *Zen* masters are called in Japanese *Chinzō*, and the great demand for them stimulated portrait artists to produce many splendid works throughout the Kamakura and Muromachi periods. The portrait of *Shoichi Kokushi* by Mincho (1352–1431) in the Kōfuku-ji and the portrait of *Daitō Kokushi* (Plate 78) in the Daitoku-ji show the heights reached by *Chinzō* portraiture. They fully reflect the spiritual force of *Zen* art.

From the Heian to the Kamakura periods the influence of religion on all aspects of life considerably decreased, or rather took a new turn. The emergence of warrior statesmen who ruled the country by force of arms and strength of personality created a demand for portraits of them to establish their fame in the minds of the people. After the establishment of the *Baku-fu* (military government) at Kamakura such portraits became increasingly popular and, for the first time in Japanese art history, a real art of portrait painting came into being. This new style is called *Nise-e* (likeness painting) and the most eminent exponents were Takanobu (1142–1205) and his son Nobuzane (1176–c. 1268). The famous portraits of *Yoritomo* (Plate 72) and *Shigemori* (Plate 73) in their official costume are masterpieces by Takanobu. These portraits have a distinction which entitles them to rank among the world's finest. It is significant that, even in such secular works, Japanese artists were not content with realism alone but aimed at idealized forms.

Such idealized portraits became objects of veneration and created a vogue among intellectuals which resulted in a more decorative and stylized series of portraits known as *Kasen-e* (portraits of 'sacred' poets and poetesses). This unusual portrait form became very popular from the Kamakura period onwards. A love of poetry is instinctive in the Japanese and from ancient times they venerated special poets as 'sacred' beings. Some even had shrines built in their honour. The 'Six Chief Poets' or 'Thirty-six Poets and Poetesses' were models for all who aspired to poetic fame. During the Kamakura period the practice of seeking poetic inspiration from such portraits created a great demand for them. The master in this field of portraiture was Nobuzane who, as we have already seen, was equally famous for his *Nise-e* (likenesses). Another famous painter of poets was Tameie (1197–1275), son of the great poet Teika. Nobuzane, like his father Takanobu, was an outstanding portraitist. His poets and poetesses were creations of his imagination but nevertheless he treated them with just enough realism to convince Japanese intellectuals of the time. The scroll of the *Thirty-six Poets*, which was cut and is now divided among many collections, is his most representative work (Plates 74, 75). However, Tameie who devoted himself exclusively to portraits of poets was not so much a portrait artist in the true sense of the word as a creator of fanciful images partly symbolical and partly decorative in intent. They followed a pattern in which the figures are more doll-like than human. His successors still further simplified the formula to such an extent that even the most cursory drawing of a poet or poetess in a set pose passed for a *Kasen-e*. The fashion for such drawings persisted among dilettantes of poetry for many years and produced sketches which were little more than amateur products of skilled calligraphers or of simple lovers of poetry. The evolution is in itself illuminating. From being religious or literary objects of veneration, portraits in Japan became decorative and idealized and finally charming but unreal doll-like creations with some symbolical overtones.

From about the end of the Muromachi period a definite change took place in Japanese portraiture. For the first time a real portrait art emerged which aimed at a realistic representation of a living person without any of the previous religious or literary implications. In the years from the end of the Muromachi to the Momoyama period the country was torn by feudal warfare and many heroic military leaders emerged. A victorious general would commission portraits of himself and his family in order to impress his followers. Power during this period was concentrated in the hands of clans, with their roots in particular places, which became centres of commerce and trade. The new class of powerful merchants which, as a consequence, gradually emerged, demanded a simple art form which it could understand and the *Ukiyō-e* (the genre painting) and portraits with personal interest arose to meet it. Early *Ukiyō-e* faithfully represented the life and customs of the day, while portraits depicted real people.

During the periods of feudal warfare, Japan also had its first contacts with the west and the first experience of western realistic modes. These stimulated in the Japanese an interest in the literal representation of nature in art and prepared the public for portraiture in the true sense of the term. The new spirit which emerged in the Momoyama and Early Edo periods, however, did not triumph completely over the older modes, and portraits of women remained to a great extent pictures of ideal feminine beauty, and those of men represented idealized heroic figures.

True realistic portraiture did not appear until in the nineteenth century a movement was led by Kazan (1793-1841). By this time the isolationist policy of the feudal Tokugawa régime had sufficiently broken down to enable books on human anatomy to reach the country together with the medical works officially imported from Holland. The realism of the copper-plate illustrations in these books profoundly impressed Japanese artists—especially the portraits of such historical figures as Hippocrates. Kazan diligently studied such models and succeeded in producing some portraits of a realism hitherto unknown in Japan. Even so, an unbiased critic would hardly rate Kazan's work very highly by comparison with western products in the field. The basic qualities of Japanese art reveal themselves in other forms which are far removed from realism.

Plate 68
PORTRAIT OF RYŪCHI
Artist Unknown. Early Heian Period. 9th Century A.D.
Colour on silk. Size 83 in. × 59 in.
Kyōōgokoku-ji, Kyoto

In A.D. 806 Kōbō Daishi returned from his mission to China and introduced into Japan the esoteric Buddhism to which we have frequently referred in the plates illustrating Buddhist painting. He brought with him a series of seven portraits of the great patriarchs of the *Shingon* sect painted by the Chinese artist Rishin (Chinese: Li Chên). Two of these portraits were damaged and, according to tradition, Kōbō Daishi himself painted replacements of which this portrait of Ryūchi is one. Kōbō Daishi's fame as a calligrapher is well established but his skill as a painter is not so well substantiated. The masterly inscriptions on various parts of this painting are attributed to the priest and I have no reason to doubt the attribution. Ryūchi was a great Indian theologian but in this idealized portrait painted in Japan no traces of his racial characteristics can be seen. The type is Chinese rather than Japanese—understandably so since the artist modelled his work on a much damaged Chinese portrait by Rishin. Such questions aside, this important painting is a most impressive representation of a powerful religious personality.

Plate 69

PORTRAIT OF GONZŌ

Artist Unknown. Heian Period. Late 11th Century A.D.

Colour on silk. Size 66 in. × 54 in.

Fumon-in, Kōyasan, Wakayama-ken

Priest Gonzō of the Sekien-ji Temple (died A.D. 827) was the teacher of Kōbō Daishi. The latter wrote an eulogy of his master which is inscribed in the upper part of the painting. The work here illustrated must be after a lost original but it is a faithful copy which preserves something of the technique of the ninth-century original. It gives a vivid impression of a great priest in the act of delivering a sermon.

Plate 70

PORTRAIT OF JION DAISHI
Artist Unknown. Heian Period.
11th Century A.D.
Colour on silk.
Size 63 in. × 50 in.
Yakushi-ji, Nara

Jion Daishi, a famous priest of the T'ang Dynasty, was highly venerated by the Japanese *Hossō* sect of Buddhism. The Yakushi-ji Temple, a centre of the sect, has since ancient times held a ceremony in his honour, when special prayers are offered to this painting. The portrait must have been modelled on a Chinese original but its Japanese creator was an artist of individual talent and most accomplished technique. This life-like figure is the product of a powerful imagination summoning up an outstanding personality of the past. The work has an added interest in that it shows a small table for writing materials, a water jar and a low seat, thus providing evidence of the style of accoutrements used by a T'ang Dynasty priest.

Plate 71
PORTRAIT OF ZENMUI
Artist Unknown
Heian Period
12th Century A.D.
Colour on silk
Size 63 in. × 30 in.
Ichijo-ji, Hyogo-ken

This portrait of Zenmui is one of a series of portraits of the Ten Patriarchs of the *Tendai* sect preserved in the Ichijo-ji Temple. Zenmui was an Indian priest who renounced all worldly considerations, studied esoteric Buddhism under Ryūchi (see Plate 68), became a priest and, in the T'ang Dynasty, travelled to China. He is even said to have visited Japan. This painting is so completely un-Japanese in conception that the artist must have closely followed a continental original brought to Japan during the Heian centuries. The strange profile of an old foreign priest seated in an unusual posture on a chair must have shocked the Japanese sense of beauty but gained power by that very feature. The composition includes some curious disproportions. The Guardian God *Bishamonten* is shown as a miniature warrior in attendance on the old priest and adds to the stature of the patriarch. Such unexpected compositions show how Japan, the eastern terminal of the spread of the Buddhist faith, inherited ideas gathered from the various countries through which it passed on its way to Japan.

Plate 72

PORTRAIT OF YORITOMO

By Fujiwara Takanobu (A.D. 1142–1205). Kamakura Period
Colour on silk. Size 54 in. × 44 in.

Jingo-ji, Kyoto

This is one of the best-known portraits in the whole of Japanese art.
The portrait of Shigemori in the next plate belongs to the same set
which originally comprised four portraits of men who were friends
of the ex-Emperor Goshirakawa. The set was painted by Takanobu
(1142–1205) to decorate the Sendōin, the ex-Emperor's palace, a
new building erected in 1188 to house the abdicated monarch. Such
outstanding works of portraiture could only have been created by an
artist with the high standards suggested by what we know of
Takanobu. The composition is extremely simple and conceived in
sharp, angular, straight lines. These are crowned with a handsome
head of compelling energy and masculinity. Yoritomo was the creator
of the *Baku-fu*, the military government of Japan centred at Kamakura.
Under his virile direction a new epoch, the Kamakura period, began.
A powerful administration swept away the pleasure-loving court society
of the Heian period and the realistic taste of the newly victorious *samurai*
or warrior class imposed itself on the arts.

The powerful conception and execution of the Yoritomo portrait have brought it a well-deserved fame but its companion work, the portrait of Shigemori, is artistically by no means inferior. Its softer lines faithfully reflect the character of Shigemori, a man well known for his filial piety. Shigemori possessed neither the fighting powers nor the administrative genius of Yoritomo but he was an attractive personality with a warm heart and a sympathetic nature. The gentleness and grace of this man so faithfully portrayed here are perhaps more attractive qualities than the haughty military bearing of the dictator Yoritomo.

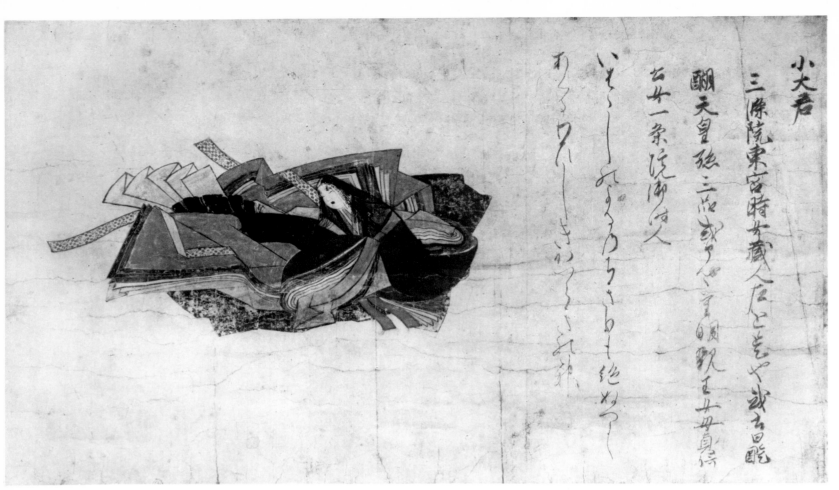

すゝしさはきえもやしつるいそのうへにいそしくもみをくたくはかりすみそめのありあけつきの三條院東宮時女蔵人庭とをさや或古旦眠醍天皇孫三品或う性書與る女一条院御文

小大君

Plates 74 and 75

PORTRAIT OF KO-ŌGIMI

Attributed to Fujiwara Nobuzane (A.D. 1176–c. 1265).
Kamakura Period. 13th Century A.D.
Colour on paper. Size 14 in. × 23 in.
Museum Yamato Bunkakan, Nara

This painting originally formed part of a set of two scrolls containing thirty-six portraits of poets and poetesses. They are attributed to Nobuzane, the son of Takanobu and a painter of portraits as famous as his father. In recent years these scrolls were cut up and mounted as thirty-six individual paintings which are now distributed among various museums and private collections.

The poet here represented is Ko-ōgimi, more popularly known as Kodai-no-kimi. It is one of the finest in the whole series.

Poetry has always played a large part in the development of Japanese culture; it remained for centuries the basis of education and intellectual life. Thus, during the Heian period thirty-six poets and poetesses were chosen, their work established as classics, they themselves raised almost to the position of deities and worshipped as protectors of the craft. Devotees raised shrines to them where aspiring poets would offer up prayers for their mastery of poetry. The portraits were often painted to serve as noble examples to students of literature. During the Heian and Kamakura periods these portraits were so popular that they became through repetition somewhat stereotyped and lifeless. The portrait here reproduced is outstanding and shows all the artistry to be expected of a painter with the reputation of Nobuzane.

Plate 76
CHIGO DAISHI—detail
Artist Unknown. Kamakura Period. Late 13th Century A.D.
Colour on silk. Size 18 in. × 15 in.
Collection Mr Murayama, Mikage

According to an old legend, when Kōbō Daishi, the founder of the
Shingon sect, was a young boy he had a dream in which he was seated
on a pedestal of eight-petalled lotus flowers discussing with various
deities the principles of Buddhism. From this legend sprang a theme
popular among Kamakura painters, that of Chigo Daishi (Kōbō
Daishi as a Young Boy). They depicted him as a child endowed
with supernatural wisdom. The painting reproduced is an exception-
ally fine example of its kind in which his wisdom and beauty are most
skilfully represented. The elegant floral designs of the costume were
painted in silver on a white background and the oxidization of the
metal has changed the silver into delicate tones of silvery grey.

Plate 77
MYŌE SHŌNIN MEDITATING AMONG
MOUNTAINS
Attributed to Jōnin. Kamakura Period. 13th Century A.D.
Ink and colour washes on paper. Size 54 in. × 23 in.
Kōzan-ji, Kyoto

The priest Myōe Shōnin (1173–1232) was famous for his self-discipline. He used to practise meditation in the wooded mountains
which rise behind the Kōzan-ji, the Buddhist temple he founded in
Kyoto. This picture is attributed to Jōnin, a priest-painter and pupil
of Myōe Shōnin in the Kōzan-ji. Myōe Shōnin believed that he
might best find enlightenment amidst the peace of nature far from the
cares and distractions of the world of men. The aim of the painting is
simply to depict the great priest in meditation but at the same time the
artist has added an Impressionist-like landscape. The wooded
mountains with birds and animals were directly observed by the
painter and freely rendered. By the Kamakura period artists were
prepared to observe nature directly and, as in this painting, to record
their impressions in a completely new way.

Plate 78

PORTRAIT OF DAITŌ KOKUSHI

Artist Unknown. Kamakura Period. Dated on the
picture A.D. 1334
Colour on silk. Size 44 in. × 22 in.
Daitoku-ji, Kyoto

Daitō Kokushi was the founder and first abbot of the
Daitoku-ji temple in Kyoto. *Zen* Buddhism was
introduced into Japan in the Kamakura period and the
Daitoku-ji has remained from that time the most active
Japanese centre of this sect. Images of Buddhas and
Bodhisattvas are of little importance in the ceremonies
of *Zen*, and the art of making such images declined from
this period. Artists turned their attention to portraits of
high priests and teachers which might serve as sources of
inspiration to their pupils. Such signed portraits sometimes served as a kind of diploma to prove that a man
had studied with a famous priest. This demand for
portraits combined with the Kamakura love of realism
to bring the art of portraiture to its height.

In the Daitō Kokushi portrait the artist has firmly
grasped the religious personality of the famous abbot.
The inscription on the painting is by Daitō Kokushi
himself and dated 1334.

Plate 79

SKETCH FOR PORTRAIT OF IKKYŪ

By Shōsai. Muromachi Period. Late 15th Century A.D.
Ink with light colour wash on paper
Size (picture only) 17 in. × 10 in.
Tokyo National Museum

This is a rare early example of a painter's sketch from
life. It is by a priest-painter named Shōsai, a pupil of the
eminent *Zen* priest Ikkyū (1394–1481). Shōsai obviously
made this sketch of the head of his master while he was
still alive. After his death he added the inscription and
mounted the sketch as a hanging scroll. The technique
is somewhat rudimentary but the approach is honest and
direct. The artist has endowed the features of the *Zen*
master with power in keeping with his severe character.

筆與而孫不知禪

墨雲画寄誰説禍

三十年来肩上重

前住大徳　休和る

一人荷擔松源禅

頂相自賛誽謹拜書

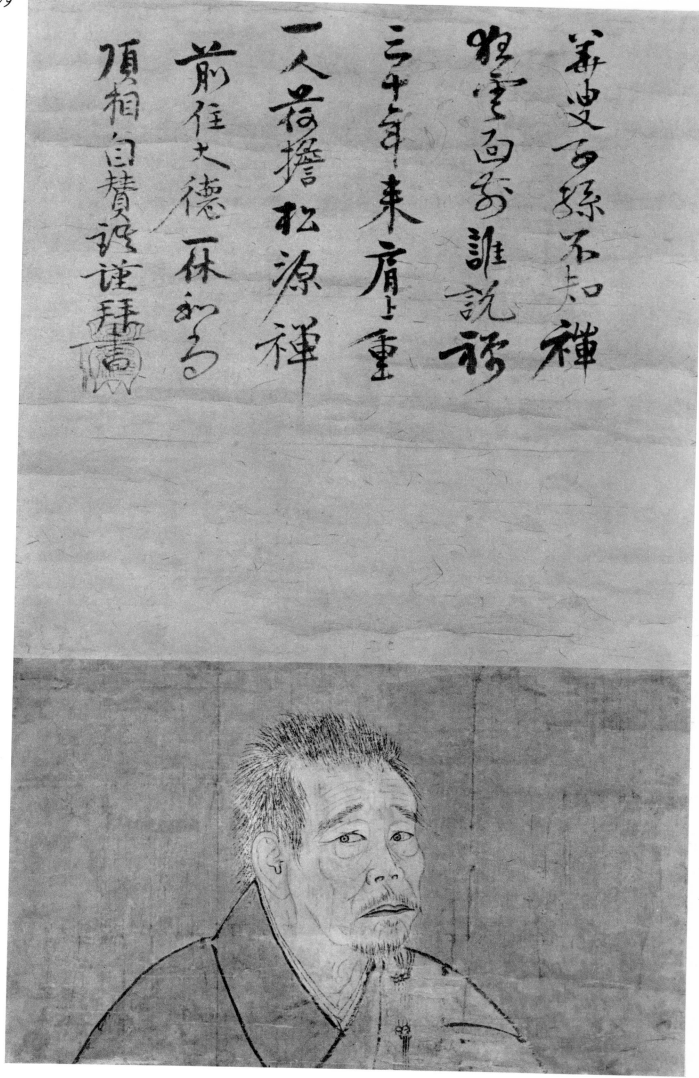

令兹藤信盈季三十六預定殁後之號曰心光院
常照興夕居士且今画其肖像自筆一句遺于屋
漏於是手識其歳月云
元禄十七祀在甲申三月
平埠元伸

信盈若遁世而號凮竹居士寓居洛北野馬
享保庚戌年四月廿五日六十有餘歳而寂
幕下樋口善尊寺也矣
信盈編
信逸書

瘦かしと
脈ちよう
春乃山
藤原伝凞

Plate 80

PORTRAIT OF NAKAMURA KURANOSUKE

By Ogata Kōrin (A.D. 1658–1716). Edo Period. Dated on the picture A.D. 1704
Colour on silk. Size 43·6 in. × 16·5 in.
Museum Yamato Bunkakan, Nara

This portrait from the hand of Kōrin was one of the most important discoveries of recent years. Until then it was thought that this outstanding decorative artist never attempted portraiture. The requirements of a portrait artist seemed far removed from his talents. When this portrait was discovered in a small shop nobody doubted its authenticity for every detail pointed unmistakably to the hand of Kōrin. It shows that, although somewhat unaccustomed to this type of painting, Kōrin's genius rose to the task of producing an extremely fine portrait. Traces of Kōrin's decorative abilities appear like a trade-mark in such details as the plum tree by a stream painted on a small folded fan. His greatness as an artist appears in his grasp of the complete personality of the sitter. The body is convincingly represented and with a few simple lines he has successfully captured his personality. The inscription records that the portrait is of Nakamura Kuranosuke, the wealthiest banker in Kyoto and Kōrin's most notable patron. They became intimate friends through their common love of the *Noh* drama. Indeed the whole painting evokes the atmosphere of the *Noh* stage.

Plate 81

PORTRAIT OF A LADY

Artist Unknown. Momoyama Period. About A.D. 1600
Colour on paper. Size 21 in. × 15 in.
Museum Yamato Bunkakan, Nara

Unfortunately the identities of both the artist and his distinguished sitter are unknown. A number of inscriptions on the background have been erased—either because they detracted from the general appearance of the painting or because, for some unknown reason, they caused offence. The handsome lady is the Momoyama ideal of feminine beauty. This was the period in which the *Noh* drama was the main pastime of the educated classes and a striking resemblance can be seen between her face and that seen in the many *Noh* masks which equally represented the period's ideal of beauty. The costume she wears is a fine example of a woven textile decorated with designs produced by a combination of dyeing and applied gold-foil (*suri-haku*) with embroidery. Here is a portrait of a noble lady from the brush of a great master.

Plate 82

PORTRAIT OF TAKAMI SENSEKI
By Watanabe Kazan (1793–1841). Edo Period. Painted
about A.D. 1837
Colour on silk. Size 46 in. × 30 in.
Tokyo National Museum

With this portrait of his friend and teacher, the distinguished *samurai*
and scholar Takami Senseki, Kazan must have surprised his countrymen. Realistic portraiture allied to a firm grasp of personality had
appeared almost for the first time in Japanese art. Kazan was one of
the forerunners of modern Japan. He was convinced of the foolishness

of the Edo government's policy of strict isolation for Japan and,
impatient of their strict laws to enforce it, he was courageous enough
to pursue whatever knowledge he could gain of western civilization.
These studies were prohibited. Kazan was arrested and finally
committed suicide.

Kazan's artistic personality was two-sided. He upheld the spiritual
objectives of oriental painting while at the same time insisting on a
serious study of nature. He was deeply impressed by the realism
achieved by western art which he saw in small copper-plate illustrations
mostly of medical books imported from Holland. Taking these as his
models he made his own individual studies of nature through which
he produced works notable for their integrity and accuracy.

We have frequently had occasion to show how Japanese art acquired its national characteristics in the Heian period. The national painting style which originated in these centuries is called *Yamato-e*. The foundations of the style are Chinese of the T'ang Dynasty but the peaceful years of the Heian period inspired an art which reflected the elegance and grace of the court life of the time just as it led to the creation of a distinctively native literature. The *Yamato-e* tradition has remained the main stream of Japanese painting down to the present day. Parallel with this is *suiboku* which was introduced from Sung China during the Kamakura period. The subsequent history of Japanese painting can be explained as the interaction of these two fundamental modes. The term *Yamato-e* means simply 'Japanese painting' while the Chinese methods were known as *Kara-e* or *Kanga*, i.e. 'Chinese painting'. It is significant that, although *Yamato-e* sprang from Chinese styles, it became so thoroughly assimilated in the Heian period that nobody could think of it as anything other than purely Japanese. The Chinese *suiboku*, a later style of ink painting introduced in the Kamakura period whose exponents place great emphasis on brushwork, was considered as the only completely Chinese style, and the continental origin in the T'ang period of *Yamato-e* was almost completely forgotten. In a sense the term itself is misleading, but it makes a justifiable distinction which provides a reasonable framework for an historical survey.

The colourful decorative style of the T'ang painting from which sprang *Yamato-e* suited the Japanese artistic sense. Japanese artists in the Heian period immediately responded to its elegance and lyrical qualities. *Suiboku* painting was the complete opposite of T'ang painting and, although the Japanese found some of its qualities congenial, they could not completely assimilate others. They regarded the spiritual austerity of the style, its repudiation of almost all colour, the strong brushwork derived from calligraphy, and the antipathy to decorative beauty and sentimentality as too severe and even bleak. We shall take up this subject in the chapter devoted to *suiboku* painting but suffice it here to say that, although the Japanese did produce an interesting style of *suiboku* with native characteristics, some aspects of the Chinese style were not thoroughly absorbed. It may well be that the style became popular for its exotic and even pedantic character. That the Japanese always recognized the alien quality of *suiboku* painting partly explains why it was never regarded as purely Japanese. Those very elements which refused to be Japanized gave it an added prestige. *Kanga*—which literally means Chinese painting of the Han Dynasty, that is, of great antiquity—was considered far superior to the common-place traditional style of Japan and its supporters lauded it as something rare and profound imported from China, the birthplace of eastern civilization. In a period of enthusiasm for all things Chinese, this was to be expected.

However, the alient elements of the *suiboku* style did fill an aesthetic gap left by the traditional *Yamato-e* styles. For example, *Yamato-e* with its grace of line and use of delicate colour so eminently suited to the scroll-paintings could not have provided structural compositions broad enough to fill the large areas of the screens which decorated the halls of the *samurai* of the Muromachi and Momoyama periods. These large spaces demanded the more powerful brushwork and the deeper contrast of dark and light which the *Kanga* style imported from the China of the Sung and Yüan Dynasties provided.

Yamato-e produced two great families of painters, the Tosa and Sumiyoshi, who were appointed official painters to the Imperial court and were responsible for the ceremonial paintings commissioned by the court and nobility. In times of national difficulty a return to Japanese ideals is always advocated and artists always returned to the *Yamato-e* tradition. This is an added indication of the depth of *Yamato-e* roots in Japanese culture.

However, *Yamato-e* is a product of the Japanese national character in its strictest sense and conse-quently tended to a narrowness of vision and a limitation of scope. During its first flowering from the Heian to the Early Kamakura period it produced some magnificent works but, after the Muromachi, it declined into a state of inertia. Yet this deep Japanese sensibility was quickly revived when a new spirit appeared to stimulate it. After many centuries of stagnation it quickened into new life during the Edo period. The movement which produced the great exponents of the decorative school of

Japanese painting, in particular Kōetsu, Sōtatsu, and Kōrin, was a reassessment and restatement in decorative and lyrical terms of the *Yamato-e* traditions. When new art movements appear, the ancient *Yamato-e* always provides a source of inspiration for Japanese painters and probably always will do so.

Yamato-e embraces many types of painting. We have already discussed Buddhist and portrait painting. The *e-makimono* (scroll-paintings) are its most important manifestation but this highly specialized form is more conveniently treated in a separate chapter. Here we shall discuss aspects of it not treated elsewhere—namely the landscape painting of the old *Yamato-e* school.

The early beginnings of landscape painting in the history of Japanese art possibly spring from certain ceremonies and teachings of Buddhism, combined with the innate Japanese love of nature. The Japanese were originally nature worshippers but Buddhism, after its introduction, rapidly became the leading religion. In the Asuka and Nara periods it was used to unify Japan and great temples were built in the capital cities to serve as centres of the State cult.

As opposed to this form of Buddhism centred in the cities, the esoteric Buddhism which came to Japan from the Late T'ang to the Early Heian periods laid stronger emphasis on a mystical approach which demanded of its adherents spiritual discipline. This could best be found in the solitude of the mountains and valleys away from the distractions of the cities. The Japanese call esoteric Buddhism *San Rin Bukkyō* (Buddhism of the Mountains and Forests). This explains why Kōbō Daishi built his main temple on the top of Mount Kōya-san, and Kōbō's great rival, Dengyō Daishi, established his headquarters deep in the Hie mountains. The importance attached to natural surroundings for esoteric Buddhist practices made an immediate appeal to the Japanese love of nature and led to two important developments in painting.

The first was the invention of the *Senzui Byōbu* (landscape screen). This indispensable accessory of esoteric Buddhist ceremonies was intended to create the impression that the ceremonies of the sects were being conducted amidst natural scenery. The practice began in the Early Heian period, and its most outstanding example is the *Senzui Byōbu* of the Kyōōgokoku-ji (Plates 83, 84). Although the screen is a work of the Late Heian period, its style belongs to a much earlier period. The figures are dressed in T'ang style, indicating that the screen was based on an earlier work which itself was strongly influenced by T'ang painting. The equally famous *Senzui Byōbu* of the Jingo-ji is a work of the Late Heian or Early Kamakura period but unlike the previous work, the figures and buildings are entirely Japanized. It provides an interesting example of the rapid and powerful process at work in the Heian period whereby the Chinese T'ang forms were nationalized. Some more examples of *Senzui Byōbu* can be found in other great temples of esoteric Buddhism and provide an interesting commentary on the early development of landscape painting in Japan.

The second and stronger influence working on *Yamato-e* landscape painting was that of *Honchi Suijaku,* the doctrine in which Shinto and Buddhist deities were identified.

From ancient times the Japanese had a large body of deities which reflected the nature worship of the native religion. When the Buddhist pantheon reached Japan, friction between them naturally occurred. *Honchi Suijaku* was the theory evolved to harmonize and incorporate the two beliefs. According to it the deities of Shintō were originally Buddhas and Bodhisattvas who had assumed native forms on Japanese soil. The two faiths thus came closer together and Shinto shrines and Buddhist temples were either incorporated or built on adjoining sites. Special *Mandara* paintings (Sanskrit: *Mandala*) based on Buddhist forms depicted the layout of the buildings within their sacred precincts, in order to show the relationship between the Buddhist deities and the Shintō gods. This type of painting encouraged the early development of landscape in Japan. *Mandaras* were produced at important shrines such as the Kasuga in Nara and the *Hie Shrine* near Kyoto (Plate 85). The landscapes in these paintings were the most important elements but for explanatory purposes small figures were added by the side of the various shrines. Most of the native gods were personifications of various aspects of nature such as deep mountains, great waterfalls, and beautiful islands. Thus these *Mandara* paintings were in effect little more than landscape paintings of beauty spots. In time, the artists of the *Mandaras* based on the *Honchi Suijaku* doctrine omitted the deities, and the paintings became indistinguishable from pure landscape paintings. The famous *Nachi Waterfall* (Plate 87) is a typical work whose origins are religious but which became purely an expression of the Japanese love of nature. The waterfall itself is the deity and, although the painting gives the impression of being a pure landscape, it is in fact a religious painting. In earlier times the Buddhist deity might have been shown above the waterfall but in the Later Kamakura period when this work was made, it was no longer considered necessary and the painting merely depicts a waterfall. The bright sun above it indicates the religious aspect. Although it simply shows a long waterfall, the painting has a dignity and a depth which is intended to inspire religious feelings in the spectator.

Plates 83 and 84
SENZUI BYŌBU
Artist Unknown. Heian Period. 11th Century A.D.
Folding Screen. Colour on silk. Size 58 in. × 102 in.
Kyōōgokoku-ji, Kyoto

The ceremonies of the *Shingon* sect include a baptism
(*Kanchō*). It is held in an area surrounded by this type of
screen painted with landscape scenes (*senzui byōbu*). The
example reproduced was inspired by the life of a hermit.
Such screens are intended to simulate a natural setting
for the ceremony. According to tradition, a Chinese
Emperor of the T'ang Dynasty gave this screen to Kōbō
Daishi who brought it back to Japan. Unfortunately
for such an attractive story, the screen is certainly Japanese
work and probably of the eleventh century. However,
the tradition has some truth in so far as Chinese T'ang
elements persist in it. In all probability it is a Heian copy
of an original Chinese screen painted in the T'ang era.
Other great centres of the *Shingon* sect such as the
Daigo-ji Temple and the temples on Mount Kōya own
similar screens but this example is the oldest and the
most interesting.

Plate 85

HIE MANDARA

Artist Unknown. Kamakura Period

Late 13th Century A.D.

Colour on silk. Size 45 in. × 21 in.

Reiun-in, Tokyo

This curious map-like painting displays the various Shintō Shrines at Hie, near Kyoto. As explained in the notes to Plate 36, Shintō shrines are now separated from Buddhist temples, whereas in the Middle Ages they were closely connected. The author has explained in his text the doctrine of *Honchi suijaka* (Identification of Buddhas and Shintō Deities), by which this union was achieved (see p. 154). This painting shows the shrines in their various positions among the Hie mountains. By the side of each shrine is also a picture of a Buddha to indicate that the two are in fact aspects of one and the same deity. This doctrine resulted in many paintings of Shintō shrines, including paintings of Buddhas. Gradually these Buddhas were omitted until Shintō shrines were shown simply in their natural surroundings. Since Shintō worshippers generally chose places of particular beauty for their shrines, these paintings played a significant part in the development of landscape painting. Sometimes Buddhist temples were similarly shown in their individual settings. The early beginnings of Japanese landscape painting are thus closely connected with religious paintings.

Plate 86

KASAGI MANDARA

Artist Unknown

Kamakura Period. Late 13th Century A.D.

Colour on silk. Size 30 in. × 22 in.

Museum Yamato Bunkakan, Nara

This painting shows the Buddhist temple at Kasagi near Nara before it was destroyed by war and fire in the fourteenth century. In the living rock at the summit of Mount Kasagi was carved a huge image of *Miroku* (Sanskrit: *Maitreya*). According to legend it was made by angels and had miraculous powers. The noble image is now destroyed and although the buildings have been reconstructed they are very much simplified. However, the same huge rock towers high above the steep valley and a few faint traces of the *Miroku* figure can still be distinguished to stimulate the imagination. The precincts of the temple still remind one of this old painting. It provides further evidence of the manner in which paintings, which began with religious aims, ended by faithfully representing real landscapes.

Plate 87
NACHI WATERFALL
Artist Unknown. Kamakura Period. 14th Century A.D.
Colour on silk. Size 63 in. × 23 in.
Nezu Museum, Tokyo

This representation of the Nachi Waterfall is more than a straightforward landscape painting. It is also a sacred image made in the light of the worship of nature—an essential ingredient of Shintō beliefs. By the Kamakura period, the paintings of landscapes with Shintō shrines, which had been so popular in the Heian period, developed into pure landscape with less religious feeling and more of the innate Japanese love of nature. This painting of the *Nachi Waterfall* was made at the interesting moment of transition from religious to realistic and secular landscapes. The impressive waterfall is situated among steep, darkly wooded mountains. To see it plunging almost from the peak of the mountain is to be moved far more deeply than one would expect of simple natural beauty. This overwhelming spectacle makes it easy to understand the power of nature worship and how the great waterfall could be identified with a god or interpreted as an expression of divine power. Although the painting was made in the fourteenth century when pure landscape painting was about to appear, nature worship was still strong. Thus the Nachi Waterfall was conceived as a pure landscape with the golden sun as the only remaining iconographical element. The religious dignity which pervades the work stems from this combination of pure landscape and ancient nature worship.

The finest expression and the fullest development of *Yamato-e* are the *e-makimono* (scroll-paintings). The form on which they are based originated in China but the Japanese developed it to a degree unknown in the country of its origin. These scrolls appealed greatly to Japanese taste; without doubt they constitute the most characteristic and interesting of all Japanese painting types.

In very early times Chinese books often took the form of writing on horizontal scrolls of silk or paper. As soon as artists conceived the idea of adding paintings to such scrolls they became true *e-makimono*. The oldest surviving examples in Japan are the *Ingakyō* sutra scrolls of the Nara period (Plate 88), dating back to the eighth century. These scrolls are divided horizontally, the upper half containing the illustrations to text written in the lower half. The pictures were meant to add interest to narratives and help simple people to understand them. It is a form of painting which, after having been imported from China, immediately appealed to the Japanese love of stories. The Chinese, it is true, painted scrolls to illustrate stories but they never developed such a special art form as the Japanese *e-makimono*, which was surely an ingenious device springing from the excessive love of the Japanese for picture-stories.

The *e-makimono* are intended to be unrolled section by section from right to left so that the stories they tell are revealed part at a time. Far-eastern writing is, of course, also read from right to left. It is important for the westerner to appreciate that the direction in which the painting is to be read is the same—the opposite, in fact, of that to which he is accustomed.

The basic form of the *e-makimono* depends for its success on an art of fluid movement and it requires that the spectator shall be prepared to participate actively in his viewing of it. The scrolls are designed in such a way that they hold the attention from one section to the next and their effectiveness is in direct proportion to the dynamic movement the artist displays, through which the story with its changes of scene is developed. The German philosopher Lessing in discussing western painting said that painting is the representation of nature or of an event seen at one glance or at one moment. This is a theory which, however true it may be for western art, is not valid for the art of *e-makimono*. Their fluidity of composition and sense of movement has led many critics to see in them the forerunner of the technique of the cinema.

In this depiction of a continuous story, the arrangement of the text which they illustrate created its own problems. The *Ingakyō* style was too limited and the artists soon discarded it. More often they used a form in which a section of text was followed by a section of painting. However, this was not so very different from a series of separate pictures and it detracted from the intrinsic desire to represent continuous movement. With scrolls of Heian romances, such as the *Tale of Genji* (Plates 95, 96), the artists had the text written in as fluid a style as possible, so that in its linear and rhythmic beauty each text part would not interfere with the continuity of the pictorial sections. But more often the artists overcame this difficulty by making the sections long enough to give themselves scope for showing changes of scene and development of narrative.

Japanese painting has always shown a predilection for sensitive line, and artists were highly trained in free line-drawing. In the section on Buddhist painting we have already pointed out how the study of Buddhist iconography and religious figures formed an important part of the religious discipline and training of the priests of the esoteric sects. Through it these painter-priests became highly skilled in the arts of draughtsmanship. Important esoteric temples like the Hōrin-in of the Mii-dera housed large libraries of iconographic scrolls and drawings. The priest-painters, under the guidance of a head of a monastery like Toba Sōjō Kakuyu (1053–1140), occupied themselves with copying them. One can imagine that in their moments of relaxation from the duties of strictly iconographical copying, these priest-artists might well have amused themselves by painting more lively scrolls to illustrate Buddhist legends. The Kōzan-ji, another famous temple of esoteric Buddhism, houses the *Animal Scrolls* (Japanese: *Chōjū-giga*) which are as remarkable for the skill of their line-drawing as they are for their subject (Plates 100, 101). Although traditionally attributed to Toba Sōjō of the Hōrin-in, it is impossible to determine who actually painted them. However, their masterly draughtsmanship and what seem to be caricatures of the priests of the time suggest that their spirited author must have been a priest of some esoteric sect.

As the Heian period gave way to the Kamakura, compositions of scroll-paintings became increasingly dynamic. The civil wars of the period and the instability of the government produced more dramatic themes. The illustrations to Buddhist legends and Heian romances were replaced by illustrations of political intrigues, wars, and civil disturbances. It was quite possible for artists to illustrate the slow tempo of such superb Heian romances as the *Tale of Genji* (Plates 95, 96), or the *Nezame Monogatari* (Plate 97), in individual sections. However, the *Shigisan Engi* (Plates 98, 99) and the *Animal Scrolls* demanded a more continuous style in which all transitions of time and place were smoothly made. Even these proceed at a leisurely pace compared with the drama and dynamism of the *Ban Dainagon Scrolls* (Plates 102, 103). In the scroll depicting the *Burning of the Gate of the Imperial Palace*, frightened people rush to the scene of the fire. The second scroll shows the quarrel between children which led to the discovery of the plot. The third scroll shows the capture of the culprit and ends with scenes of the despair of his family. These are all acts in a vivid drama in which the spectator is swept along by the speed of the composition and the energy of the line-drawing. In this splendid set of scrolls dramatic interest and fluid composition are perfectly matched, and the tragedy unfolds itself majestically.

The Japanese development of the art of scroll-painting was very original but it had its limitations. The providing of illustrations to a continuous narrative runs counter to the instantaneous nature of plastic art, and, except for the most notable works, scroll-painting tended to become mediocre. Great masterpieces were produced in the Late Heian and Early Kamakura periods but, after the thirteenth century, signs of deterioration soon appeared. They ended by being little more than mere picture scrolls. However, excellent examples of the art occasionally appeared even in later times.

In the second half of the Kamakura period and towards the end of the great period of scrolls production, a special and interesting type emerged which illustrated the travels of famous priests. The rise of new Buddhist sects which aimed at popularizing the faith among common people led priests to travel throughout Japan in search of converts in the provinces. Their activities provided a particularly suitable theme for scroll-paintings. The finest example of this type of *e-makimono* is the *Ippen Shōnin Eden* painted in 1299 by En-i. The travels of this priest take us to distant parts of Japan and give us a graphic impression of how they looked at the end of the thirteenth century. Fascinating scenes of mountains and rivers, towns and buildings, the country people and their daily lives unfold before us as if in a procession.

These 'travelogues' of the wandering priests gave a new lease of life to what had become a stereotyped form. Meanwhile in China *suiboku* landscape scrolls had been steadily growing in popularity. This type of landscape scroll reached Japan, and in the Muromachi period we see outstanding work in the mode by Sesshū dated 1486. Sesshū (1420–1506) undoubtedly owed much to his study of the paintings of the Yangtze River by the Southern Sung painter Kakei (Chinese: *Hsia Kuei*). However, Sesshū's interpretations reveal both his own peculiar gifts and the Japanese reaction to this scroll form. His mastery of line and composition seem to carry the spectator along from one beauty spot to another in an endless panoramic journey.

The travel and landscape scrolls did not mark the end of scroll-painting. It appeared in other forms and was put to other uses. Artistically the most important of these are the poem scrolls of the seventeenth century in which Sōtatsu (active, first half of seventeenth century) painted graceful designs in gold and silver and Kōetsu (1558–1637) added poems in his masterly calligraphy. Outstanding among these are the *Deer Scroll* (Plate 148), the *Flowers and Grasses of the Four Seasons*, and the *Lotus Pond Scroll* (Plate 150). In these scrolls the decorative brilliance of Sōtatsu's painting and the graceful freedom of Kōetsu's calligraphy unite to pay a last tribute to this favourite art form of Japan.

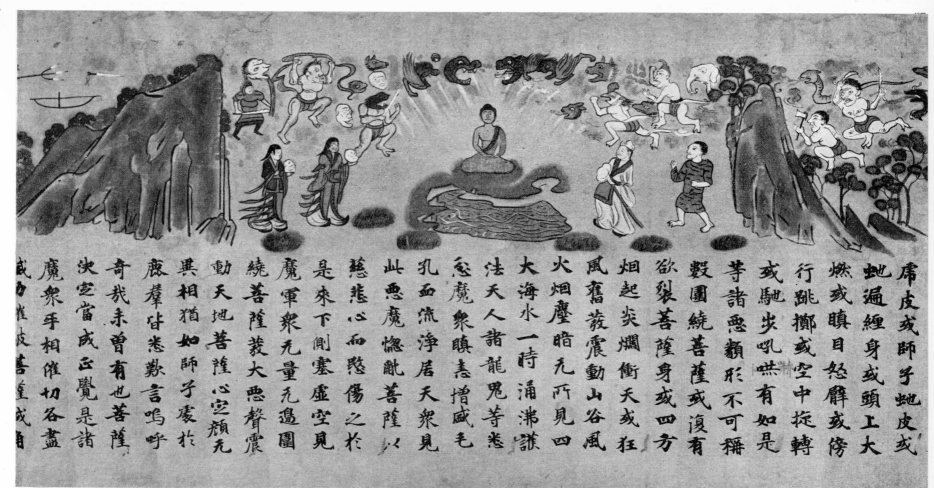

庸皮或師子虵皮或
虵遍繞身或頭上大
燃或瞋目怒齘或傍
行跳擲或空中掟轉
或馳步吼嚇有如是
等諸惡類形不可稱
觳圍繞菩薩或復有
欲裂菩薩身或四方
烟起炎爛衝天或狂
風奮蓊震動山谷風
火烟塵暗无所見四
大海水一時涌沸諸
法天人諸龍鬼等卷
怒魔衆瞋恚增盛毛
孔面流淨居天衆見
此惡魔惆悵菩薩以
慈悲心而愍傷之於
是來下側塞虛空見
魔軍衆无量无邊圍
繞菩薩茲大惡督震
動天地菩薩心宏顏无
異相猶如師子震於
鹿羣甘卷歎言嗚呼
奇我未曾有也菩薩
決定當成正覺是諸
魔衆手相推攞切各盡
咸力推攞菩薩咸自

Plate 88

INGAKYŌ SUTRA SCROLL

Artist Unknown. Nara Period. 8th Century A.D.
Colour on paper. Size (height) 11 in.
Hōōn-in, Daigo-ji, Kyoto

The *Ingakyō* is a rare example of one of the earliest forms
of scroll-painting in which the various scenes illustrate
a text written below. Examples of this type were found
at Tun-huang in the extreme west of China dating from
the T'ang Dynasty and several have survived in Japan,
the eastern terminal of the spread of T'ang culture. The
Ingakyō is a *sutra* which relates events in the lives both
past and present of the Buddha. The section illustrated
represents attacks on the Buddha by the powers of evil,
some of which threaten him while others tempt him.
The style is very simple as befits illustrations intended to
make an appeal to a wide public. It is interesting to see
how the Japanese faithfully studied the T'ang style but
how in the painting as well as in the calligraphy they
added their own artistic characteristics.

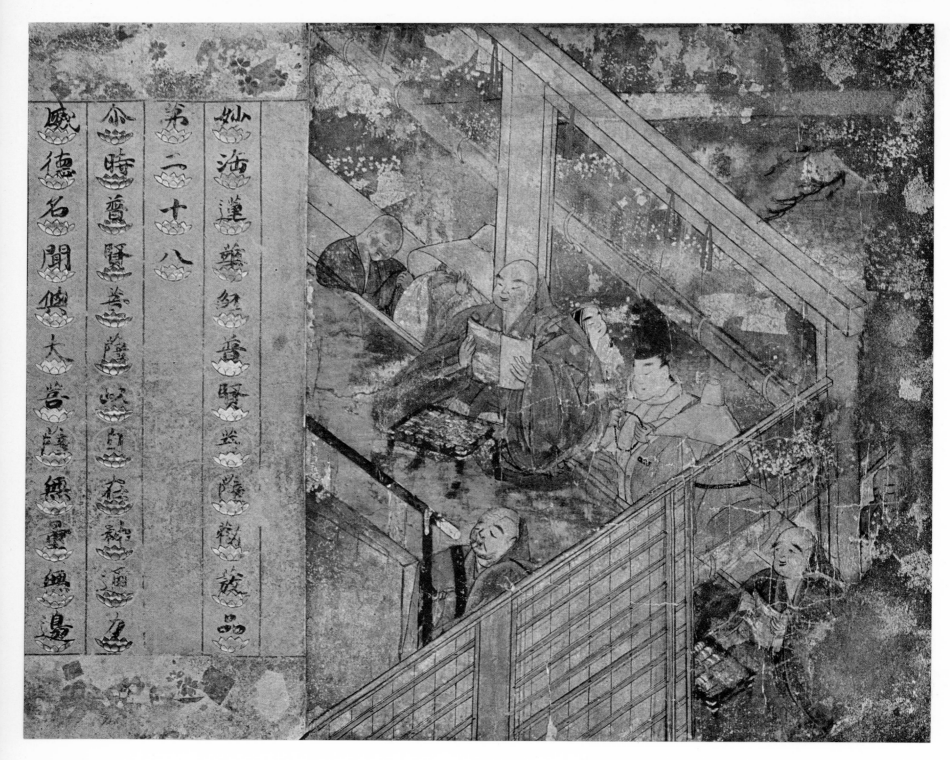

Plate 89
ICHIJI RENDAI HOKEKYŌ SUTRA SCROLL
Artist Unknown. Heian Period. Late 12th Century
Colour on paper. Size (height) 10 in.
Museum Yamato Bunkakan, Nara

This *Hokekyō sutra* scroll is popularly known as the Ichiji Rendai Kyō because each character of the sutra is written on a lotus-flower pedestal. This is intended to indicate that even a single character of the sutra should be considered sacred. Here the over-decoration of Buddhist sutras to suit the taste of hedonistic Heian society reaches its climax. The frontispiece of the scroll shows a small private hall of worship where priests, noblemen and ladies are gathered together to recite the holy scripture. The personalities are observed with such a remarkable degree of realism that they create the impression of being accurate portraits. There is a tradition concerning this scroll according to which the text was written by the ex-Emperor Goshirakawa who, after his abdication, entered the priesthood. The imagination is stimulated to see here a sutra reciting party in the ex-Emperor's private hall of worship.

Plate 90

KEGON GOJŪGOSHO SCROLL
Artist Unknown. Kamakura Period. 13th Century A.D.
Sumi drawing with light colour wash on paper. Size (height) 12 in.
Tokyo National Museum

The *Kegon Gojūgosho* scroll recounts in pictures the story of a pilgrimage which Zenzaidōji (Boy of Good Fortune), made to the fifty-five holy saints of the *Kegon* sect. The illustrations form a continuous composition and now occupy the whole width of the scroll. The text was cut into short passages and interspersed among the pictures where they apply. The fitting of text to illustrations was one of the major problems of the creators of scrolls and it was here solved very neatly. Most of this long scroll is owned by the Tōdai-ji Temple in Nara which was the centre of *Kegon* Buddhism. However, parts have been cut out and are now in other collections. The scene here illustrated is the last and one of the finest in the whole scroll. It shows Zenzaidōji's visit to the Bodhisattva Fūgen. The Boy of Good Fortune, here at the end of his pilgrimage, comes to the Bodhisattva who greets him with a smile and a gesture of welcome. This scroll is one of the most exquisite examples of the fluent line-drawing for which Japanese scrolls are justly famous.

90

Plate 91
KUNŌJIKYŌ SUTRA SCROLL
Artist Unknown. Heian Period. Finished A.D. 1141
Colour on paper. Size (height) 10 in.
Collection Mr Muto, Sumiyoshi

In A.D. 1141, noblemen and ladies of the court of Emperor Toba donated a set of *Hokekyō* sutra scrolls to the Kunō-ji Temple in Suruga province. The section illustrated forms the frontispiece to the Yakusō Yubon Scroll of this set which is intended to illustrate the Buddha's kindness to man. It shows two friends sheltering under an umbrella from rain and symbolizes the blessing of rain.

166

やくかくのときやしやうに
直天をもしか枚

Plate 92
JIGOKU SŌSHI (HELL SCROLL)
Artist Unknown. Early Kamakura Period. About A.D. 1200
Colour on paper. Size (height) 10 in.
Tokyo National Museum

Although scroll-paintings were first made as illustrations to sutras, their wide appeal
led to their being adapted to all forms of literature. This art reached its climax from
the end of the Heian period and lasted throughout the Kamakura period. Many
types of scroll were produced ranging from Buddhist miracle stories to romances
inspired by popular literature. The *Jigoku Sōshi* (Hell Scroll) is a masterpiece among
the earlier examples. According to the Buddhist faith there are a number of different
hells where humans are punished according to their particular sins. The hell in this
scroll comprises eternal flames into which devils drive the unfortunate naked sinners.
The huge red flames in sweeping linear rhythms fill the whole scroll and create an
impression of beauty combined with terror.

Plate 93
YAMAI-NO-SŌSHI (SCROLL OF DISEASES) - I
Artist Unknown. Early Kamakura Period. About A.D. 1200
Sumi drawing with light colour wash on paper. Size (height) 10 in.
Collection Mr H. Okura, Tokyo

The *Yamai-no-Sōshi* (Scroll of Diseases) was probably inspired by Buddhist thought
to depict the various misfortunes, both physical as well as spiritual, which can befall
mankind. It takes the form of a series of illustrations of various diseases—which
incidentally gives it an added interest to historians of medicine. The artist was
attracted by curious deformities and abnormalities which could be treated
humorously. The various scenes thus form extremely interesting caricatures. Two
examples of this interesting scroll are shown here. Plate 93 shows a soldier and his
family. The father is afflicted with a black nose, a deformity inherited by all his
children even down to the baby at his mother's breast. The scene has a strange
mixture of humour and pathos.

Plate 94
YAMAI‑NO‑SŌSHI (SCROLL OF DISEASES) · II
Artist Unknown. Early Kamakura Period. About A.D. 1200
Sumi drawing with light colour wash on paper. Size (height) 10 in.
Collection Mr Murayama, Mikage

This scene which is taken from the same scroll as the preceding plate gives a most graphic picture of mental derangement. It shows an emaciated man lying on a low bed, his eyes shut and his head tightly bound to suggest the pain. The text states that his malady takes the form of hallucinations in which he sees hordes of pigmy priests about five inches tall dressed in white paper robes and carrying long sticks. They come towards him and flock around his pillow. The artist has most skilfully represented the man's mental torment, his frightened face with his eyes shut tightly as if to keep out the scene.

The scroll has a further sociological interest in that it shows the miserable conditions in which the poorer sections of the community lived. This is seldom seen in the majority of scrolls which are concerned more with classical subjects or with aristocratic society.

94

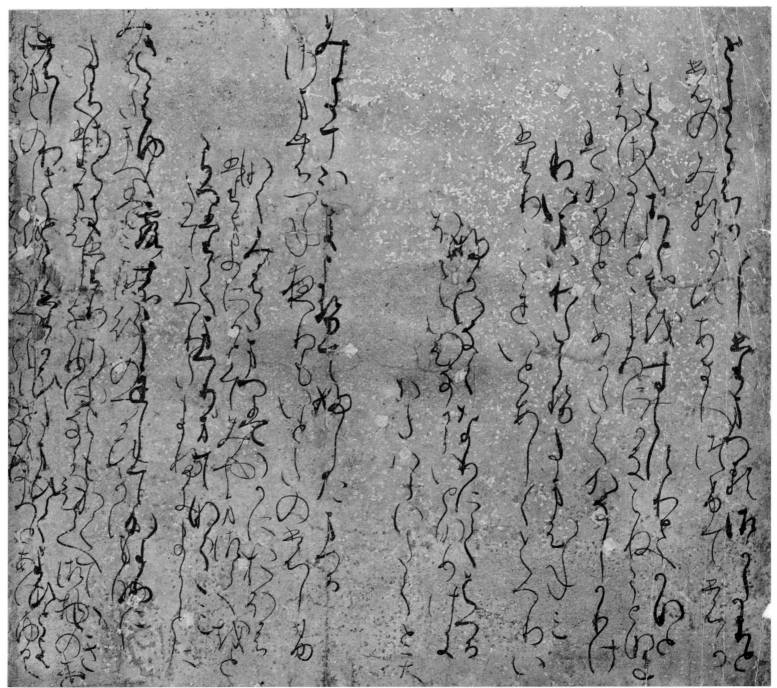

GENJI SCROLLS—CHAPTER OF SUZUMUSHI
AND THE TEXT PART OF CHAPTER MINORI
Artist Unknown. Late Heian Period. 12th Century A.D.
Colour on paper. Calligraphy on decorated paper
Size (height) 8 in.
Collection Mr Masuda, Odawara

The *Tale of Genji* is a long series of romantic stories in many chapters. If all the incidents there recorded had been made into pictures, the set of scrolls would have been very large indeed. Of the present twelfth-century set only four scrolls have been preserved—three in the Tokugawa Museum, Nagoya, and one in the collection of Mr Masuda, Odawara. Two sections of the Masuda scroll are here reproduced.

Plate 95 records an incident from the chapter entitled Suzumushi. The setting is the Imperial Palace on a moonlit night when the Emperor ordered his courtiers to make music. This is the *Yamato-e* style of painting at its best carried out in the most effective harmonies of delicate colour. The hazy moonlight, so typical of Kyoto, bathes the scene in light and shadow of romantic silvery grey. The parallel straight lines of the building—which could easily become monotonous—are effectively broken by the curved lines of the music-making courtiers in their billowing robes. Whether or not this work was made by the famed Takayoshi to whom it is attributed, it is masterly—the very essence of the Japanese sense of rhythm in art.

Connoisseurs of scroll-painting appreciate the calligraphy they contain as highly as the painting and the calligraphy of the *Genji* scroll is an outstanding example of the art of the period. The names of the three greatest calligraphers of the time are associated with the scroll—Korefusa, Masatsune and Jakuren. It is possible that all three contributed since more than one hand can be distinguished. More important than the problem of authorship is an appreciation of the beauty of line and the rhythms expressed by this form of writing unique to the Japanese. If the text had been written in the usual Chinese characters, the stiffness and formality of the script would have interrupted the flow of the scroll. The Japanese in their love of scroll-painting gradually developed a particular type of flowing linear calligraphy which is as much a decoration as a form of writing. The gentle gossamer-like lines between the scenes seem rather to unite than to separate them.

Plate 97

NEZAME SCROLL
Artist Unknown. Late Heian Period. 12th Century A.D.
Colour on paper. Size (height) 10 in.
Museum Yamato Bunkakan, Nara

The *Genji* scrolls and the *Nezame* scroll here reproduced rank high among the masterpieces of pure *Yamato-e* style in scroll-painting. They are both the oldest and the finest. The frontispiece to the *Nezame* scroll is also the best surviving representation of a garden in Heian style. The cherry trees are in full bloom and slender branches of willow trees wave gracefully in the breeze. The willows are treated in a very decorative manner yet, strangely enough, without losing any of their truth to nature. They can be seen thus in Kyoto to this day. The old *Yamato-e* style was the natural expression of Japanese taste born of the atmosphere of Kyoto. It remained the source of inspiration for many later masters from Sōtatsu and Kōrin downwards. The *Nezame* tales present many problems for historians of Japanese literature since their original form is now lost. Many scroll-paintings must have been made to illustrate them but this is the only survivor and further studies based on it are needed.

97

Plate 98
SHIGISAN ENGI—I
Artist Unknown. Late Heian Period. 12th Century A.D.
Ink and slight colour on paper. Size (height) 12 in.
Chōgosonshi-ji, Nara-ken

Although quite different from the *Genji* and *Nezame*
type, the *Shigisan Engi* scroll marks another peak in the
art of Japanese scroll-painting. The type is distinguished
by the most accomplished use of line-drawing almost to
the complete exclusion of colour. In its present form, the
work comprises three scrolls from which two scenes are
here reproduced. Plate 98 shows the *Scene of the Flying
Granary*. This shows how the full granary of a rich man
of Yamazaki suddenly took to the air, crossed a river and
headed for a distant mountain. The family and servants
pour out of the house to see what is happening to the
precious granary. The master of the house mounts his
horse to set out in pursuit. People by the riverside road
cry out in surprise and raise their arms; a priest with
rosary in hand prays to heaven to bring the building
back to earth. It would be difficult to find a parallel to
this masterly depiction of the consternation of a crowd
of people in the face of a supernatural happening.

Plate 99
SHIGISAN ENGI—II
Artist Unknown. Late Heian Period. 12th Century A.D
Ink and light colour on paper. Size (height) 12 in.
Chōgosonshi-ji, Nara-ken

This plate reproduces part of the *Scroll of the Nun*. I
illustrates the experiences of a nun from Shinano province
who came to Nara to search for her lost brother. She
visited the Great Buddha to entreat its help and spent
the night in front of the huge statue. In her sleep she
dreamed that the Great Buddha told her to go towards a
mountain which had a purple cloud over its summit
and that there she would find her brother. Waking up,
she set off with her heart full of hope. The picture shows
the Great Buddha, and the nun in several positions—
praying, sleeping and then departing as the story recounts.
The work has an historical interest in that it shows the
Great Buddha and its temple as they were in the twelfth
century. Soon after this scroll was painted both were
ravaged by civil war and sometime later they were very
badly reconstructed and restored. Thus, in addition to
their artistic merits, these scrolls sometimes provide very
valuable information which is not available in another
form.

99

Plates 100 and 101
CHŌJŪ GIGA (ANIMAL SCROLL)
Artist Unknown. Late Heian Period. 12th Century A.D.
Ink on paper. Size (height) 12 in.
Kōzan-ji, Kyoto

This extremely well-known set of four scrolls owned by the Kōzan-ji Temple, Kyoto, is known as the *Animal Scrolls*. In fact only one of the scrolls concerns the activities of animals. However, it is the most interesting and enigmatic of the whole set. Throughout its length animals are shown playing, quarrelling and making mischief in general. A number of the scenes suggest that they are intended to satirize the foibles and hypocrisy of the priests of the time. Rabbits, monkeys and frogs play leading parts. We do not know the meaning of the rabbits but the large-mouthed frogs may well be intended to represent talkative priests mouthing empty doctrines with loud voices. Monkeys, on the other hand, are notorious for their cunning and hypocrisy. They are also considered to be the servants of the Hie shrines which are closely connected to the Enryaku-ji Buddhist temples. Here the monkeys may well represent the Enryaku-ji priests. The Enryaku-ji and the Kōzan-ji which houses these scrolls are situated fairly closely together. As head-quarters of the rival *Tendai* and *Shingon* sects, there was little love lost between them and it is possible that the artist caricatured the priests of the Enryaku-ji as

monkeys. Nevertheless, much of the charm of this scroll comes from a simple good humour and real malice forms only a small ingredient. In my opinion, a master priest-painter is here simply amusing himself by depicting his favourite animals disporting themselves as his fertile humour directed the brush.

These *Animal Scrolls* have long been attributed to a priest-painter Toba Sōjō. I cannot accept this popular attribution. Toba Sōjō (1053–1140), whose real name was Kakuyū, was a high priest and a distinguished painter, the head of the Hōrin-in Monastery of Mii-dera. This temple, the repository of many esoteric Buddhist iconographical drawings and scrolls, acted as a training ground for aspirant priest-painters. The histories tell us that Toba Sōjō was pre-eminent among priest-painters and many early writers praise his draughts-manship, especially in humorous subjects. The *Animal Scroll* is technically one of the finest pieces of drawing which Japan has produced and its humour cannot be disputed. Naturally the name of Toba Sōjō became associated with it. However, recent research has brought to light some iconographical drawings signed by Kakuyū in a style which has little resemblance to that seen here. Thus, while admitting that an artist with a talent no less than that of Toba Sōjō must have made them, in the present state of our knowledge it would be wise to leave the question of their authorship to be decided by further research.

Plates 102 and 103
BAN DAINAGON SCROLLS
Artist Unknown. Late Heian Period. 12th Century A.D.
Ink on paper. Size (height) 12 in.
Collection Mr Sakai, Tokyo

The three *Ban Dainagon* scrolls illustrate a conspiracy
planned by a courtier and high official known as
Ban Dainagan (more correctly Tomo-no-Dainagon).
The detail reproduced is from the Burning of the
Ōtenmon Gate of the Imperial Palace which *Ban Dainagon* set on fire. Here all the dramatic qualities of Japanese
scroll-painting are shown at their best. Courtiers and
citizens rush towards the Imperial Palace. Each figure is
an individual study in excitement, astonishment, fear
and confusion. As the threatening black smoke rises to
the sky, they recoil from the flames which, enveloped in
smoke, shoot upwards. This masterpiece is attributed to
the genius of Mitsunaga. Although this may one day be
proved correct, sufficient evidence is still lacking to
enable us to accept it.

The art of *suiboku* painting, commonly known in Japan as *sumi* painting, was introduced from China during the Sung and Yüan periods (960–1368). It gained great popularity in Japan during the Kamakura period and became a thoroughly assimilated mode during this and the succeeding Muromachi period.

It is a distinctly far-eastern art form and has produced both in Japan and China a long tradition which is still very much alive. The special qualities of this form of painting spring from a combination of three elements—the use of *sumi* (Chinese ink) with its range of tones from white to black, the sensitive eastern brush which can produce not only linear drawing but also many different types of brushwork, and the special paper which has been developed to take the ink. These materials and techniques were all directed to the expression of the spirit of man in painting.

The *sumi* (Chinese: *mo*) is an ancient Chinese invention used originally for writing and subsequently for painting. The earlier Chinese paintings were generally coloured and *sumi* was used only for outlines. But from the close of the T'ang period, under the influence of freer and more vigorous calligraphic styles, *sumi* was gradually becoming the principal material for painting. In the Sung period all Chinese culture reflected a highly spiritualized quality and *sumi* painting, sometimes with the addition of slight colour-washes, became the most favoured mode. This *suiboku* style (Chinese: *shui-mo-hua*) was in direct contrast to the colourful styles which had been popular from earlier periods. The two schools of painting, the one in colour and the other in ink, form the two main divisions of far-eastern painting and laid the foundation for all subsequent developments. As we have seen, the Japanese first imported the colourful T'ang style and developed it into *Yamato-e*, which was so completely naturalized that the Japanese took it as their own style, even forgetting its Chinese origin. Then the new *suiboku* style arrived in Japan from the China of the Sung and Yüan Dynasties and gained more and more popularity during the Kamakura and Muromochi periods. It is true that both these styles, the coloured and the *suiboku*, show the subjective and spiritual nature of far-eastern painting, for after all both the Chinese and the Japanese consider painting to be the finest expression of the

5 Suiboku Painting

spirit. But when they became more keenly conscious of the spirituality in their culture, that is in the Sung and Yüan Dynasties in China and in the Kamakura and Muromachi periods in Japan, artists found that the tones which could be obtained with ink offered a most sensitive instrument for the expression of this spirituality.

The Kamakura period experienced a complete reaction against the sybaritic life of the Heian court which *Yamato-e* so perfectly expressed. The fighting men of Kamakura who had usurped the power of the Imperial court were essentially simple in their tastes. In religion they turned to the discipline of *Zen*. They naturally spurned the decorative and sentimental aspects of Heian social life, and their artistic tastes were for the uncoloured, austere, and spiritual art of *suiboku* painting. The same spirit animated the austere ritual of the tea ceremony.

Suiboku painting was also admirably suited to depict one aspect of the Japanese countryside. The semi-tropical seas surrounding Japan bring sharp changes of atmosphere to the islands. When the sun shines the colours are brilliant but the clouds and rain quickly change the landscape into a misty, grey world. These changes are reflected in the character of the Japanese people—at one moment excitable and gay but quickly depressed and sentimental. The lavish *Yamato-e* style is the expression in painting of one side of their character while *suiboku* painting expresses the more melancholy and subdued aspects. The two modes provided the Japanese with a full range for the expression of their character. The full development and fusion of the two produced the finest flowering of Japanese painting in the Muromachi period. *Suiboku* painting can be characterized first as an art of line and second as the art of tonal values. The many different ways in which artists have combined these have produced a wide variety of styles. These are naturally influenced by period, locality, and individual taste, but we can conveniently divide all *suiboku* painting into two main schools, one of which emphasizes line and brushwork, and the other tone.

The great Chinese painter and critic of the Ming period Tōkishō (Chinese: Tung Ch'i-ch'ang), was responsible for the theory which divided Chinese painting into Northern and Southern schools. His historical grounds for such a division cannot always be defended and it has aroused much opposition, but the author is convinced that his classification is fundamentally sound. Any traveller in China coming from the north to the south is immediately struck by the contrast not only between the landscape and climate but also between the ways of life and customs of the two areas. The peoples of the north and south differ in ideas, feelings, and in artistic sensitivity. In the north the air is dry and clear and tall mountains stand out in strong relief. There is little foliage and the mountains have sharp outlines which are visible for many miles. Northern school painting with its strong contours and realistic detail thus reflects the qualities of this landscape.

Southern China, however, especially along and south of the Yangtze River has a damp climate. The sky is often cloudy and the air hazy. The countryside is rich and well-wooded and everywhere are canals and lakes. Southern school painting tends towards a softness in which the mountain masses, the forests and villages are expressed in tones and nuances of ink rather than in clear-cut lines. It is essentially a lyrical painting.

The north of China along the Yellow River is the birthplace of its old civilization and in early painting artists used what they called 'lines like steel wires' or 'like the strings of a harp' for the outlines and then filled in the areas so defined with rich colours. Later these lines became more and more emphasized and accentuated like the brushwork of calligraphy. This was the style which best represented the characteristic northern landscape and it became the 'orthodox' style during the Sung period. It also formed the basis of the Academic style of the Sung court and was followed by all professional painters. However, it made little appeal to southerners. When the Sung court, under pressure from northern invaders, moved from K'ai-fêng to Hang-chou in the south and established the Southern Sung Dynasty (1127–1280) the south became the artistic centre of China. The Academic style continued even in the south but the artists of the area reacted against it and created their own individual style. This is what is known as the *Bunjin-ga*, or 'poet-painters' style, which is also popularly called

Nanga or Southern Painting. Its characteristics were a free and poetic treatment of subject and soft tonal brushwork. This, unfortunately, is perforce an all too brief summary of a very complicated problem but it is important for a westerner to have some idea of these fundamental differences of styles since they affected not only Chinese but also Japanese ink painting.

The first style of *suiboku* painting to reach Japan was that of the Northern school—especially that of the Academies of both the Northern and Southern Sung Dynasties. The powerful and precise brushwork of such Chinese masters as Baen (Chinese: Ma Yüan), Kakei (Chinese: Hsia Kuei), and Ryokai (Chinese: Liang Kai) formed the basis of Japanese *suiboku* painting. Great artists like Josetsu, Shūbun, Sesshū, and Motonobu all worked in this tradition. Motonobu in particular was responsible for incorporating this Northern style into the Kanō school which became the main current of Japanese *suiboku* painting.

One of Japan's greatest masters Sesshū, is an outstanding example of the Japanese adherence to the Northern school as it survived in Japan from the academic tradition of the Southern Sung. He went to China in 1467 and stayed there till 1469. That was in the Ch'êng-hua era of the mid-Ming period and in his autobiographical writings he records that he could find no Chinese master at the time whom he could admire. He himself gained a great reputation in China; he was even commissioned to decorate with murals an official building in Peking. Sesshū achieved fame in China, not only because he was a gifted painter in his own right, but because he was a master of the Southern Sung Academic style—a much admired tradition which in China itself during the Ming period had degenerated into conventionality. To the Chinese he must have seemed a reincarnation of one of the great masters of the past. Sesshū wrote that, after his disappointment with contemporary Chinese artists, he looked back with renewed appreciation to his Japanese teachers Josetsu and Shūbun. His criticisms imply that Japanese *suiboku* painting was still faithfully keeping to the precious tradition of the Southern Sung which had already been lost in China.

Despite the beauty of its colours, *Yamato-e* could never meet the requirements of large-scale compositions. It was the *suiboku* styles with their powerful brushwork that reflected the masculine spirit of the Kamakura Age which added to the repertoire of traditional painting a style well suited to decorate the large sliding screens in the castles and palaces which the lords henceforth began to build for themselves. Without the powerful brushwork of *sumi* painting the magnificence of Momoyama painting is inconceivable.

The fact that these Chinese styles were of alien origin seems to have given them a novelty value and increased their popularity. Starting as an alien form, the Japanese slowly incorporated them into what eventually emerged as the Kanō school styles which were to dominate Japanese painting throughout the three hundred years of the Edo period. Gradually they lost their early vitality and retained only the strong calligraphic element. With the rise of modern Japan, the Kanō styles disappeared.

We have hitherto been concerned with the Japanese reaction to the Northern school painting in China. But it was perhaps the *suiboku* painting of South China that appealed most warmly to the Japanese artistic temperament. Its soft brushwork and hazy tones were so congenial to the Japanese that they could assimilate them with ease. Many of the eminent Chinese painters who used the Southern style were not professional painters but more often priests, philosophers, poets, or *littérateurs*. They were essentially amateurs who believed that painting was the purest means whereby a man could express his nobility of spirit. They cared nothing for the display of mere technique ability. The Chinese painter most popular in Japan was Mokkei (Chinese: Mu Ch'i). His misty southern landscapes of the Yangtze River greatly influenced Japanese painters and inspired them to produce a style notable for superb effects of light and shade and for softness of line. The Muromachi period painter Sōami (died 1525), was the most important early exponent of this style. It is strange that, although Mokkei is perhaps the best appreciated Chinese painter in Japan, the Chinese histories hardly mention his name. Almost all his works were brought to Japan and have been treasured to this day. The fact that Chinese and Japanese evaluations of his importance differ so greatly is an indication of the different standards of the two peoples in their approach to *suiboku* painting. The Chinese Academy painters, following their preference for strong decisive brushwork, completely disregarded the soft brush of Mokkei.

We have already mentioned how most Japanese *suiboku* painters followed the Northern styles, but even such a great exponent of them as Sesshū occasionally turned to the Southern styles for inspiration. Sesshū wrote that while he was in China he wished to learn something new. He was attracted by the Chinese *Haboku* (Chinese: P'o-mo), the 'splashed ink' technique of the Southern style which dispensed completely with outlines and attempted to indicate form simply by areas of black and grey. This was, of course, a technique which lent itself admirably to depicting hazy or rainy landscapes. The fact that even Sesshū, the most outstanding exponent of the Northern style, could not on occasions resist the Southern style is a measure of its appeal to Japanese sensibilities.

The desire to establish a truly national *suiboku* style led the Japanese to emulate Mokkei rather than any other Chinese artist. After the early works of Sōami in the Muromachi period, the most important exponent was Tōhaku (1539–1610) of the Momoyama, whose screen masterpiece, the *Pine Wood* (Plates 123, 124) shows a consummate gift for adapting the Chinese use of light and shade to the Japanese taste. The steady nationalization of the Chinese style from the Momoyama to the Early Edo period produced many interesting works. However, it was possible here to indicate only the broad outlines of this movement and the reader will find further information in the notes to the plates.

The *suiboku* painting of the Edo period was in essence a continuation of the styles created in the Muromachi and Momoyama periods. The closing of the country resulted in a considerable degree of artistic inbreeding and the lack of external stimulus tended to reduce all the traditional arts to conventionalism. *Suiboku* painting shared this fate.

From ancient times the Chinese considered that *sumi* or black ink could express 'the five colours'. The conception of *sumi* as a means of producing colour effects was inherited by Sōtatsu (active, first half of seventeenth century) and Kōrin (1658–1716), who used it for large-scale decorative painting. Sōtatsu was responsible for a special technique called *tarashikomi*. In this the artist applies the *sumi* thickly on silk or paper and, while it is still wet, drops spots of water on to it. As the water spreads on the thick ink it produces random effects and designs which can be most effective. This is a technique which the Chinese never consciously developed, though Sōtatsu may well have been inspired to invent such devices by the varied *sumi* effects of Mokkei's work. He used it to brilliant decorative effect.

Plate 104
BAMBOO AND SPARROW
By Kaō. Late Kamakura Period. 14th Century A.D.
Ink on paper. Size 36 in. × 12 in.
Museum Yamato Bunkakan, Nara

Practically nothing is known about the life of the artist Kaō who painted this *Bamboo and Sparrow*. A few of his works have survived with reliable seals. He must have been a priest-painter who devoted his masterly calligraphic brushwork to the subjects beloved of the *Zen* sect which he served. *Sumi* or ink painting was developed in China during the Sung Dynasty to the highest form of spiritual expression and it entered Japan with the *Zen* (Chinese: *Ch'an*) sect of Buddhism. Kaō, working as early as the Kamakura period, emerges as one of the earliest painters to attempt the technique. The simplicity of his style is an indication of its early date. His paintings are distinguished by a *Zen*-inspired symbolism which gives as much if not more significance to what is not as to what is represented. In this famous masterpiece, Kaō has painted only two small branches of bamboo and a sparrow—nothing else. The spectator responds to the limitless expanse of sky directed there by the sparrow's pose and to the free movement of the wind as it sways the bamboo branches.

Plate 105
HYŌNEN ZU (CATFISH AND GOURD)
By Josetsu. Early Muromachi Period. Early 15th Century A.D.
Ink and slight colour on paper. Size (painting only) 40 in. × 30 in.
Taizō-in, Myōshin-ji, Kyoto

Attached to this painting are inscriptions by thirty famous *Zen* priests who lived in the Ōei era (1394–1427). One of these states that the painting was made by Josetsu on the order of the *Shōgun* or military governor of Japan who wanted a small screen painted in a new style to stand by his side. This was probably about 1410. The inscription establishes the important fact that *sumi* painting in black and white only was still considered to be a 'new style' in Japan. Apart from this very important painting we know almost nothing about Josetsu and can only accept the obvious facts, i.e. that he was a priest-painter and a close friend of the thirty priests.

The composition of poems or belles-lettres in appreciation of a painting was the fashion of the time among educated men. Thus the literary content of a painting was highly appreciated. The subject of this work, *Hyōnen Zu* (Catfish and Gourd) is a well-known *Zen* problem of how to catch a slippery catfish with an equally slippery gourd.

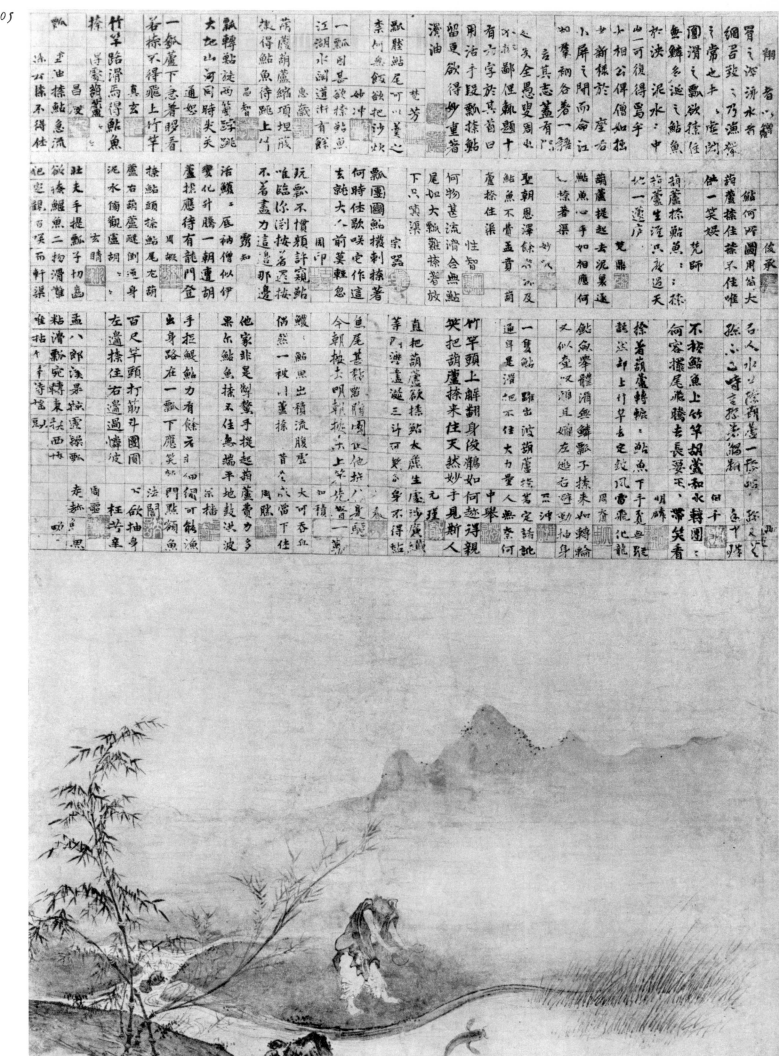

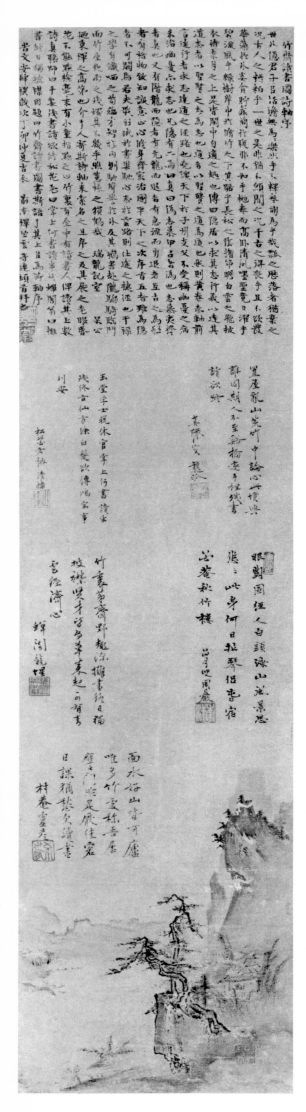

106

Plates 106 and 107

CHIKUSAI TOKUSHO (READING IN A BAMBOO STUDIO)

Attributed to Shūbun (active A.D. 1423–1448). Muromachi Period
Dated on the painting A.D. 1448
Ink on paper. Size 53 in. × 13 in.
Tokyo National Museum

So many *Zen* priests of the time added inscriptions to this painting that the composition itself seems to have shrunk into a small corner of the paper. Indeed, the painting seems to have served as little more than a pretext for poets and writers to display their literary talents. It provides a further illustration of the way in which the evocative power of a work was of major importance and *sumi* painting was the medium which appealed most strongly to the taste of the period. It gave infinitely more freedom to the imagination of the *littérateurs* of the time who preferred simplified brushwork to the detailed and realistic manners. In this work suggestion rather than straightforward representation is the keynote. In the background stand a few high rocky peaks; a copse of pine trees grows on a rock; a sparse bamboo grove half hides a small hut in which a hermit sits reading before an open window. Below is a broad lake whose far shore is only hinted at by means of grey washes. The painting is attributed to the priest-painter Shūbun and I have no reason to doubt the identification of this highly evocative picture as the work of this genius.

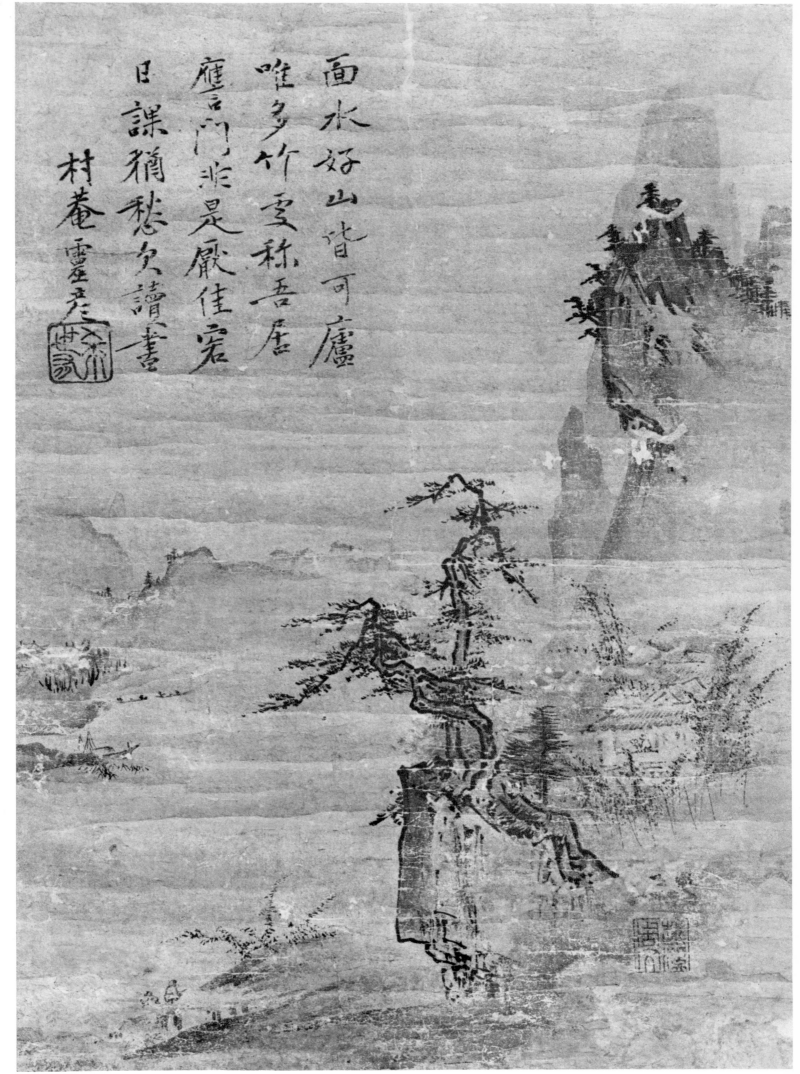

面水好山皆可廬
唯多竹雪稱吾居
塵言門非是巌佳宕
日課猶愁負讀書
村菴靈□是

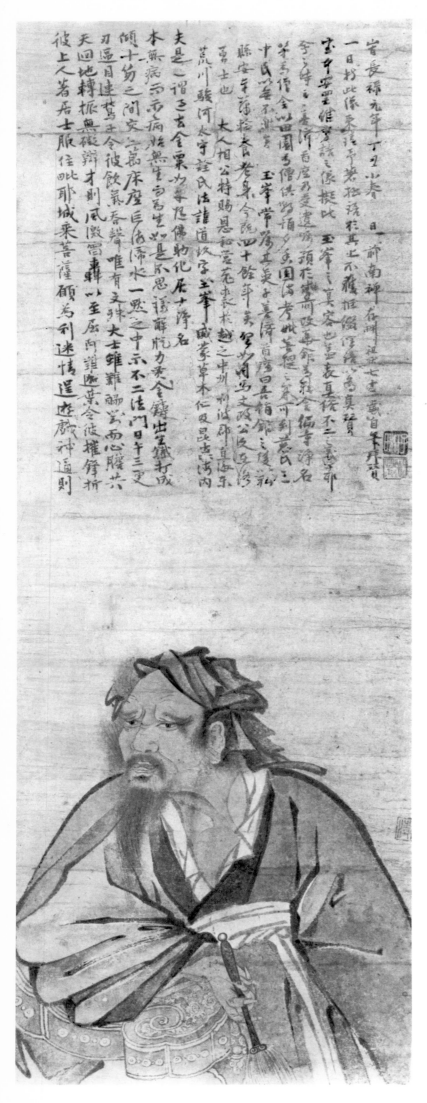

Plates 108 and 109

YUIMA

By Bunsei. Muromachi Period. Dated on the painting A.D. 1457
Ink on paper. Size 36 in. × 13 in.
Museum Yamato Bunkakan, Nara

Abbot Somoku of the Nanzen-ji Temple in Kyoto wrote a long inscription
on this painting which is dated 1457. In it he states that a *Zen* priest named
Zensai, the son of a *samurai*, converted his father's house into a Buddhist
monastery and ordered the artist to paint this portrait of *Yuima* in the likeness
of his father intending that it should serve as the main devotional image of
the temple. *Yuima* (Sanskrit: *Vimalakirti*) was a disciple of *Shaka*. He was a
man of great wisdom who never joined the priesthood but remained a
layman the better to propagate Buddhism among the people. The painter
Bunsei was a priest-painter belonging to the Daitoku-ji in Kyoto. So skilled
were his ink landscapes that he was often confused with the great master
Shūbun. A number of portraits of priests by Bunsei have survived but they
are of less interest since they follow very closely the conventional styles used
for *Zen* portraits. This *Yuima* is a masterpiece of very different stature. Here
with ink alone he has produced a painting which reveals the dignity of a
great man's innermost soul.

Plate 110
LANDSCAPE
Artist Unknown. Muromachi Period
15th Century A.D.
Sliding Screens. Ink on paper. Size 70 in. × 112 in.
Shinjuan, Daitoku-ji, Kyoto

Large numbers of screens in ink on paper were produced
during the Muromachi and Momoyama periods and
many have survived in Kyoto. None are so impressive in
their nobility of inspiration as these screens owned by the
Shinjuan, a monastery founded by Ikkyū (1394–1481)
the famous *Zen* priest renowned for the severity of his
religious discipline. The austere spirit of Ikkyū still
seems to dominate the temple and especially the room
which houses these screens. The painting here reproduced
is, in its composition, the essence of simplicity worked
out with a minimum of brush strokes and nuances of
dark ink. The result at the hand of a great artist is a
masterpiece of spiritual landscape—a world untouched
by any taint of the commonplace and far removed from
that of man. The identity of the artist is completely
unknown. An old tradition attributes it to Dasoku who
was a close friend of Ikkyū but, in the absence of any
supporting evidence, this remains nothing more than a
tradition.

Plate 111

AMANO HASHIDATE
By Sesshū (A.D. 1420–1506). Muromachi Period
Ink and light colour on paper. Size 30 in. × 66 in.
*National Commission for the Protection of Cultural
Properties, Tokyo*

Amano Hashidate has for many centuries been praised
as one of the three most famous beauty spots of Japan.
Sesshū was here deeply moved by its soft beauty and
made this large sketch—one of the very rare examples of
a preliminary sketch by a great master which has
survived. The finished work for which it served is said
to have been in the collection of the Tokugawa *Shōguns*
but is now lost. Research into the names of the buildings
which Sesshū added to his painting has revealed that
the artist made the sketch between 1501 and 1506 when
he was at least eighty-two years old. The knowledge that
he made a journey to such a distant place in his old age
thus adds a new detail to what we know of his life. The
work is a masterpiece in which the old master has un-
erringly grasped the very essence of nature. His command
of detail is matched by his understanding of the most
important aim of far-eastern landscape painting—the
deep appreciation of the grandeur of nature. The result
is a work of overwhelming beauty.

111

Plate 112

WINTER LANDSCAPE
By Sesshū (A.D. 1420–1506). Muromachi Period
Ink and light colour on paper. Size 18 in. × 11 in.
Tokyo National Museum

Sesshū originally made a set of four paintings to represent the four seasons of the year. Of these only two have survived representing Autumn and Winter. They are without doubt by the master.

At the time of Sesshū, traditionalism was perhaps the strongest force in art. A painter was expected to follow the style of outstanding masters of the past. It was rare for a landscape painter to take his inspiration direct from nature. In this work Sesshū was faithful to the traditional styles created by the Academic school of the Chinese Southern Sung Dynasty. In particular he had closely studied the work of Baen (Chinese: Ma Yüan) and Kakei (Chinese: Hsia Kuei). From these classical masters he derived his strong calligraphic brushwork and the powerful structure of his compositions.

The author, together with most modern critics, prefers the works inspired by a direct approach to nature as seen in the *Amano Hashidate* sketch in the previous reproduction but this traditional style has its virtues. The technical accomplishment and the dignity of these works laid the foundation of the Japanese Academic style which Kanō Masanobu, whom Sesshū patronized, was later to establish.

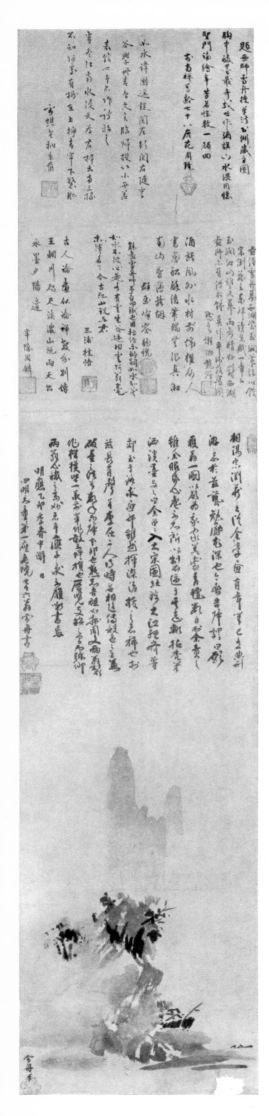

Plates 113 and 114
HABOKU SANSUI (LANDSCAPE IN HABOKU STYLE)
By Sesshū (A.D. 1420–1506). Muromachi Period. Dated on the painting
A.D. 1495
Ink on paper. Size 58 in. × 14 in.
Tokyo National Museum

In a long inscription on this painting Sesshū records some of the impressions he gained during his journey to China. He was deeply impressed by the breadth and grandeur of Chinese landscapes but he remarks that he looked back with great admiration to his Japanese teachers Josetsu and Shūbun. It is very interesting to read that Sesshū, who was brought up in the tradition of the Southern Sung painting, then prevalent in Japan, held a poor opinion of contemporary Chinese painting, i.e. the styles popular in the Ming period. Nevertheless he was determined to learn something new during his stay in China and studied with Chinese teachers to master the *haboku* (Chinese: *P'o-mo*) 'splashed-ink' style. This style of ink painting dispenses with outlines and creates its forms by splashes of ink in various shades. The technique is admirably suited for creating the impression of a cloudy or rainy landscape. Japan is an island with a very moist atmosphere and Sesshū found the 'splashed-ink' style very suited for recording the landscapes of his native country. Although his most characteristic works are in the powerful, angular, calligraphic style in the tradition of the Southern Sung academy, a few very effective *haboku* studies by him have survived.

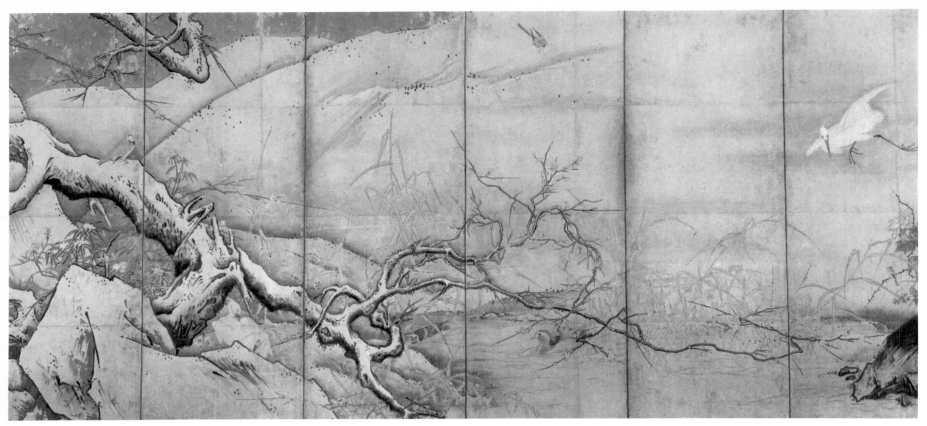

Plates 115 and 116
FLOWERS AND BIRDS
Attributed to Sesshū (A.D. 1420–1506). Muromachi
Period
Pair of six-fold Screens. Ink and light colour on paper
Size (each screen) 64 in. × 148 in.
Collection Mr J. Kosaka, Tokyo

The pair of screens here reproduced is incomparably the
finest of a number attributed to Sesshū. He placed
neither seal nor signature on these paintings but the
present author accepts them as genuine works. The
compositions are unparalleled in their grandeur of conception. The gnarled trunk and branches of an old plum
tree which reach out from the left are full of the vital
power of nature. The stately crane is the focal point of
the whole composition and brings together the tortuous
lines of the foliage. The pair of screens depicts the four
seasons of the year. Camellias on the right denote the
spring, lotus flowers represent summer, the dead reeds
by the waterside, autumn, while the bamboo and snow
covered plum tree are the symbols of winter.

Plates 117 and 118 (pages 196, 197)
LANDSCAPE
Attributed to Sōami (died A.D. 1525). Muromachi Period
Sliding Screens. Ink and light colour on paper. Size (each screen)
69 in. × 48 in.
Daisen-in, Daitoku-ji, Kyoto

This landscape is by Sōami, a remarkable artistic talent whose influence on
Japanese ink painting was far reaching. The majority of Japanese ink painters
of the Kamakura and Muromachi periods favoured the powerful, angular
style of the Southern Sung academy which was itself the inheritor of what is
known as the Northern school of Chinese painting. Sōami, however,
preferred the so-called Southern school with its smooth brushwork and soft
tones. Sōami may well have admired the work of the Chinese Yüan Dynasty
painter Mokkei (Chinese: Mu Ch'i) whose paintings reflected the hazy
landscapes of the Yangtze River and its lakes and were very popular in Japan.

In Sōami's work lay the true direction of Japanese ink painting. Starting
from the hard brushwork of the Northern school it graduated to the softer,
more free manners of the Southern school, which were better suited to
Japanese taste.

In addition to his gifts as a painter, Sōami was the leading connoisseur of
Chinese paintings in his day. His taste and experience resulted in his being
made keeper of the large collection of Chinese paintings assembled by the
art-loving Shōgun Yoshimasa. Thus Sōami was in a unique position to
study the various Chinese currents of painting. From these he chose for
himself and incidentally for future generations of Japanese painters the soft-
toned style of the Southern school as seen in the work of Mokkei. The
significance and wisdom of his choice will become evident in the paintings
of the Momoyama period.

Plate 119

SHŪMOSHIKU ADMIRING THE LOTUS
FLOWERS

By Kanō Masanobu (1434–1530). Muromachi Period
Ink and colour washes on paper. Size 36 in. × 13 in.
Ex-collection Mr Ogura, Tokyo

One of the most revered Chinese philosophers of the Sung
Dynasty was Shūmoshiku (Chinese: Chou Mao-shu). Apart
from his philosophy he is famous for his love of lotus flowers,
which according to him were the 'saints among flowers'.
He provided a popular subject for painters who generally
show him seated quietly in a boat admiring the flowers of a
lotus pond. Masanobu has here used the theme as an excuse
for painting a marshy pond. Although he shows a number
of lotus flowers his real interest is in the large willow trees
which dominate the scene. This Masanobu was the first
painter of the Kanō family and a man whose gifts were said to
have been discovered by the great Sesshū. Masanobu's son,
Motonobu, was even more talented than his father and as one
great master followed another in this Kanō line, the school
became established as the Academic school. It was to
dominate the Japanese art world throughout the Momoyama
and Edo periods down into the nineteenth century.

Plate 120

WATERFALL

By Kanō Motonobu (A.D. 1476–1559). Muromachi
Period

Ink and colour washes on paper. Size 18 in. × 34 in.
Museum Yamato Bunkakan, Nara

In the versatility and breadth of Kanō Motonobu's
talents most of the elements characteristic of Muromachi
painting were synthesized. In addition to the training
he acquired as the son of Masanobu, he inherited the
strong brushwork and the powerful sense of composition which distinguish the work of Sesshū. However,
having acquired this experience, he greatly extended the
scope of his work to embrace more than just *Zen*
subjects.

In the years leading up to the Momoyama period it
became the custom for the more powerful and independent warlords to build huge palaces and castles. Motonobu adapted the various elements of his training to
meet the demands which these rich patrons made on
his decorative abilities. He used not only the black and
white ink techniques but also the rich colours characteristic of *Yamato-e*. Occasionally he combined the two
styles, thereby initiating a new movement in Japanese
decorative painting.

The painting reproduced here is known as *The
Small Waterfall*. Motonobu twice painted waterfalls and
on both occasions produced works of outstanding merit.
His powerful brushwork seems admirably suited to
depicting the swirl and force of a falling mass of water.

Plate 121
WIND AND WAVES
By Sesson (A.D. 1504–after 1589). Muromachi Period
Ink on paper. Size 9 in. × 12 in.
Collection Mr Nomura, Kyoto

Behind the work of Sesson is an artistic personality of great individuality. His independence may partly be due to the fact that he lived and worked completely in the provinces. He passed almost his whole life in Hitachi province and never visited Kyoto where the art and culture of the period were concentrated. Like many of his contemporaries he greatly admired the work of Sesshū and may have seen examples of it in the temples of Kamakura. Yet, living away from the forces which shaped the arts of Kyoto, he rapidly developed a personal style and in it produced works which can compare with those of any master of the time.

In this small painting Sesson's gifts are freely displayed. He shows a sea whose calm horizontals are thrust out of balance by the buffeting of a storm. As the waves sweep down from the right a small sailing boat seems to run down before them. The force of the wind is suggested by the bare tree stripped of its leaves and by the bamboos which bend beneath its onslaught. Through them Sesson perhaps tried to symbolize man's efforts to resist the overwhelming powers of nature.

Plate 122

RODŌHIN
By Sesson (1504–after 1589). Muromachi Period
Ink on paper. Size 47 in. × 23 in.
Museum Yamato Bunkakan, Nara

Sesson has here applied his talents to a very different subject—the Chinese Taoist sage Rodōhin (Chinese: Lu Tung-pin) who is said to have had command over the dragons. Sesson shows him standing on the head of one formidable creature swimming throughout the stormy waters and calling to another dragon coiled among the distant dark clouds. The figure is transfigured as it stands with arms outstretched releasing a tiny dragon from a bottle held in his left hand. No Japanese painter of this time was capable of producing a figure of such energy and sublime appearance. Again, it would have been beyond the experience of an academic painter to reproduce waves which are more than just waves and are perhaps the very essence of the power of dashing water. In the development of his individual talents Sesson was fortunate in being free from the restricting influence of the formal training which the Kyoto professional painters underwent.

Plates 123 and 124
PINE WOOD
By Hasegawa Tōhaku (A.D. 1539–1630). Momoyama Period
Pair of Folding Screens. Ink on paper. Size (each screen) 61 in. × 137 in.
Tokyo National Museum

During the Kamakura period relations with China were once more firmly established. As a result, during the following Muromachi period a flood of Chinese art entered Japan. As previously noted, the most popular styles of painting during these centuries were those of the Sung and Yüan Dynasties in which the strong brushwork of the Academic style was the most important feature. As the Momoyama period progressed a new spirit appeared in Japanese painting. The native Japanese sense of beauty, nurtured by the soft qualities of the landscape, began to reassert itself.

The genius of this new period was Tōhaku. He was the painter who convinced the Japanese that their own landscape could be expressed most beautifully in terms of black and white. It was he who reawakened the native landscape sensibilities.

His masterpiece is reproduced here. These two screens represent the pine woods in Kyoto—possibly on a hazy morning when, to the delight of passers-by, the trees seem to play hide-and-seek in the mist. The scene and atmosphere is familiar to every Japanese but as yet no artist had expressed its beauty with the same soft charm as Tōhaku. Ink painting had hitherto been considered a lofty vehicle fit only to convey the philosophical ideas of China. Tōhaku was the first to appreciate the nuances of grey in Japanese landscape and to open the eyes of his compatriots to the possibilities in a medium hitherto reserved for Chinese themes. It is important to give some credit for this to Tōhaku's admiration of the Yüan Dynasty painter Mokkei (Chinese: Mu Ch'i) and to his Japanese predecessor in the Muromachi period, Sōami, who was almost alone in following Mokkei's style.

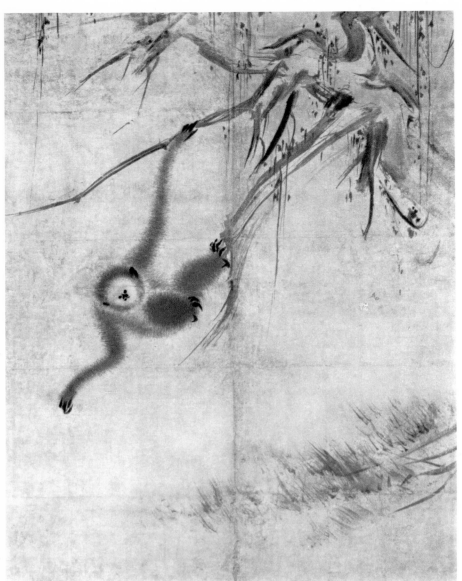

Plate 125
MONKEYS
By Hasegawa Tōhaku (A.D. 1539–1630). Momoyama Period
Ink on paper. Size (each painting) 60 in. × 44 in.
Ryūsen-in, Myōshin-ji, Kyoto

Tōhaku's paintings of monkeys here reproduced are now mounted as hanging
scrolls but originally they formed parts of folding screens in the possession of the
Maeda family. An amusing story ist old of how the warlord Maeda Toshinaga
while sleeping by these screens imagined that one of the monkeys was stretching out
an arm and about to snatch at his hair. The warrior quickly drew his sword and cut
off the monkey's arm. The damaged screen was repaired and they were mounted
in their present form. The painting subsequently became famous and is popularly
known as *The Picture of the Monkey with an Arm Cut Off*.

The style of the paintings owes much to the example of the Chinese artist Mokkei
(see Plate 124). Through Tōhaku's enthusiam for Mokkei's work, this particular
Chinese painter was one of the strongest formative influences on Japanese ink
painting in the Momoyama and later periods.

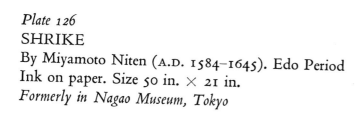

Plate 126

SHRIKE

By Miyamoto Niten (A.D. 1584–1645). Edo Period
Ink on paper. Size 50 in. × 21 in.
Formerly in Nagao Museum, Tokyo

The outstanding amateur painter Niten was by profession a
master of fencing and swordsmanship. His command of
these weapons, for which he was pre-eminent in Japan, seems
to have contributed to his powerful artistic personality. He
preferred to paint birds of prey with bodies poised ready to
strike. Their sharp eyes, powerful beaks and weapon-like
claws give his studies a peculiar power. The observation, in-
sight and precision with which he depicted these birds have
no parallels in Japanese painting. His strong brushwork is as
clean and decisive as a sword stroke. The painting here
reproduced of a *Shrike* is perhaps his most famous work and
clearly shows how he achieved his power by single accurate
brush strokes.

Niten's style can be traced back to the Chinese Southern
Sung artist Ryōkai (Chinese: Liang Kai) whose simplicity
and precision he greatly admired. The art of Ryōkai was
inspired by *Zen* Buddhism and Niten, using the minimum
of brush strokes similarly tried to reproduce the evocative
manner of *Zen* painting. The sharpness of Ryōkai's work
made an immediate appeal to a man like Niten whose
training and experience were with the sword.

Momoyama Screen Painting

Plates 127 and 128
PLUM TREES BY WATER
Attributed to Kanō Eitoku (A.D. 1543-1590). Momoyama Period
Sliding Screens. Ink and colour washes on paper. Size (height) 68 in.
Jukō-in, Daitoku-ji, Kyoto

This series of sliding screens painted with huge plum trees and attributed to Eitoku decorate a room in the Jukō-in Monastery. This was built in 1556 and the screens must be roughly contemporary. They show such a powerful, individual style that the author is inclined to accept the attribution.

Eitoku was the grandson of Motonobu and lived during the heroic years of the Momoyama period. Nobunaga and Hideyoshi, who united and repaired the ravages of a war-torn Japan, were his patrons. They decorated their palaces and castles in the most luxurious style, as much to suit their own bombastic taste as to overwhelm their followers and guests with the outward appearance of their wealth and power. Eitoku became their artistic prophet. His decorative paintings on screens, with their large-scale subjects and rich colours, are unmatched in the whole of Japanese decorative art.

No authenticated works by the artist have survived and we are forced to derive some idea of his achievements from works attributed to him such as the screens here illustrated. The outstanding features of the Jukō-in paintings are their heroic proportions and the powerful brushwork for which Eitoku was famous. It is said that he considered the usual brushes made of animal hair to be too soft and weak to produce the very strong lines which his compositions demanded. He therefore devised stronger brushes tipped with pointed straw with which he could produce whatever strength of brushwork he needed. The plum trees in this painting seem to have been created with just such 'straw brushes'.

Plate 129
HINOKI BYŌBU
Attributed to Kanō Eitoku (A.D. 1543–1590). Momoyama Period
Folding Screen. Colour on gold paper. Size 67 in. × 182 in.
Tokyo National Museum

Here, too, it seems reasonable to accept this as a genuine work by
Eitoku. The sweeping composition, powerful brushwork and rich

colours applied in large areas seem to point to the hand of this master.
The brown trunks of the old trees are shaded with black ink, dark
green leaves stand out against the golden clouds which envelop the
valley, brilliant blue water flows by the hard rocks of the sea-shore.
These are typical of the brilliant decorative effects at which Eitoku
was aiming. No truer reflection in art of the taste of the Momoyama
warlords is possible.

Plate 130
PEONIES
Artist Unknown. Momoyama Period. Early 17th Century A.D.
Sliding Screens. Colour on gold paper. Size (height) 69 in.
Daikaku-ji, Kyoto

These paintings provide another illustration of the love of nature for
which the Japanese are famous. It led them to decorate their rooms
with garden scenes of flowers and birds so that even within their
houses they could enjoy the illusion of being in a garden surrounded
by their favourite flowers, birds and animals. The visitor to this
Room of the Peonies in the Daikaku-ji Temple in Kyoto will
immediately appreciate the conscious effort which the painter has
here made to bring the garden into the house. The artist has not been
identified but the style closely resembles that of Kanō Sanraku
(1559–1635) who inherited the artistic traditions of Eitoku and who
worked well into the Edo period.

13

The Momoyama period was of short duration but its brief forty-two years saw momentous political changes and the flowering of a magnificent decorative art which formed a brilliant prelude to and laid the foundations for the modern painting of Japan. During the period Japan made its first contacts with the west. Western culture found a footing and Christianity gained many converts. The first western nation to have important relations with Japan was Spain and Spanish Baroque art of the sixteenth century with its vivid colours and strong contrasts of tone, was the first European influence to reach these shores. The Baroque spirit met with a welcome response in the heroic atmosphere of the Momoyama and strengthened the grandiose character of the art of the age. The domination of men like Nobunaga and Hideyoshi brought to an end the long period of feudal warfare. The huge castles they built with their dazzling rooms were intended to impress upon other feudal lords, the emissaries of foreign powers, and the powerful merchants, a sense of the dictators' grandeur and power. The decoration of these castles called for a completely new art of overwhelming brilliance and vast scale.

The entire decoration of magnificent rooms was entrusted to artists like Eitoku (1543–1590) and Sanraku (1559–1635). Kanō Eitoku worked for Nobunaga, the first warlord finally to subdue the local chieftains. Later he and Sanraku also decorated the Jurakutei Palace and the Momoyama Castle built by Hideyoshi, who continued Nobunaga's work and completed the unification of the country. Other great artists like Tōhaku (1539–1610) and Yūsho (1533–1615) appeared, both skilled in the *suiboku* styles and the ornate decorative modes. With the emergence of this galaxy of great painters, Japanese art attained a new magnificence.

It is important, when putting the art of Japan in its context as a part of the art of the world, to appreciate that for the first time since the days of Nara, Japan now created a truly grand style. One mentions this in order to counter the usual western conception of Japanese art as the dainty art of *Ukiyo-e* or of the intricate applied miniature art of *inrō*, *netsuke*, and *tsuba*. These tourist objects do not reflect the finest qualities of the Japanese spirit. To appreciate the true achievements of Japanese art it is essential to consider the Buddhist sculpture of the Asuka, Nara and Early Heian periods, and the screens of the Momoyama period where the powerful plastic qualities which Japanese art was capable of expressing are most apparent. Because of the preoccupation of Western art critics with the more familiar objects of Japanese art and style a surprising neglect of these periods has characterized their treatment of Japanese art.

It was the adaptation of *suiboku* brushwork to *Yamato-e* styles that made possible the powerful large compositions needed to meet the monumental challenge of the huge areas to be covered. This was largely the work of Kanō Motonobu (1476–1559) in the Muromachi period. His school, the Kanō school, by amalgamating the two fundamental Japanese painting modes, provided a foundation for the following three hundred years of painting. Motonobu, however, was mainly a *suiboku* artist and it was not until the Momoyama period that colours were fully combined with ink brushwork. This was the achievement of Motonobu's son, Eitoku.

It is said that Eitoku invented a brush made of straw to enable him to execute the broad and sweeping strokes necessary for decorating the large areas these castle and palace walls provided. Unfortunately few works can be ascribed to Eitoku with any certainty. The sliding screens of the Jukō-in of the Daitoku-ji (Plates 127, 128) and the folding screens in the Tokyo National Museum (Plate 129) are generally attributed to him. Here we find gnarled tree-trunks and boulders outlined in particularly strong brushwork which suggests the use of such a straw brush. The structural composition is a very important element in these works.

In addition to the new strength of brushwork, the screens relied for their effect on a display of brilliant colours. Indeed the screens are often called *Konpeki Shohekiga* (Gold and Blue Screens) which gives an indication of what was expected in the genre. Artists painted flowers, birds, and sometimes landscapes in brilliant colours with blues and greens predominating. These were shown off against a rich gold background. I find it difficult to visualize an art of this brilliance as coming from a union of *suiboku*

209

and *Yamato-e* simply at the desire of the great lords for a display of their wealth. There must have been some decisive influence from Spanish Baroque art.

The great Spanish missionary Xavier reached Japan in 1549 and Nobunaga and Hideyoshi were at first friendly towards the Christians. A foreign temple, the Nanban-ji was built in Kyoto. Here the Japanese must have seen religious paintings and objects. Hideyoshi later decided that these foreign missionaries harboured political ambitions and he gradually suppressed Christianity until, in the beginning of the Edo period, the authorities completely prohibited it. Christians who refused to surrender their faith were cruelly punished, and the works of art which the Christians brought to Japan were completely destroyed. For this reason little remains of this art in Japan, and it is difficult to assess its importance or to trace whatever influence it may have had. But it is certain that in its vivid colours, strong contrasts of light and shade and its grandiose, mystical qualities, Spanish art of the period must have appealed to the spirit of the Momoyama.

The old temples of Kyoto still preserve some of the finest examples of the Momoyama art, the most important being the sliding screens of the Chishaku-in known as the *Cherry Tree* screens (Plates 132, 133) and the *Maples* screens, and the *Willow Trees* (Plate 131) in the Sanbō-in of the Daigo-ji and the *Peonies* (Plate 130) belonging to the Daikaku-ji. It is difficult to ascertain their authorship with any certainty, but they are all representative products of the period and in direct line of descent from the heroic compositions of Eitoku.

There is another aspect of the screen-painting of the Momoyama period to which we have not yet referred. Whereas the lords used the brilliant colourful style mainly for the outer reception rooms of the palaces and castles where they intended to impress their visitors, they usually decorated their inner, private rooms in the more restful black and white styles. This new, monumental *suiboku* acquired a thoroughly national character in this period. Hitherto the Japanese had kept close to the Northern Chinese styles; they now began to use the foreign medium to paint what they themselves felt to be true and beautiful, and to draw inspiration, as I have already described in the previous chapter, from the Southern Sung styles. Tōhaku's masterpiece, the *Pine Wood* (Plates 123, 124), is perhaps the finest example of this Japanese development in *suiboku* painting on a large scale.

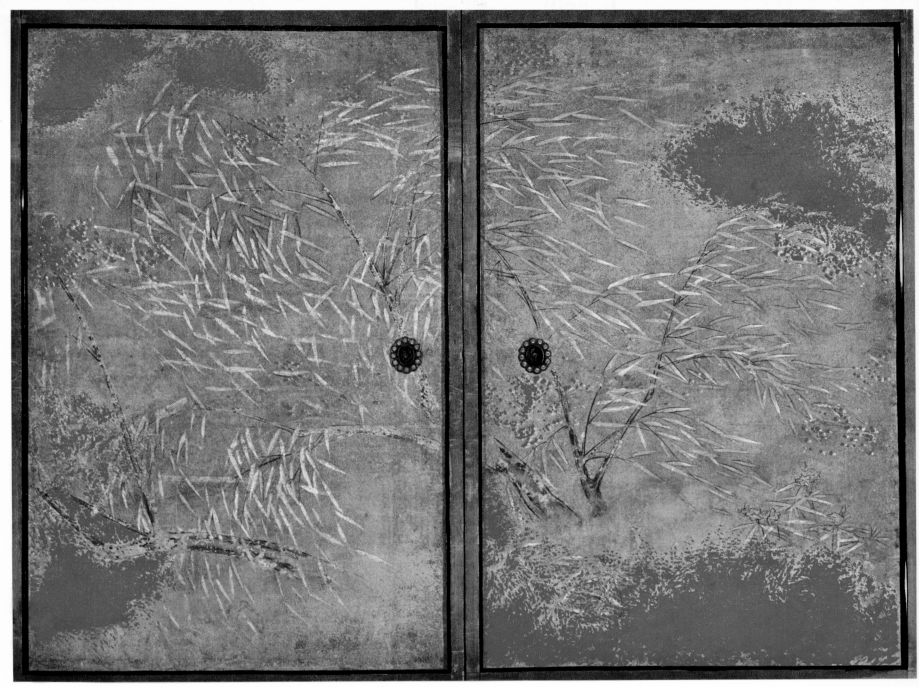

Plate 131
WILLOW TREES
Attributed to Kanō Eitoku (A.D. 1543–1590). Momoyama Period
Probably painted in A.D. 1598
Sliding Screens. Colour on paper. Size (height) 68 in.
Sanbō-in, Daigo-ji, Kyoto

The Sanbō-in buildings of the Daigo-ji Temple in Kyoto were built in 1589 when Hideyoshi was at the height of his power and supreme ruler of the whole of Japan. In the spring the cherry trees in its famous garden and in the surrounding hills are visited for their beauty. The temple garden in particular is one of the finest of its type in Japan and it was here that Hideyoshi held his vast garden party to admire the trees. Eitoku was already dead by this time but, as he was always closely associated with Hideyoshi and responsible for so many of the dictator's paintings, it is natural that the screens which decorate the Sanbō-in should be attributed to him. Although it is impossible to accept them as the work of Eitoku, the Sanbō-in is the one place above all others in which the atmosphere of Hideyoshi and his favourite painter has been preserved. The painter of the *Willow Trees in the Wind*, here reproduced, has faithfully preserved the characteristics of Eitoku's style. An artist of great decorative genius has observed the growth of the slender willow branches and their free movement in the early summer breeze. He has translated a common road-side scene into a colourful masterpiece of its kind.

Plates 132 and 133
CHERRY TREES
Artist Unknown. Momoyama Period. Painted about 1591
Sliding Screens. Colour on gold paper. Size (height) 69 in.
Chishaku-in, Kyoto

Fire has often damaged the Chishaku-in Monastery which houses these screens and its history is therefore very complicated. It would appear that these imposing *Cherry Tree* screens originally belonged to another Buddhist temple, the Shōun-ji which Hideyoshi built in 1591 to commemorate the death of his favourite son Sutemaro. The paintings later came into the possession of their present owner.

The year 1591 is slightly after the death of Eitoku and, although his style still prevailed, younger artists, of whom Tōhaku was the foremost, were introducing new elements of Momoyama taste. It is understandable that the screens have sometimes been attributed to Tōhaku, but there is no documentary evidence to support this attribution. The cherry trees are already somewhat removed from the manner of Eitoku in which a firm understanding of the structure of natural objects was the main feature. More realism and more decorative approach is seen in these paintings. This is notable in the cherry blossoms with their thick layers of Chinese white in relief on a gold background. The artists who followed Eitoku seem to have been content to develop his innovations and to seek more decorative effects.

Plate 134
COCK'S-COMB, MAIZE AND MORNING GLORY
Artist Unknown. Early Edo Period. First half of 17th Century A.D.
Folding Screen. Colour on silver foil. Size 55 in. × 63 in.
Freer Gallery of Art, Washington

It is now some sixty years since Charles Freer, the founder of the Freer
Gallery of Art in Washington, came to Japan to collect paintings.
During his stay he was greatly influenced by the taste of some of
Japan's most eminent collectors of the time, notably by Mr Hara of
Yokohama. Through these friends he became interested in the works
of what they then called the Kōetsu school, and he subsequently took
back to America some genuine examples of the paintings of Sōtatsu
and others of their type. Historically and artistically they provide some
very interesting material.

This screen *Cock's-Comb, Maize and Morning Glory* is one of the
best he acquired. The wind-tossed movement of the long leaves, the
heavy flowers on their slender stems and the maize are most carefully
observed and skilfully translated into a decorative composition.

However, this painting is extremely difficult to date. The style in
general is that of the Momoyama period, but the background is of
oxydized silver. This technique, in which the gold foil usually fixed
to the paper was replaced by silver foil, was introduced in the Early
Edo period when Sōtatsu was active. In the author's opinion, this
delightful screen is an Early Edo version of the Momoyama style in
which the influence of Sōtatsu is already beginning to make itself felt.

7 Early Ukiyō-e Painting

The most important social development during the Momoyama period was the emergence of a rich and powerful class of commoners. Art had hitherto been the monopoly of the court nobility and the educated priesthood. Henceforward it was required to satisfy the taste of uncultured *samurai* and *nouveaux riches* commoners who had the leisure and means to enjoy it.

A successful *samurai* would commission a portrait to commemorate a notable victory; the commoners demanded paintings depicting the manners and customs of their own class. In this way the repertoire of classical subjects for painting was greatly enlarged. Hitherto it had been restricted to religious, historical, and literary themes. The demand for paintings of everyday life gave rise to the beginnings of *Ukiyō-e*. The term 'Early *Ukiyō-e*' is here used to distinguish it from the *Ukiyō-e* prints of the later Edo period which are, of course, internationally well known. Although both depict scenes of everyday life, the early *Ukiyō-e* receives special attention on account of its particular artistic merit and its brilliant portrayal of the spirit of the important Momoyama and Early Edo periods.

It is difficult to identify the artists who first freed themselves from the pedantic, classical subjects and looked for inspiration to the world around them. We know the Eitoku's younger brother, Kanō Naganobu (1577–1654) painted the screen *Dancing under the Cherry Trees* and that Kanō Yoshinobu (1532–1640) painted the Kita-in screens of the various *Professions*, but educated men considered such genre subjects as unworthy. There is reason to suppose that good artists worked in the field but, on account of this peculiar artistic snobbism, they often left their works unsigned. The famous *Hikone* screen (Plates 141, 142) has a landscape which betrays the hand of a most competent Kanō artist. On the other hand, the popular movement produced its own prophets, the most famous being Iwasa Shoi Matabei (1578–1650). He claimed to be a descendant of the Tosa school and his style indicates that he had some justification for claiming the connection. Many *Yamato-e* artists seem to have worked in the field of popular art—a not altogether surprising development when one remembers that *Yamato-e*, the most Japanese of all styles, was most suited for such essentially Japanese subjects. The only difference was that the subjects of *Ukiyō-e* were taken from contemporary life.

Generally speaking, artists of the established schools such as the Kanō, Tosa, and Sumiyoshi were too bound by their conventional training to paint with the freedom and ease which the new subjects demanded. Many of the Early *Ukiyō-e* artists were probably renegades from the traditional schools. 'Matabei' to whom most of the early works are attributed, is little more than a generic name to describe a number of such artists.

Western figure painting which reached Japan after the Momoyama period may also have influenced the creation of *Ukiyō-e*. The subjects of European paintings, especially those which depict ordinary people in their various activities, were conspicuously different from the traditional landscapes, flowers, and birds of far-eastern painting. The merchants who demanded the new art were the very people who, through trade, had most contact with the west and doubtlessly they had opportunities to meet westerners and see their art. The Japanese *Namban Byōbu* (Foreigners' Screens), a type of screen painting which depicts foreign ships and people, are later than the Momoyama period but critics generally consider them as Early *Ukiyō-e* and they show a connection between European genre painting and the beginnings of a similar art in Japan.

In addition to renegade Kanō and *Yamato-e* painters, entirely unschooled popular artists also shared in the creation of *Ukiyō-e*. What they lacked in technique they compensated for by a refreshing originality and freedom of approach. Real *Ukiyō-e* came from these untutored painters. Their art was an indigenous and pure expression of the Japanese artistic sense.

It is interesting to consider the respective merits of the two outstanding examples of Early *Ukiyō-e* painting, the *Hikone* screen and the *Matsuura* screens. The *Hikone* screen (Plates 141, 142), as previously mentioned, was probably a work by a gifted Kanō artist. His training shows itself not only in the masterly composition but also in a stiffness which is typical of the Chinese inspired brushwork of the Kanō school, and which detracts from the spontaneous charm of the scene. However, the *Matsuura* screens (Plates 135, 136, 137, 138) show no such pedantic restraint. The artist must have been outside the academic circles. Other popular artists painted the small screen of *Dancing Girls* (Plates 139, 140), and the *Nawa Noren* (Rope Curtain) (Plates 145, 146) which depicts a scene typical of the gay quarters.

The painting *Yuna* (Women of the Hot Baths) is worthy of particular mention in that it was not simply a portrayal of beautiful women but rather because it contained a strongly satirical quality. The choice of such a subject for traditional art would have been inconceivable. The anonymous master has here shown a decadent interest in the ugliness and vulgarity of these low-class courtesans. With some justification critics have compared the painting with the work of Toulouse-Lautrec.

Although Early *Uikyō-e* was essentially a people's art, it reacted to the large-scale brilliance of the Momoyama—Early Edo spirit. With the increasing prosperity which the Edo period brought to the commoners, so the demands for *Ukiyō-e* expanded. However, its rapid development did not necessarily imply an improved quality. The opposite was true. Although the artists refined and perfected their techniques and increased the delicacy and subtlety of their work, they did not deepen their inspiration or develop their artistic sensibilities. During the climax of the Edo period, during the Genroku era (1688–1703), many designers achieved fame but the demand for their work became too great and the quality began to show unmistakable signs of deterioration. After the Genroku years, hand-painted *Ukiyō-e* could no longer satisfy the tremendous demand and the publishing houses, perhaps inevitably, began to rely increasingly on mass production by means of wood-block printing.

The prints of the Late Edo period depict a charming but decadent society. Their nervous sensitivity and sensuous beauty remind one of European *fin-de-siècle* art. Although the colour-prints influenced western Impressionism and were the first Japanese art to gain international recognition, it is not my intention here to consider them, although I do not deny their special charm. They represent, however, only one special aspect of Japanese art and the interested reader will find an extensive literature on them in European languages.

Plates 135 and 136
MATSUURA BYŌBU—I AND II
Artist Unknown. Early Edo Period. First half of 17th Century A.D.
Pair of Folding Screens. Colour on gold paper
Size (each screen) 60 in. × 144 in.
Museum Yamato Bunkakan, Nara

This brilliant pair of screens originally belonged to a Northern Kyūshū feudal family named Matsuura, and hence they are known as the *Matsuura Byōbu*. These and the *Hikone Byōbu* (Plates 141, 142) are the most famous examples of figure painting on screens in Japanese art. Both are the work of Early *Ukiyo-e* masters and are masterpieces in the skill with which they show aspects of contemporary life. Unfortunately their painters have not been identified. According to a typically far-eastern aesthetic, for an artist to make a study of people for the sake of their beauty of figure or dress, and if such a work contained no religious or literary significance, it was not considered worthy of the art of painting. Painters of such genre scenes had no artistic standing.

However, from the Momoyama period onwards it occasionally happened that, from interest or from popular demand, an artist with a classical training painted such a screen. However, he would take care to remain anonymous. The painter of the *Matsuura Byōbu* could hardly have had this classical training. The style and details point rather to a craftsman, possibly a designer of textiles and costumes. His achievement springs entirely from a native instinct for beauty and from an unsophisticated technique which is all the fresher for its lack of classical restraint.

Experts in the history of textile design recently made a study of the robes of the women who fill these screens. They concluded that they were painted in the early seventeenth century, the period of transition from the Momoyama to the Edo period in which the arts of weaving, dyeing and embroidery were greatly enriched. These years, before Japan was closed to all contact with foreign countries, were a time of great luxury of taste. Objects imported from abroad were eagerly sought and greatly admired. The master of the *Matsuura Byōbu* shared fully in this curiosity for foreign objects and customs. He shows a woman smoking tobacco in a long pipe, others wearing western costumes and necklaces, while yet another plays a three-stringed instrument imported from the Ryūkū Islands. The artist was so absorbed by these fascinating details that he paid less attention to the needs of an integrated composition. Indeed, he may not have had the training which would have enabled him to handle such large figures. Thus the paintings become a parade of beautiful women adorned with all the novelties of the time. This may detract from its value judged by classical standards, but it shows a new inquiring spirit and a fresh enjoyment of life which herald the approach of 'modern art'.

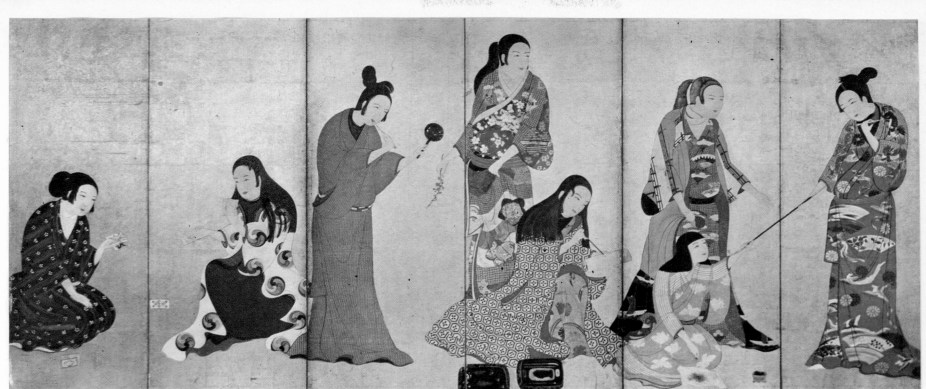

Plate 137
MATSUURA BYŌBU—III—detail of Plate 136
Artist Unknown. Early Edo Period. First half of 17th Century A.D.
Pair of Folding Screens. Colour on gold paper
Size (each screen) 60 in. × 144 in.
Museum Yamato Bunkakan, Nara

This detail shows a young girl wearing an overcoat decorated with many-coloured circles over a dark green costume tailored in western style, obviously a great novelty at the time. She is playing a card-game called by the Japanese 'Un-sun Karuta', a Japanese transcription of the Portuguese 'um sum carta'.

The rich costume worn by the girl in this detail is in typical Momoyama style. It shows the Japanese art of textile design and manufacture at its finest moment. Both in technique and design the robes of the Momoyama period were never surpassed.

Plates 139 and 140
DANCING GIRLS
Artist Unknown. Early Edo Period. 17th Century A.D.
Folding Screen. Colour on gold paper
Size (height) 25 in.
Kyoto National Museum

The screen is one of the best preserved of what must originally have been a series of similar screens of *Dancing Girls*. Another is in the Museum of Fine Arts, Boston, and yet a third from a Japanese collection was cut and remounted as separate hanging scrolls. The flowers and birds on the fans carried by the girls point to the hand of a Kanō school painter. Thus, as in the *Hikone Byōbu*, a painter with a classical training has been unable to resist the inspiration provided by the fascinating aspects of the world which surrounded him.

Plates 141 and 142
HIKONE BYŌBU
Artist Unknown. Early Edo Period. First half of 17th Century A.D.
Folding Screen. Colour on gold paper. Size 37 in. × 101 in.
Collection Mr Ii, Hikone

This screen has always remained in the possession of the Ii family which is descended from a feudal household of Hikone. The tradition, and even the popular songs which attribute it to Matabei, are unfortunately quite without foundation. The landscape elements show the hand of an artist trained in the Kanō school and it is quite possible that an artist with a classical training was here tempted to portray some interesting aspects of contemporary life which attracted him. The work is unsigned, probably because, as previously explained, cultured society would have considered such a subject to be unworthy of the attentions of a serious artist. The *Hikone* screen is of particular interest in that it shows the conflict between classical traditions and the new forces making themselves felt in the art world of the time. New standards of realism and beauty were to triumph over the pedantic manners of a classical art whose conventionality had robbed it of all vitality. The variety of pose and figure in this screen is most striking. It is in a bad state of preservation. This work and the *Matsuura Byōbu* are the finest surviving works of the Early *Ukiyo-e* movement.

Plates 143 and 144
HONDA HEIHACHIRO ESUGATA
Artist Unknown. Early Edo Period. First half of 17th Century
Folding Screen. Colour on paper. Size 28 in. × 62 in.
Tokugawa Museum, Nagoya

The subject of the painting on these screens—an exchange of letters between two shy
lovers—is very rare in Japanese art before the eighteenth century when it appeared in
Ukiyo-e. The design of the brilliant dress worn by the heroine incorporates a three-
leaved hollyhock *mon* or crest and this suggests that she belonged to the noble

Tokugawa family. The lovers have often been identified as a beautiful widow of the Tokugawa named Senhime and Honda Heihachiro a gallant and handsome *samurai*. No evidence exists to prove or disprove this attractive tradition and the author sees no reason to dispute it. On stylistic grounds it must have been painted in the first thirty years of the seventeenth century and thus may well have been made at approximately the same date as the romance. The composition, with its skilful placing of figures, is well calculated to suggest the nuances of such a relationship. The subtlety indicates a painter of outstanding talent but he, too, preferred to remain anonymous.

Plates 145 and 146
NAWA NOREN (ROPE CURTAIN)
Artist Unknown. Early Edo Period. 17th Century A.D.
Folding Screen. Colour on gold paper. Size (painting only) 63 in. × 35 in.
Collection Mr K. Hara, Tokyo

Nawa Noren can be translated into English quite simply as 'Rope Curtain'.
Such curtains hang at the entrance doorways to Japanese restaurants or tea-
houses. A glimpse of a beautiful female figure passing through the swinging
lines of a rope curtain was a familiar experience for the visitor to the gay
quarters of Kyoto. It inspired many a genre painting among which this is
outstanding. The woman's graceful poise and delicate expression, the tasteful
elegance of her dress, show an artist who was accustomed to and skilled in
dealing with figure painting. Her robes in particular are most effectively
painted with long sprays of wisteria hanging from the shoulders and waist
in harmonious parallel lines which follow the soft, curved contours of her
body. Thus, true *Ukiyo-e,* an art which specialized in genre subjects and in
the portrayal of human beauty, had started.

The other half of this screen has a painting of a bamboo curtain worked
out in horizontal lines. This is a much later addition and has nothing to do
with the painting illustrated. However, the use of a horizontal theme to
contrast with the verticals of the older work is a striking illustration of one
aspect of Japanese taste.

Plate 147
YUNA
Artist Unknown. Early Edo Period. 17th Century A.D.
Colour on paper. Size 28 in. × 31 in.
Atami Museum, Shizuoka-ken

Yuna were women who worked in hot spring resorts and catered for the pleasures of visitors. They were, in fact, little more than low-class prostitutes with neither the education nor the refinement of their more elevated sisters in the profession. The painter has here, somewhat in the manner of a Toulouse-Lautrec, revealed them as they were—ugly in face and body, dressed in flashy bad taste, haughty of bearing and quite indifferent to their surroundings. He was concerned neither with sympathy nor scorn. His state of mind, in its enjoyment of distorted and decadent beauty, may even reflect the morbid sensibilities of some modern art trends.

The most interesting form of painting in the Edo period was undoubtedly that produced by Sōtatsu and his school. Like *Ukiyo-e* and the arts of the Heian period in general, it was completely Japanese in inspiration.

Sōtatsu's style, which can be most briefly characterized as the art of *Yamato-e* enlarged and rein-forced by the grandeur and decoration of Momoyama taste, can be traced back to the *Yamato-e* of the Heian period. Sōtatsu was active in the Early Edo period and his successor Kōrin produced his finest works in the Genroku era.

This notable school of painting is often called the Kōetsu school from the name of its spiritual founder Kōetsu (1558–1632). However, comparatively recent studies have shown that Kōetsu rarely painted and that he was principally a calligrapher. His very considerable influence on the movement probably derived from the fact that he established an artistic community at Takagamine on the out-skirts of Kyoto. There he acted as the artistic leader of a number of artists and craftsmen active in various fields. Sōtatsu (active first half of seventeenth century) belonged to this circle and seems to have expressed in painting the ideals of Kōetsu. Thus it is more correct to refer to the Sōtatsu school.

The origins of Sōtatsu are obscure but, artistically speaking, he undoubtedly belongs to the long and illustrious line of *Yamato-e* painters. According to tradition, he was by profession a fan painter and the large number of his fans which have survived seems to support this. There are reasons to suggest that he was connected by marriage with Kōetsu, which would further suggest that Kōetsu influenced him. The fact that they collaborated in art is proved by a number of works in which Sōtatsu did the painting and Kōetsu the calligraphy (Plates 148 and 150). A number of works in lacquer also show their joint efforts.

Sōtatsu's great achievement lay in his adaptation of *Yamato-e* to the large-scale compositions demanded by his period without resort to the style of the Kanō masters. His screens *Thunder-god and Wind-god* (Plates 153, 154), *Genji Monogatari*, and *Bugaku* show how completely he could dispense with the Japanese interpretations of Chinese ink painting. The power of his soft and supple lines sustains them over the large canvases in a manner which is completely new for *Yamato-e*. The free and lavish use of the traditional *Yamato-e* colours is in marked contrast with the sparseness and stiffness of the Kanō line. By such means Sōtatsu was able to breathe a new life into this most Japanese of all painting styles.

It may seem a paradox but, in my opinion, Sōtatsu's breadth of colour effects owes much to his special study of the *suiboku* or *sumi* ink techniques. Occasionally he did work in *sumi* but, even in this medium, he shows a completely Japanese taste. He seems to have studied the *suiboku* art of the Chinese artist Mokkei (Chinese: Mu Ch'i) which he came to know through Tōhaku, who may have been Sōtatsu's teacher in painting at one time and who was the most enthusiastic admirer of the Chinese artist. This may account for Mokkei's influence on Sōtatsu's ink works. The subtlety of this Chinese master's ink style seems to have influenced Sōtatsu's use of colour by enriching and deepening it. His treatment of colour tones was thus inspired by his appreciation of the tones possible in *sumi*. *Yamato-e* artists had hitherto used ink only sparingly; Sōtatsu revolutionized this practice by using it in a daring manner as seen in the black clouds on a gold background in his *Thunder-god and Wind-god* screen (Plates 153, 154). His understanding of the artistic possibilities of *sumi* ink enabled him to develop it along original decorative lines.

The distinctively Japanese *tarashikomi* technique (see p. 180) was also an invention of Sōtatsu. It again shows his interest in the exploration of *sumi* techniques. In the hands of Kōrin and his followers this technique was responsible for many original and striking effects.

This new interpretation of *Yamato-e* decorative painting was further developed by the Genroku era artist Kōrin (1658–1743). The latter's international reputation as being the most representative Japanese painter is certainly well founded, for he developed and explored every possibility in the style initiated by Sōtatsu. He was not necessarily a greater artist than Sōtatsu. The earlier painter was the pioneer, Kōrin was the perfector. The age in which Kōrin worked, one of undisturbed peace and great prosperity, gave his talents full scope. He became the leader of taste in a gracious, wealthy society whose principal pursuits were beauty and pleasure.

Kōrin was the son of a Kyoto *kimono* maker named Kariganeya who, incidentally, was also a relative of Kōetsu. In his youth he was surrounded by beautiful robes and decorative objects and his family was sufficiently wealthy to give him a training which fitted him for the artistic leadership of a brilliant and sophisticated world. His younger brother Kenzan (1663–1743) applied his equally brilliant artistic talents to the art of ceramics.

The screen of *Waves* (Plate 152) in the Metropolitan Museum of Art, New York, is a typical Kōrin product. Kōrin has modelled the huge waves directly on nature which is unusual for him. But the rich blue colour and the gold background add the decorative element for which he is famous. The impact of the oncoming waves is almost overpowering. The *Iris* screen with its wealth of flowers in lapis lazuli and their brilliant green leaves shows the same masterly combination of the realistic and decorative. He includes no shores or indications of water but manages to create the impression of a sea of flowers against the golden light of early summer. His intention is not to paint realistically but idealistically and decoratively. Kōrin's genius is seen at its best in the screens of *Red and White Plum Trees* (Plates 155, 156). Here a silver stream ripples quietly across a golden background with, on one side, a red and on the other side, a white flowering plum tree. The curious lines of the water, the gnarled old tree-trunks and the large flowers evoke an image of springtime. These 'Kōrin waves' and 'Kōrin plums' became stock designs for later works of applied art. Kōrin caught the essence of their life and created a pattern which at once enchants and dazzles the spectator. The greatness of Kōrin's art lay in his ability to reach beyond naturalistic representation into a world of ideal beauty.

His taste is illustrated by a story of how the rich bankers of Kyoto arranged a *kimono* contest for their wives. They all arrived in scintillating robes but the wife of the most eminent banker, Nakamura Kuranosuke, whose portrait Kōrin himself once painted (Plate 80), staged her entrance late wearing a *kimono* designed entirely in black and white. The impression she created, so we are told, was that of a white crane descending into a flock of hens. She made the rest of the ladies look like her maids. She gained first prize and, so the story goes, Kōrin had been responsible for her choice of costume. The story is interesting in so far as it gives some idea of Kōrin's innate gift for masterly effects and his appreciation, like Sōtatsu before him, of the possibilities of black and white. He, too, produced a few *suiboku* paintings.

Kōrin's younger brother Kenzan devoted his remarkable talents to pottery making. He painted only for relaxation and we see in his works a casual quality, a freedom and freshness of approach which is perhaps of greater significance than the work of his illustrious brother. His painting on applied art objects have a bold sense of design and an originality of composition. Of his painting, the famous *Flower Baskets* (Plate 158) is his masterpiece. It could only have been made by a designer.

The last great painter of the movement was Hōitsu (1761–1828) who greatly admired Kōrin and studied his life and works. He even erected a monument to his memory. Hōitsu's paintings show a close dependence on Kōrin, but he lived in a different age and could not simply repeat the Genroku taste. He came under the spell of the naturalistic painting and his great contribution to the art of the period lay in his gifts for infusing the decorative style of Kōrin into the realistic nature studies of the time. The elements were not always easily reconcilable and many of Hōitsu's works are not of the highest artistic merit. However, occasionally he combined the broad decorative approach with a sensitive appreciation of detail. The rain-drenched summer grasses and the wind-swept *Summer Rain and Autumn Wind* (Plates 159, 160) which he painted on the back of his copy of Kōrin's *Thunder-god and Wind-god* screens are perhaps his finest achievement.

Plate 148
DEER SCROLL
Calligraphy by Hon-ami Kōetsu (A.D. 1558–1637)
and painting by Tawaraya Sōtatsu
Early Edo Period. Early 17th Century A.D.
Gold and silver on paper, calligraphy in ink
Size (height) 13 in.
Seattle Art Museum

Yet another notable example of the joint work of
Kōetsu and Sōtatsu is this *Deer Scroll*. Originally it was
a long scroll but in recent years it was cut into sections of
which the Seattle Art Museum was fortunate to obtain
a large portion. Kōetsu and his artistic circle often used
deer motifs. The reason for this may be found in Kōetsu's
interest in the *Noh* drama and his friendship with the
Noh masters of the Kanze family in Nara from whom he
himself studied the art. Nara was as famous then as it is
now for its deer park where herds of deer, sacred to the
Kasuga shrine, wander freely among the woods surrounding it. This *Deer Scroll* is one of the most important of the
many works with deer executed by the Kōetsu school.
Here all the aspects of the life of deer are carefully observed
and incorporated into a fascinating decorative composition.

Plate 149

FAN SCREEN—detail

By Tawaraya Sōtatsu. Early Edo Period. Early 17th Century A.D.

Folding Screen. Colour on fan-shaped paper. Size (height) 7 in.

Sanbō-in, Daigo-ji, Kyoto

Very little is known about the life of Sōtatsu. According to the most interesting tradition, he was by profession a fan maker. This is supported by a number of fan-shaped paintings which are without doubt his work. These paintings may originally have served as fans but were later mounted on screens to make what the Japanese call *Senmen Byōbu* (Fan Screens). The fan here reproduced is taken from a well-known fan screen by Sōtatsu owned by the Daigo-ji Temple where the artist lived for a time.

The Japanese fan is a difficult shape for the purposes of composition. Sōtatsu, however, overcame the difficulty in a masterly way, instinctively making use of optical corrections. In this fan, by skilfully distorting the architecture of three thatched farm-houses, he has produced a most successful composition. The blossoming plum trees provide a pleasant spring-time atmosphere and at the same time unite and balance the composition.

Plate 150
LOTUS POND SCROLL
Calligraphy by Hon-ami Kōetsu (A.D. 1558–1637)
and painting by Tawaraya Sōtatsu
Early Edo Period. Early 17th Century A.D.
Gold and silver on paper, calligraphy in ink
Size (height) 13 in.
Collection Mr S. Ōhara, Kurashiki

Two great artists, Kōetsu and Sōtatsu, co-operated to
produce this scroll. Sōtatsu, using only gold and silver
pigments, covered the whole length of the scroll with
representations of the four seasons of the year on a lotus
pond, while Kōetsu, the outstanding calligrapher of his
time, wrote a hundred famous poems over the painting.
The scroll synthesizes the beauty of fine rhythmic calligraphy in ink and the elegance of lotus flowers and
leaves in gold and silver. Evidence exists to suggest that
Kōetsu and Sōtatsu were closely related. Certainly they
were intimate friends and each influenced the art of the
other.

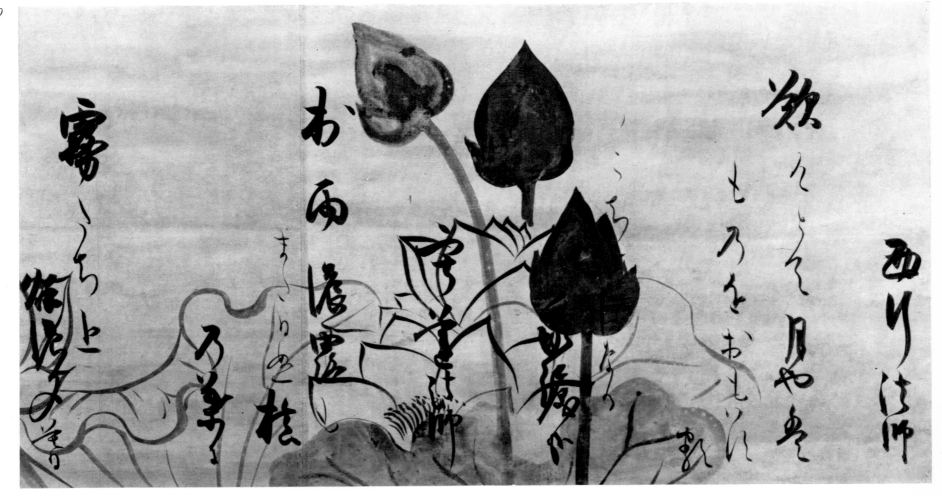

Plate 151

WATER FOWL ON A LOTUS POND

By Tawaraya Sōtatsu. Early Edo Period. Early 17th Century A.D.

Ink on paper. Size 45 in. × 20 in.

Formerly in the Collection of Mr Magoshi, Tokyo

Sōtatsu based his art on *Yamato-e* and, as one would expect, its main characteristic is the use of colour. Nevertheless he also produced a type of ink painting which is almost unique. Until about twenty years ago, historians regarded all black and white paintings attributed to Sōtatsu with suspicion. They doubted that an artist in whose work colour played such an important part could show such abilities in the field of monochrome painting. However, since then, studies in the work of this artist have greatly progressed and new material has slowly come to light. From this it seems clear that Sōtatsu worked equally well in both media.

The painting here reproduced, *Water Fowl on a Lotus Pond* is considered his best work in the ink style. When Chinese painting of the Sung and Yüan periods entered Japan during the Kamakura and Muromachi periods, Japanese artists studied it closely and gradually absorbed it. Over the centuries they began to evolve their own styles which reflected the native Japanese taste. These ink works of Sōtatsu are the clearest illustration of the way in which Chinese modes were completely taken over by the Japanese. His soft brushwork in this style is most remarkable. He also used what may be called a very 'wet' ink made by mixing water very freely into the ink. This 'wet' ink can produce an infinite variety of nuances in black and a most decorative effect. Sōtatsu developed this technique, called in Japanese *tarashikomi*, and it was extensively employed by his great successor Kōrin.

Plate 152
WAVES
By Ogata Kōrin (A.D. 1658–1716). Edo Period
Folding Screen. Colour on gold paper. Size 58 in. × 65 in.
Metropolitan Museum of Art, New York

Kōrin is acknowledged to be the greatest decorative genius that Japan has produced. But he was also a most remarkable painter in the fullest sense. His best-known style is, of course, conspicuously decorative. Trees, flowers, mountain streams, waves and even animal and human figures are all transformed by his powers into effective ornamental designs. However, the painting here reproduced shows a rare side of his artistic gifts. In this *Wave Screen* he has abandoned his usual manner to paint the surging waves of the sea with as much realism as he could command. In his younger days he has studied the Kanō style and mastered its powerful calligraphic brushwork. Later, his

admiration for Sōtatsu led him to prefer a more decorative approach and a softer more curvilinear brushwork. It comes as a surprise to find him painting such a striking screen in a style which he had once abandoned. Overwhelmed by the power of the sea, he perhaps felt that the Kanō manner was more suited than the decorative style to depict its threatening power. At the same time his gifts as a colourist still stand out. He used only three colours but with masterly effect; gold for the background, white for the crests of the waves and an ominous blue, thickly applied, which makes the waves stand out in strong relief and at the same time produces an impression of a deep stormy sea.

Plates 153 and 154
THUNDER-GOD AND WIND-GOD
By Tawaraya Sōtatsu. Early Edo Period. Early 17th Century A.D.
Pair of Folding Screens. Colour on gold paper. Size 60 in. × 66 in.
Kennin-ji, Kyoto

Sōtatsu was without doubt the most outstanding painter of the Early Edo period. His early training was in the *Yamato-e* style and whatever direction his artistic development took him this always remained the basis of his work. He grew up during the Momoyama period and absorbed its decorative manner and grand style. The influence of his relative Kōetsu, as previously noted, was another strong formative

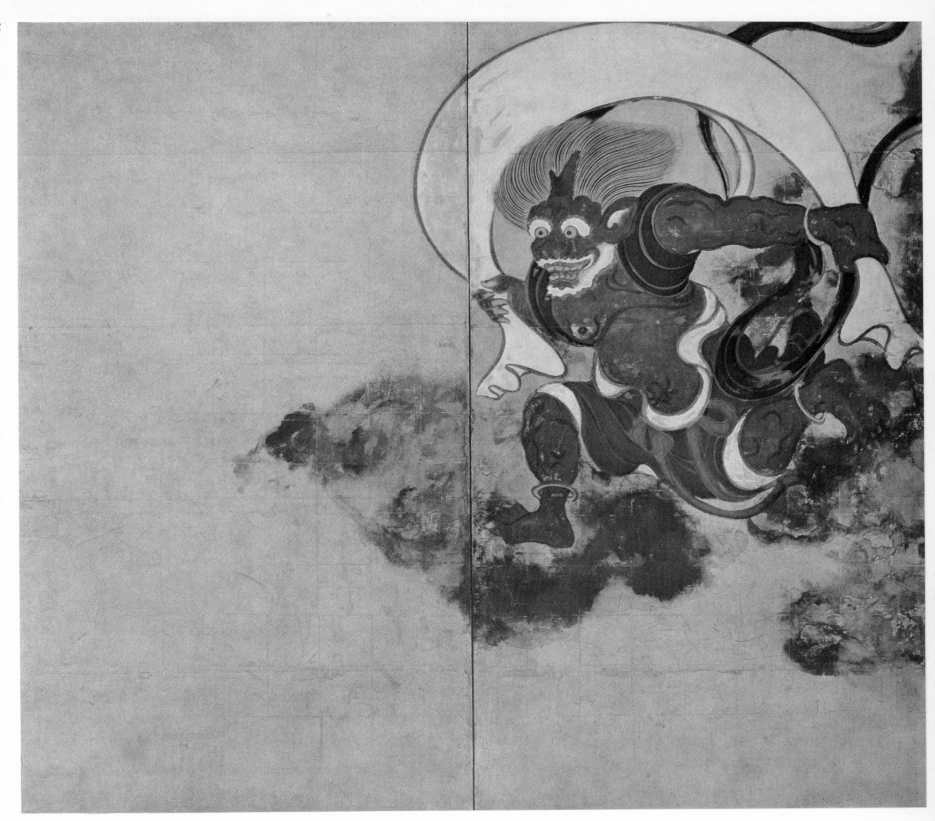

influence on his work. Under Kōetsu's guidance and, as we have seen in Plates 148 and 150, often with his active collaboration, the genius of Sōtatsu blossomed. He founded the modern school of decorative painting which was to produce such remarkable artists as Kōrin, Kenzan and many others.

In these famous screens Sōtatsu has represented the Thunder-god and the Wind-god in the old *Yamato-e* style. However, he has translated it into a grander scale. His more eloquent manner inherited from the Momoyama atmosphere has an added quality of humour which is essentially modern. In the black clouds he shows a new use of ink. Thus he synthesized the arts of the past for decorative purposes and laid the foundation for the future development of this aspect of Japanese art.

Plates 155 and 156
RED AND WHITE PLUM TREES
By Ogata Kōrin (A.D. 1658–1716). Edo Period
Pair of Folding Screens. Colour on gold paper. Size (each screen) 62 in. × 68 in.
Atami Museum, Shizuoka-ken

This famous pair of screens is perhaps the finest surviving example of Kōrin's decorative style. The design was inspired by early spring-time and is imbued with a true Japanese sensibility and feeling for beauty. The old plum trees bear large

flowers decoratively treated in red or white; a full stream swollen by the spring waters slowly flows through the scene in playful eddies. The fragrance of blossoms seems to fill the air. Such scenes stir the imagination of the Japanese and satisfy their love of nature in art.

This pair of screens became the pattern for all similar designs of the Kōrin school. The plum-blossoms became known as *Kōrin Ume* 'Kōrin's plum-blossoms'; the stylized waves as *Kōrin-nami* 'Kōrin's waves'. Artists seem never to have tired of repeating them on lacquer, pottery and textile designs down to the present day.

Plate 157
YUIMA
By Ogata Kōrin (A.D. 1658–1716). Edo Period
Ink on paper. Size 15 in. × 21 in.
Collection Mr Sorimachi, Tokyo

This simple, charming painting shows a side of Kōrin's genius which is not represented by his more ornate works. It is a study of *Yuima* (Sanskrit: *Vimalakirti*) the lay-disciple of the Buddha. According to Buddhist lore, *Yuima* was once engaged in a discussion by the Bodhisattva *Monju* (Sanskrit: *Manjusri*) who was renowned for his learning and eloquence. While Monju poured forth his wisdom *Yuima* remained completely silent. Yet *Yuima* emerged victorious from the discussion. From this the silence of *Yuima* was said to be 'like thunder', or in other words that his silence was more impressive than *Monju's* eloquence. *Yuima* thus gained the reputation for being a wise cynic and as such became very popular.

Kōrin lived during the Genroku era (1688–1903) of the Edo period when the *Haiku* poem (the short seventeen syllable verse form) was a popular literary fashion. Wit, humour, and sarcasm were highly appreciated and Kōrin, the most popular artist of the Genroku years seems to have portrayed *Yuima* with much humour and some sarcasm. The disdain or irony in *Yuima's* look is known as *Yuima no Yokonirami* or 'the side-glance of Yuima'. The work is a rare example of a Kōrin work in ink, a medium he had mastered but seldom used.

Plate 158

FLOWER BASKETS

By Ogata Kenzan (A.D. 1663–1743). Edo Period

Colour on paper. Size 44 in. × 20 in.

Collection Mr Matsunaga, Odawara

Kenzan's artistic gifts matched those of his elder brother Kōrin. He specialized in pottery manufacture and most of his painting takes the form of designs on ceramics. Occasionally he painted but then entirely for his own pleasure. On these occasions he produced unaffected, unpretentious works which show a complete disregard for the requirements of a technical finish. They reflect his free attitude to life and art. An amusing story is told of how he once met his great patron the Abbot of the Tōeizan who so admired the artist's genius that he took off his own cloak and gave it to Kenzan. So unmindful was Kenzan of this high mark of esteem that he returned to his pottery studio and started to work with his clay, wiping his muddy hands on the precious garment which he was wearing.

The *Flower Baskets* here reproduced is far removed from the work produced by professional painters. Theoretically one would expect the strong black lines of the pattern he made of the baskets to clash with the naturalistic flowers they contain yet both are effectively harmonized through the genius of this individual artist.

Plates 159 and 160
SUMMER RAIN AND AUTUMN WIND
By Sakai Hōitsu (A.D. 1760–1828). Late Edo Period
Pair of Folding Screens. Colour on silver paper. Size (each screen) 61 in. × 71 in.
National Commission for Protection of Cultural Properties, Tokyo

The last great master of the Sōtatsu-Kōrin school was Hōitsu who continued to
work into the nineteenth century. By this time artistic taste had changed. Modern
realism had made a deep impression and the somewhat artificial stylization of

natural objects for the sake of their decorative beauty was no longer universally
accepted. Hōitsu's merit lies in his close observation of the summer and autumn
grasses beaten by the rain or blown by the wind. He had a remarkable gift for
composing screens of great decorative beauty based on realistic detail. Certain con-
ventions of the Sōtatsu-Kōrin school survive, notably in the curved blue area of
water which cuts across one corner of the screen *Summer Rain*. This might seem
illogical in a realistic composition. In the nineteenth century the dominating force
of Japanese painting, regardless of schools was realism. These screens are the last
masterpieces of a long Japanese tradition.

Plates 161 and 162
PINE TREES IN SNOW
By Maruyama Ōkyo (A.D. 1733–1795). Edo Period
Pair of Folding Screens. Colour on paper
Size (each screen) 60 in. × 140 in.
Collection Mr Mitsui, Tokyo

This famous pair of screens shows the art of Ōkyo at its best. In Japan the day following a snow-fall is generally crystal clear. The old pine trees with their new mantle of snow glitter in the golden sunshine of a bright morning. Ōkyo, with all the resources of Japanese painting at his command, has reproduced this subtle atmosphere.

The screens were ordered by the very wealthy Mitsui family who gave Ōkyo complete freedom to use as much gold dust as he liked. This he sprinkled liberally on the background to create the impression of the sparkling air of a sunny morning. On this gold background he painted in high relief his snow clad pine trees. The manner in which he has placed the snow lying on the old black trunks and the green pine needles is the result of most accurate observation.

Nevertheless, the screens fulfil most effectively their function as decorations for a large room. Ōkyo's preoccupation with truth to nature never blinded him to his responsibilities as an artist.

9 The Realistic School

The Tokugawa rulers, as I have described, banned all contacts with the west but they were powerless to prevent some knowledge of western culture reaching Japan. Through the port of Nagasaki, the one door left open to foreign shipping, some European influence did pass, particularly in the field of the natural sciences. We have seen how the Catholic art that entered Japan in the sixteenth century perished when, after about sixty years, Christianity was ruthlessly suppressed. In the eighteenth century a new type of realistic painting influenced Japanese art. As a consequence, the study of nature and its faithful representation in art became of increasing importance. The Japanese had hitherto never considered realism to be of significance. On the contrary they generally delighted in deviations from truth to nature. The affirmation of realist principles was the work of Maruyama Ōkyo (1733–1795) whom historians generally considered to be their finest Japanese exponent. The influences entering Japan through Nagasaki were formed of a combination of the arts of the west with styles of Chinese painting that had already been subject to western influences. Artists from all over Japan went to study the new modes being expounded in Nagasaki and propagated them in Kyoto and Edo.

Ōkyo came from Kyoto where he had received an artistic training along traditional Japanese lines, but his natural gifts for the faithful representation of natural phenomena stimulated his interest in the new trends. He studied the Chinese naturalists as well as examples of western realism and incorporated lessons learned from both into his work. One of the few branches of western science which the Tokugawa rulers tolerated was that of medicine which they felt to be politically harmless and of benefit to the people. However, the medical textbooks included anatomical drawings which convinced men like Ōkyo of the necessity for an intimate knowledge of the human body in figural work. From Dutch copper-plate engravings he learned the principles of perspective in paintings of landscape and

architecture. He was perhaps the first Japanese artist ever to make life studies of the nude. The realism of Ōkyo's paintings created a great sensation among a public accustomed to the traditional eastern modes. His sketches from nature show a precision and skill which entitle him to a place among the best artists of other countries in the genre.

Many stories were told to illustrate the degree of accuracy he achieved. One of the best known tells how he always wanted to paint a sleeping boar. One day he heard that one was sleeping in a near by wood and he hurried to the spot to sketch it. He returned and made his painting. A farmer who happened to see it remarked that it was extremely well painted but that the boar looked sick. Ōkyo, very much surprised, returned to the wood where he found that the boar was, in fact, dead.

Ōkyo's achievement is remarkable only if seen in the light of Japanese artistic traditions. Compared with western realism we see that, despite such accuracy as is seen in details like the fur on animals, the characteristic Japanese decorative sense still makes itself felt. This gives his work other and more valuable qualities which entitle him to a foremost place in the history of Japanese art. His masterpieces, the *Hozu River* (Plates 163, 164) and the *Pine Trees in Snow* (Plates 161, 162), do indeed show a scrupulous observation of nature, the former in the depiction of swirling water and the latter in the newly-fallen snow on the green pine needles. Yet both are fundamentally decorative in conception. The fluent lines of the *Hozu River* screen create a pattern of great beauty and the *Pine Trees in Snow* are a splendid decorative fusion of colour which produces most effective contrasts of white and green against a golden haze of morning.

Ōkyo had many followers but the realistic movement, which was radically opposed to the fundamental principles of eastern painting, produced its reaction. A remark by Soga Shōhaku, an expert

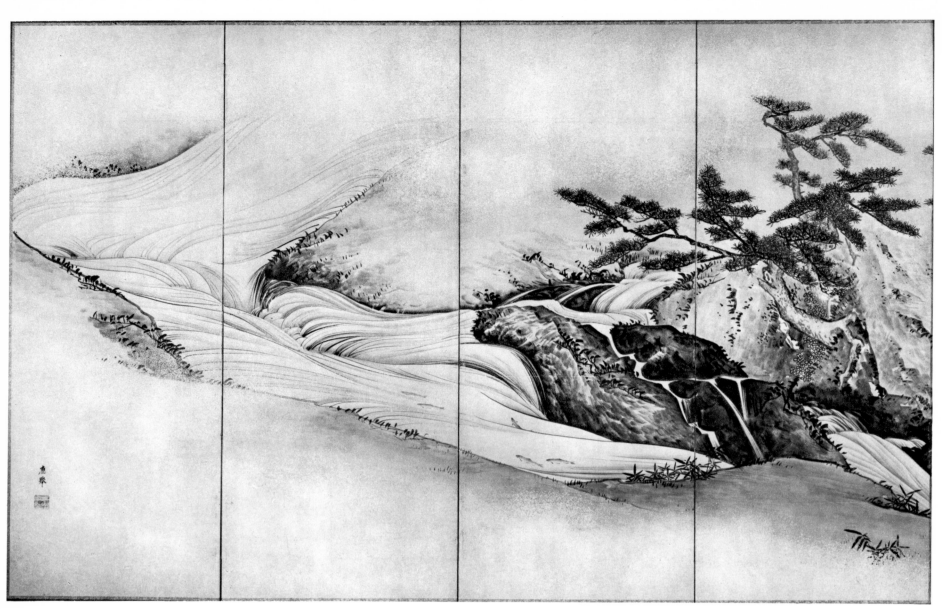

sumi painter of the time illustrates the bitter feelings Ōkyo created, 'If you want a painting (which is art) come to me; if you want just a picture (which is a play-thing) Ōkyo's will do!' To such men Ōkyo represented all the evils attendant on superficial efforts to imitate nature. In the next chapter we shall see how in the late years of the Edo period the reaction against Ōkyo's ideals led to a revival of *Bunjin-ga* ('poet-painters') work.

Nevertheless, the spirit of scientific inquiry absorbed the whole world at this time and Ōkyo was its prophet in Japan. Other schools, even the *Bunjin* painters in some way or other incorporated Ōkyo's discoveries into their work.

Matsumura Goshun (1752–1811), Ōkyo's gifted pupil, founded the Shijō school which, until comparatively recent years, dominated the art world of Kyoto. It is interesting to see how this school which inherited Ōkyo's ideas, soon became dissatisfied with straight-forward realism and turned to literary themes. This in itself illustrates the Japanese penchant for poetic allusion and for some form of subjective or spiritual expression in art. Goshun was not only a painter but also famous for his *haiku* poetry. While staying within the bounds of realistic modes he tried to introduce the highly subjective *haiku* spirit into his work. This dualism is the outstanding characteristic of the art of the Shijō school and gave it great popularity. It shows clearly how impossible it was for Japanese painting not to return to subjective and spiritual forms of expression.

Plates 163 and 164
HOZU RIVER
By Maruyama Ōkyo (A.D. 1733–1795). Edo Period
Folding Screen. Colour and ink on paper. Size 60 in. × 188 in.
Collection Mr Nishimura, Kyoto

Despite all the efforts which the Tokugawa rulers made to isolate Japan and exclude western civilisation, Japanese art could not escape the wave of realism which was sweeping the art of the world. This new movement filtered into the country mainly with western scientific knowledge through Nagasaki, the one port partly open to foreigners. It ended by revolutionizing Japanese art.

The leading artist among the many who were to a larger or smaller extent in-fluenced by western realism was Maruyama Ōkyo. He had a particularly keen eye for the close observation of facts and a tireless gift for the study of every aspect of realism which might improve his accuracy in the representation of natural objects; contemporaneous Chinese painting in a realistic manner, European copper-plate engravings, even illustrated books on anatomy imported from Holland. His paintings are without parallel in Japan and it is said that his countrymen found them so life-like that they confused them with the real thing.

Nevertheless, Ōkyo was after all a product of the Japanese artistic spirit and, although he studied nature far more closely than any painter before him, his works do not carry realism as far as those of say Dürer, Holbein or Courbet. The *Hozu River*, for instance, owes its manner of depicting a magnificent flow of water to a most accurate study of a stream and rocks but the painting, despite its life-like detail, still succeeds in creating a decorative effect. It marks the highest degree of realism reached by any Japanese artist before the introduction of oil painting.

Plate 165
SKETCHES OF HARES
By Maruyama Ōkyo (A.D. 1733–1795). Edo Period
Sketch Book. Ink and light colour on paper
Size (height) 12 in.
Collection Mr Nishimura, Kyoto

The sketch books of this outstanding Japanese exponent of the realistic style are of very great interest. They
show a very different mind from that which produced
large decorative or poetic pictures to the order of wealthy
patrons. Here, in these sketch books which seem to
explore the secrets of nature, we see a mind moved by
scientific curiosity and a desire for accuracy. They show
Ōkyo following his deepest interests—animals, birds
and insects, plants in the various seasons of the year and
sometimes even human figures draped or naked. Such
subjects were very rare in Japanese art of the time.
Considered purely as sketches, they compare with
similar works by the great masters of any country.

The so-called *Bunjin-ga* ('poet-painters') movement best expresses the reaction inspired by the realistic tendencies of Ōkyo and his followers. It illustrates the fundamental idealist approach which lies at the root of all eastern painting and which always reaffirms itself when art threatens to become too realistic.

The east regards life as a balance between spirit and matter. Too great an emphasis on the material aspect degrades the spirit and curbs its liberty. It was inherent in this dislike, or disregard, of the material world that a meticulous representation of nature in art denied the soul of an artist its vital freedom. The Japanese held that to dwell on the physical aspect of natural objects and to strive for technical perfection in depicting them was a deviation from the true aims of art and, as such, to be discouraged.

The *Bunjin-ga* movement, in which the opposition to realistic painting was formulated, strove to express the lofty spirit of art. As a consequence it followed naturally that an artist must be a cultured man, perhaps a writer or a poet, and not a professional painter skilled only in techniques. Without the expression of the spirit a painting was not entitled to be considered as art. The *Bunjin-ga* movement was a cult of the amateur painters which used nature only as a means of conveying spiritual values.

The ideas underlying *Bunjin-ga* had existed for centuries in China where scholars and *littérateurs* had long practised painting for their pleasure. Their products lacked technical perfection but they had an artistic freedom, a spiritual grace and distinction. They reflected the same ideas as Southern painting in China to which I have already referred. This Southern painting is often considered as synonymous with *Bunjin-ga*. I have mentioned in the chapter on *suiboku* painting how the poetic temperament of the Southern Chinese and their misty river countryside led them to develop a distinctive tonal landscape painting, which during the Yüan and Ming Dynasties developed into what is known in Chinese as *Wên-jên hua*, transliterated into Japanese as *Bunjin-ga*. In the Ch'ing Dynasty (1644–1911) the *Wên-jên* movement became extremely popular—partly as a reaction to the western style of realistic painting which the Emperor Ch'ien-lung greatly favoured. The movement entered Japan via the port of Nagasaki together with western painting modes. It became increasingly popular among the intellectuals and formed a current running counter to that of Ōkyo's realism.

The greatest exponents were Ikeno Taiga (1723–1776) and Uragami Gyokudō (1745–1820). These two painters disliked not only the realism but also the technical perfection of Ōkyo and his followers. The more the Maruyama and Shijō schools flourished, the more the *Bunjin* painters asserted the basic eastern principles of free expression and decried mere technical perfection.

It is difficult to determine the formative influences on Taiga's angular and yet calligraphic brush-work—for he was also famed for his calligraphy. His style is in marked contrast to that of Ōkyo, but he achieved an effect which naturalism could not produce. His grasp of landscape was, I believe, due to his studies of Hsiao Chih-mu's landscape sketches which were published in wood-block form during the Ch'ing Dynasty. Taiga greatly admired the rough, broad brushstrokes of these prints and incorporated their approach into his own style. Through a seemingly almost carefree manner, he impressed his personality very strongly on his work. It gives the impression of an art which conveys more than it actually states. It hints at the depths of his understanding and the purity of his thoughts towards landscape. Such a restraint was in marked contrast to Ōkyo's facility of brushwork and explicit forms.

Gyokudō's style was in a sense the opposite of that of Taiga. His grasp of the essentials of *Bunjin-ga* approach were none the less sound but, whereas Taiga was restrained and evocative, Gyokudō was exuberant. He made every style his own and expressed his ideas by eloquent brushwork and simplified ink tones. Gyokudō had been a *samurai* but abandoned this calling to devote himself to painting and music. With his *koto* (Japanese harp) on his back he became an itinerant musician and gained great popularity. As a painter he was entirely self-taught and he only took up the art late in life for amusement. He followed no rules or school of painting and his work shows a rare freedom and spontaneity.

In following the Chinese ideal of interpreting nature according to their own individual visions, Taiga and Gyokudō were close to European Impressionist theories. It is interesting to observe how similar fundamental ideas produced similar responses and art forms which have much in common.

Historians have often compared the anti-realistic movement of *Bunjin-ga* to those of European artists. However, the eastern form is never very far removed from nature and it never expressed itself in abstract or geometric forms. It relied on the reaction of the senses to nature and it is closest to western Impressionism and post-Impressionism. Despite the obvious difference of materials and the techniques, the works of these two artists remind one of Monet and Cézanne.

Two other great exponents of *Bunjin-ga* ideals during this same period were Tanomura Chikuden (1777–1835) and Aoki Mokubei (1767–1835). Although they repudiated all rules, they nevertheless expressed the harmony with nature which was the aim of the school. They sought new spiritual interpretations of nature and new methods of expression which might bring them closer to its ultimate truth. Unwittingly their new techniques led them towards a neo-realism.

One of the great masters of the movement was Buson (1717–1783). The landscapes he painted of his native Kyoto and Osaka are extremely sensitive. He was not only a painter but also a famous *haiku* poet and he tried to introduce into his painting the very particular atmosphere of the Japanese *haiku* poem. This type of painting formed a separate sub-division of *Bunjin-ga* which is known as *Haiga* and it shows a completely new approach to the art. I have already mentioned *Haiga* in connection with Goshun, who founded the realistic Shijō school but who, being also a great *haiku* poet, painted some successful *Haiga*. This is another example showing how close the realistic painters and the poet-painters were to each other in their attachment to nature, although their main arguments were opposed to each other.

Watanabe Kazan (1793–1841) provides an interesting example of an artist who took elements from a number of schools. He came from the *samurai* class and was renowned as a deeply cultured man of high principles. He ended his life by suicide in defence of his ideals. His original and sensitive interpretations of nature represent a sincere effort to grasp the essential character of landscape in all its moods. He first studied the *Bunjin* painting of the Ming and Ch'ing Dynasties and later turned to a study of western naturalistic works from which he learned a great deal. Unlike the amateur *Bunjin* approach to landscape, bird, and flower subjects, Kazan could paint with the most meticulous naturalism. He has also painted excellent portraits, a subject in which Kazan felt the east could not compare with the west. Basing his work on a study of the illustrations in western medical works, he became the first Japanese artist to paint portraits in the western style. However, despite his portraits, he remained at heart a true *Bunjin* painter and was always suspicious of mere naturalistic methods. He is an outstanding example of the ambivalence of *Bunjin-ga*—on the one hand anti-realistic and yet on the other, always closely attached to nature.

Thus, this powerful *Bunjin* movement represents the effort of eastern ideals to reassert themselves on the one hand over the Maruyama and Shijō schools and on the other over the *Ukiyo-e* movement, all of which were strongly realistic in approach. These conditions persisted until the close of the Edo period in 1868. Japan then emerged from her long seclusion and a flood of western culture swept over the country bringing with it fundamental changes in life and art. In comparison with the youth and energy of the new art styles which arose in this period, the artistic controversies of the Late Edo period appear like the petty squabbles of a decadent era.

Plate 166

SAGES AMONG MOUNTAINS

By Ike Taiga (A.D. 1723–1776). Edo Period
Sliding Screens. Ink and colour washes on paper
Size (height) 66 in.
Henjoko-in, Koyasan

Far-eastern art, Chinese as well as Japanese, has always shown two contrasting trends, the one towards realism, the other towards spirituality. Any tendency for one to become too strong immediately seems to produce a violent reaction in the other, which serves to restore the balance.

Led by Ōkyo, the realistic movement gained great strength in eighteenth-century Japan. At the same time, among the *Bunjin* ('poet-painters') a strong anti-realistic movement developed. The poet-painters believed that painting should be a means whereby a man might express his most exalted feelings. It was the personal mirror of his soul. In their opinion, preoccupation with truth to life and the technical means necessary to represent it, destroyed the essential spiritual source of art. The basic theory of the *Bunjin* painters thus has much in common with that of post-Impressionist western art.

Taiga was one of the outstanding representatives of the poet-painter movement. His seemingly careless, almost amateurish, technique comes like a breath of fresh air in the formal atmosphere of the time. This very free style seems to burst the bonds of convention and technique fashioned by the established schools. It is tempting to see superficial similarities between Taiga's manner of depicting rocks and trees by means of series of unconnected dots and the *pointillism* of the nineteenth century in Europe. I suggest that Taiga's dotting technique owes much to his interest in a Chinese book of wood-block prints of mountains. Nevertheless, in breaking through the smooth, accomplished technique of the Academic schools with this individual dotting style, Taiga shows himself to be one of the founders of modern art.

Plate 167
VIEW OF LAKE SEIKO
By Ike Taiga (A.D. 1723–1776). Edo Period
Ink and colour washes on paper. Size (height) 77 in.
Manpuku-ji, Kyoto

Taiga's vision of the grandeur of nature and what seems to be an 'anti-technique' approach—intensely personal and regardless of truth to nature—is best understood from this landscape of Lake Seiko, a lake in China which he never visited. He uses a dotting technique extensively to represent mountains and forests. He piles cubes one upon the other in a manner reminiscent of Cézanne. This painting, unfortunately badly preserved, is owned by the Manpuku-ji Temple. The abbot of this temple was one of Taiga's patrons and the artist painted a large series of wall- and screen-paintings for the temple while he was staying there as a guest. The landscape here reproduced forms the central section of the series.

Plate 168
SAN-U SEN-I (RAIN IN THE MOUNTAINS)
By Uragami Gyokudō (A.D. 1745–1820). Late Edo Period
Ink on paper. Size 14 in. × 12 in.
Collection Mr S. Ohara, Kurashiki

Gyokudō, the painter of this *Rain in the Mountains* was the first Japanese poet-painter to gain recognition in the west. Gyokudō was a member of the *samurai* class but his love of art, especially music, led him to desert his feudal lord. With his *koto* or harp slung from his shoulder he wandered over the country. Later in life and without any training he began to paint in ink in a manner which was entirely personal.

In this small painting he reproduces an impression which he probably gained during a walk through a valley as the rain began to fall. Mountains appear and disappear amidst the changing pattern of clouds, the trees of the forest are wet with rain. To Gyokudō they appeared so fresh and green that he felt they must surely stain the rain-drops and thus dye his summer clothing. The short parallel lines of the brushwork are most impressionistic.

Plate 170
CHIKUKEI HŌIN (VISIT TO A HERMIT IN A BAMBOO GROVE)
By Yosa Buson (1766–1783). Edo Period
Ink and colour washes on silk. Size 46 in. × 16 in.
Collection Mr S. Ueno, Ashiya

The so-called 'anti-realistic' movement can be interpreted as the expression of a desire on the part of the poet-painters to communicate with the true spirit of nature more directly than was possible with what they considered to be a superficial realistic technique. The realistic and the spiritual, far from being so irreconcilable could coexist in the same artist. Buson's approach to painting was fundamentally realistic, and no artist surpassed him in depicting the countryside of Kyoto and Osaka.

170

169

Plate 169
TŌUN SHISETSU (FROZEN CLOUDS SIEVING POWDERY SNOW)
By Uragami Gyokudō (1745–1820). Late Edo Period
Ink and light colour washes on paper. Size 49 in. × 34 in.
Collection Mr Y. Kawabata, Kamakura

This masterpiece by Gyokudō shows a completely different style from that in the previous plate. It is a mountain snowscape. The trees are bare and, except for a solitary man in his hut, nothing seems to be alive. Even the clouds seem frozen.

When a powdery, dry snow falls in Japan the cold can be almost unbearable and in this painting the deathly silence which accompanies this kind of weather is given a virtually tangible quality.

It is difficult to exaggerate the significance of the changes which took place in Japan after the Meiji Restoration in 1868. Suddenly three centuries of cultural inbreeding and intellectual stagnation ended and Japan's pent-up energies were released in an effort to absorb western civilization. The aspects of western life which most impressed Japan were its science and technology. The country threw itself with enthusiasm into an effort to catch up with the west—especially in scientific matters. For a time the Japanese discarded everything and blindly worshipped the west. A vehement iconoclastic movement swept art circles and, stimulated by new nationalistic feelings, manifested itself in a sudden hatred of Buddhist art. Some of the most extreme nationalists called for a separation of Buddhism and Shintōism—rejecting the former simply because they claimed that it was a later introduction from a foreign country. For at least one thousand years Buddhism had been an integral part of Japanese life, its temples existing in perfect harmony with those of Shintōism. Now they were forcibly separated. The Buddhist temples, with all the treasures they contained were threatened with extinction. Happily this extremist movement did not last long and its effects were short-lived. It is interesting to remember the story of the Five Storeyed Pagoda of the Kōfuku-ji in Nara. This most conspicuous monument of a city of art treasures was, on the suggestion of the governor, sold at auction for only fifteen yen. The buyer wanted the fine timber but he found that it would cost him much more than fifteen yen to extract it and fortunately the pagoda survived. Many such incidents could be told of this period in which it seemed likely that the traditional culture of Japan would be completely forgotten.

Shortly after this period of national hysteria, in 1878, the American scholar Ernest Fenollosa (1853–1908) came to Japan as Professor of Philosophy in the University of Tokyo. It is fitting to pay a tribute to the part he played in saving the traditional arts of Japan which were threatened at best with neglect, at worst with wanton destruction. He recognized their value and, with the help of his assistant Okakura Kakuzō, took measures to preserve them. He was instrumental in setting up a law for the preservation of national treasures, in establishing museums, in founding the Tokyo Art School, and in furthering a system of exhibitions to foster the growth of a new art. These measures slowly brought the Japanese back to an appreciation of their own artistic heritage. Although the enthusiasm for western architecture, painting, and sculpture continued undiminished, there were men who called for a return to native traditions.

I must ignore here the oil painting which, inspired by various European movements, has grown up in Japan and limit myself to a survey of the traditional forms of art and their reaction to the new conditions. Broadly speaking four schools existed at the end of the Edo period—the Maruyama-Shijō school, the *Ukiyo-e* movement, the *Bunjin-ga* painters, and the decorative school. The narrow intellectual confines of the Edo period gave them little scope for development. The impact of western culture naturally affected them all and enriched these Japanese forms of art. Gradually the differences between the old and the new were settled and an art emerged which was in keeping with spirit of the age but based on native traditions. As was to be expected, the conditions produced many extremists but even these are interesting as expressions of the energy and vitality of the time. In the crudities they produced we see the effort of the Japanese to revive the decadent art of the last years of Edo.

The new painting was influenced on the one hand by western styles and on the other by a study of ancient art. Hitherto it had been almost impossible to study old masterpieces in the original. The study of ancient art had until that time meant copying and recopying the copies made by the Tosa and Kanō schools. Such a system could hardly give a true idea of the spirit and the styles of the old masters. The measures established by Fenollosa and Okakura for the preservation and study of the old works provided comparatively good opportunities for their close study. As a result they provided a sound basis on which the new art movements could build. In time the period of intoxication with western culture passed and the Japanese realized that, although the study of western art had its benefits, especially from the point of view of techniques, wholesale imitation was unwise.

Fenollosa's warning acted like a spark to tinder. The Japanese quickly realized how much they would lose if they repudiated their long and splendid artistic heritage. Western style oil painting continued to win many adherents but the traditional forms were strong enough to survive and develop.

Okakura's leadership in the new movement was of great significance. He reformed the Imperial Household Museum (the present Tokyo National Museum) and made it the centre for the preservation and study of ancient works of art. At the same time he established the Tokyo Art School (the present Tokyo University of Art) which became the national centre for instruction and education in the arts. Through them he tried to encourage the development of a truly national art. Okakura was not able to hold the directorship of these two bodies for very long, but under the stimulus he provided a number of talented artists emerged who were the precursors of the vigorous artists of the present day. Most of them belonged to the Nihon Bijutsu In group which gathered around Okakura after he had resigned his directorship of the Art School.

The new styles of painting to appear in these years were virtually a Renaissance in Japanese art. The artists responded to the new spirit of the time, trying at the same time to revive classical schools and techniques. The masters of this period were free and eclectic in their ideas, but their works were extremely individual. Space permits us to mention only a few of the most significant. Kanō Hōgai (1828–1888) was one of the first 'new' painters to emerge. His *Hibo Kannon* (Plate 172) is a most remarkable reinterpretation of an ancient Buddhist theme. The Bodhisattva is represented with a most naturalistic execution and, although the subject is highly idealized, the artist obviously painted from a living model. The composition is well-balanced and modern in its approach. It contains a number of western elements and one can say that is representative of the type of idealistic art which Fenollosa encouraged. Other younger artists sought inspiration from the traditional forms of painting of Japan, China, and even occasionally, India.

Shimomura Kanzan (1873–1916) produced a number of masterpieces in a style which is a true revival of *Yamato-e*. The exclusively oriental *sumi* painting found a champion in Yokoyama Taikan (1868–1958). His studies of Chinese and Japanese *suiboku* painting led him to evolve a new interpretation which is both grand in concept and delicate in execution. Hishida Shunsō (1874–1911) died young but in his short life he produced a modern style with a very sensitive and individual approach to nature. His *Black Cat* (Plate 171) is refreshingly original and most decorative.

In addition to the modern artists in Okakura's group, a number of other painters kept closer to traditional modes while at the same time endeavouring to show originality in spirit and technique. They lived and worked in Kyoto, then as now a great artistic centre away from the metropolitan, international Tokyo, which was always very open to foreign influences. In the conservative and peaceful atmosphere of Kyoto, traditional artists work even to this day.

The most representative artist of this conservative trend was Takeuchi Seihō (1864–1942) (see Plate 176). He remained faithful to the styles of the Maruyama-Shijō school but by means of a most skilful brushwork, he produced a remarkably truthful and sensitive interpretation of nature.

Of the *Bunjin* painters Tomioka Tessai (1836–1924) (Plate 177), living a secluded life, created works whose vigour and freedom cannot be found in the art of his predecessors. He grew to full maturity in his later years and some of his finest works, painted when he was nearly ninety, remind one of the breadth of the last phase of Renoir's art.

Apart from the traditional styles, oil painting developed very rapidly. It would be unjust to regard it, as have some critics, as merely a slavish imitation of western styles. As modern communications shrink the world and modern forms of industrialization bring the Japanese closer to the west, so our architecture, clothes, and even the food we eat become more western. The Japanese approach to art is being internationalized, whether we like it or not. Young Japanese artists of sensibility have come to share the same thoughts and face the same social and artistic problems as their western colleagues. In taking to oil painting, Japanese artists are not merely imitating—they are responding to an international movement which finds in oils the best means of expressing modern plastic ideas. Oil painting has become an integral and natural part of our artistic life.

In time, a distinctive Japanese oil-painting style will emerge, and there are signs of this happening already. The recognition which Fujita gained recently in Paris is an encouraging example. Modern Japan has fully assimilated oil painting, recognizing it to be one of the most suitable vehicles for the expression of native ideas.

Plate 171
BLACK CAT
By Hishida Shunsō (A.D. 1874–1911). New Japan Period
Colour on silk. Size 46 in. × 24 in.
Collection Mr M. Hosokawa, Tokyo

Fenellosa's desire to found modern Japanese art on a native tradition was inherited by his pupil and successor Okakura Kakuzō. The latter's knowledge of world art and his understanding of the art of his own country, which was naturally deeper than that of his teacher, enabled him to inspire and guide the younger generation of Japanese artists. Shunsō was a typical representative of this new broad approach and, despite an early death at the age of 37, he initiated a new trend in Japanese art.

The *Black Cat* is distinguished by a hitherto unparalleled sensitivity of observation and delicate execution. The decorative effect is in the fullest tradition of Sōtatsu or Kōrin but the interpretation is completely original. It is the outcome of a modern mind combining a close study of nature with an equally deep study of old masterpieces.

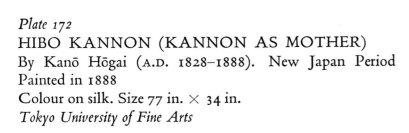

Plate 172

HIBO KANNON (KANNON AS MOTHER)

By Kanō Hōgai (A.D. 1828–1888). New Japan Period
Painted in 1888
Colour on silk. Size 77 in. × 34 in.
Tokyo University of Fine Arts

When the Emperor was restored in 1868, the government adopted an 'open-door' policy and welcomed western art and culture. Japan changed almost overnight and with the 'New Japan', there developed a new art. The early years of this change produced chaotic conditions in which the conservative forces of a nationalistic spirit struggled against the flood of western art. The new generation of artists for a time felt lost and without direction.

An American, Ernest Fenollosa, played an important part in these years. He advised the Japanese government that education in art should be based on the native traditions and that western movements should not be allowed to overwhelm it completely. He found a disciple in Hōgai who was willing to follow his advice and reject the narrow-minded nationalism of the Edo period and to study the arts of both east and west. *Hibo Kannon* (Kannon as Mother) was the outcome of this liberal approach to art. It was an ambitious work which Hōgai completed only shortly before his death. Judged by present-day standards it has its faults but it was a bold and energetic step away from the decadence of the Edo period and it gave promise of a healthy development for Japanese art. The following plates illustrate the fulfilment of this promise.

Plates 173 and 174
YOROBŌSHI
By Shimomura Kanzan (A.D. 1878–1930). New
Japan Period
Pair of Folding Screens. Colour on gold silk
Size (each screen) 74 in. × 160 in.
Tokyo National Museum

Kanzan stands out among the artists who grew up under
the guidance of Okakura. His decorative talents in both
composition and colouring enable one to compare his
large screens with the fine works of the Momoyama
period. The subject of the painting is *Yorobōshi* which is
taken from a *Noh* play. In this drama a blind boy was
lost from his home. After many years of unhappy
wandering, one spring day as the plum trees were in full
bloom he prayed to the sun for help. His father, by
chance coming to that same spot, was reunited with his
son. The colours of the painting are peculiarly beautiful,
the whole scene is bathed in golden sunshine and the
strong branches of the plum trees are dotted with
beautiful flowers. But this screen relies on more than just
decorative beauty. Its poignant story has the power to
touch deeply. The Indian poet Rabindranath Tagore
visited Japan in 1916 and was so impressed by this
painting that he ordered a very capable artist to make
an exact copy which he took back to his school at
Santiniketan.

Plate 175

CHICHIBU MOUNTAINS IN EARLY
DAWN OF SPRING

By Yokoyama Taikan (A.D. 1868–1958). New Japan
Period

Ink with some gold on silk. Size 26 in. × 44 in.
Collection Princess Chichibu, Tokyo

Taikan's technique differs from that of Shunshō and
Kanzan in that he works mainly in ink. He seems to
have explored every possibility of the medium. Through
his distinctive, delicate tones which range from the
deepest black through all the many tones of grey he
produces an inimitable sense of depth, of the distance of
mountains and rivers, of the movements of mists and
clouds and even of the appearance and disappearance
of the forms springing from his imagination. His aim
in the use of ink was to express a spiritual meaning
which in the opinion of Okakura is the essence of far-
eastern art.

Plate 176

SOSHŪ NO AME (RAIN AT SOOCHOW)

By Takeuchi Seihō (A.D. 1864–1942). New Japan Period
Ink on silk. Size 75 in. × 55 in.
Musée d'Art Moderne, Paris

Tokyo, the new capital of the country, was the centre of western influences and the
headquarters of all the new art movements. Kyoto, the old capital, remained
fundamentally conservative in outlook. Takeuchi Seihō, the best-known Kyoto
painter preserved the realism and adroit brushwork of the Maruyama and Shiko
schools until he died about fifteen years ago. He was at the same time a modern
artist and as a young man visited the museums and art centres of Europe. His
experiences enabled him to introduce fresh ideas into the ancient art of Kyoto.
Soshū no Ame (Rain at Soochow), painted after a visit to China, was exhibited in
Paris in 1922 when the Musée de Luxembourg acquired it for its collections.
Seihō has here used bold black ink tones to create the impression of summer rain. In
this he shows an appreciation of the artistic trends of Tokyo but, compared with
the manner in which Taikan used his ink, he was calm and restrained. He remained
in fact, a true Kyoto artist and basically his brushwork never deviated from the
traditional Kyoto styles.

Plate 177

SANSŌ FŪ-U (MOUNTAIN VILLA
IN A STORM)

By Tomioka Tessai (A.D. 1836–1924). New Japan
Period

Ink and colour wash on paper. Size 49 in. × 24 in.
Collection of Mr Naito, Kyoto

Despite its conservatism, Kyoto has always been an ideal
place for an artist to work. There, insulated from the
world, a great painter in the old tradition could work
well into the twentieth century. Tessai was a true poet-
painter or scholar-painter. Indeed, he never thought of
himself as a painter but rather as a scholar working in the
famous library which he built up. Painting for him was
only a means whereby he could express his innermost
ideas or illustrate his scholarly or literary meanings. He
usually wrote sentences or poems on his paintings and
would often insist that a visitor should first read the
inscriptions in order that he might better appreciate the
painting. He was completely independent and original
in his styles, disregarding all the accepted rules of ink
painting. The independence of his approach is a
modern characteristic and produces an effect of great
freedom and originality. Tessai was an extraordinary
phenomenon—a man still holding to a traditional
belief that painting should be literary and didactic
and yet painting in an individual manner which gave
him a leading place among the moderns. He continued
to work until he was nearly ninety, faithfully continuing
poet-painter traditions of the Edo period. Even the
painters in oils and other enthusiasts of modern movements appreciated his work and his fame reached
Europe and America. The bold use of ink and the powerful brushwork of the painting illustrated are typical of
his originality.